MIND AND MORALITY

Mind and Morality

An Examination of Hume's Moral Psychology

JOHN BRICKE

CLARENDON PRESS · OXFORD

1996

Oxford University Press, Walton Street, Oxford OX2 6DP

Oxford New York
Athens Auckland Bangkok Bombay
Calcutta Cape Town Dar es Salaam Delhi
Florence Hong Kong Istanbul Karachi
Kuala Lumpur Madras Madrid Melbourne
Mexico City Nairobi Paris Singapore
Taipei Tokyo Toronto
and associated companies in
Berlin Ibadan

Oxford is a trade mark of Oxford University Press

Published in the United States
by Oxford University Press, Inc., New York

British Library Cataloguing in Publication Data
Data available

Library of Congress Cataloging-in-Publication Data
Bricke, John, 1939–
Mind and morality: an examination of Hume's
moral psychology / John Bricke.
Includes bibliographical references.
1. Hume, David, 1711–1776.   2. Ethics.   3. Philosophy of mind.
I. Title.
B1499.E8B67 1996 170'.92—dc20   95-46828
ISBN 0-19-823589-5

1 3 5 7 9 10 8 6 4 2

Typeset by Invisible Ink
Printed in Great Britain
on acid-free paper by
Biddles Ltd,
Guildford and King's Lynn

ACKNOWLEDGEMENTS

A great many helped, and I am deeply grateful to each of them. Páll Árdal, George Davie, Tim George, James King, Jane McIntyre, David Fate Norton, Geoffrey Sayre-McCord, and Ted Zenzinger provided both stimulus and close criticism in the course of conversations or communications on some or other of the topics in the book, at some or other points in the past.

My colleagues in the Department of Philosophy of the University of Kansas helped by challenging, and by (at times raucously) resisting, the readings of Hume that I submitted to their rigorous scrutiny at colloquia over many years. The late Warner Morse pressed hard for clarification of the arguments in Chapters 1 and 3. The comments of Richard Cole, Anthony Genova, James Page, Russ Shafer-Landau, and Arthur Skidmore substantially affected the contours of Chapter 4. J. Michael Young, whose death has darkened the days in which I have brought the book to completion, helped tame the thicket that was Chapter 5. Ann Cudd and Rex Martin probed patiently, and constructively, my first efforts at Chapter 6.

Four philosophers who read the whole of the book in its penultimate form—Annette Baier, Richard Norman, Michael Smith, and David Raphael—combined a secure grasp of my interpretative and philosophical intentions with acute criticism, and with a wealth of invaluable suggestions for improvement of the book's argument.

My debts to others who have written on Hume will be obvious to those who peruse the notes. My debt to the philosophical stimulus of Donald Davidson's writings will be apparent in almost every section of the book.

Peter Momtchiloff was helpful and considerate at every stage of the book's production. Angela Blackburn, with keen eye and good judgement, did much to lighten and clarify my philosophical prose. Ty Barnes helped with the index and saved me, many times over, from misquoting Hume. Elizabeth Barnhill, Paula Courtney, Janice Doores, Cynthia Hodges, and Diana McKinney each came generously to the rescue when I faltered in the preparation of the manuscript.

My wife, Hodgie, and my son, Ian, endured a driven presence in the household, but remained supportive and encouraging throughout.

The University of Kansas helped by awarding me several generous grants from its General Research Fund, and by granting me sabbatical leaves for the spring semester, 1983, and the fall semester, 1990. The University's Hall Center for the Humanities made the marvellously timely award of a Faculty Research Fellowship in the spring semester, 1991. Both Andrew Debicki, formerly Director of the Hall Center, and Janet Crow, its Executive Director, ensured a continuing framework of support upon that Fellowship's completion. The University's College of Liberal Arts and Sciences offered essential word-processing assistance. Its Department of Philosophy provided unstinting secretarial and other help right from the start.

Quotations from Hume's *A Treatise of Human Nature*, ed. L. A. Selby-Bigge; 2nd edition with text revised by P. H. Nidditch (Oxford University Press, 1978), or from his *Enquiries Concerning Human Understanding and Concerning the Principles of Morals*, ed. L. A. Selby-Bigge; 3rd edition with text revised by P. H. Nidditch (Oxford University Press, 1975), are made by permission of Oxford University Press.

For Ian

CONTENTS

Introduction

To understand morality one must understand mind. To understand mind one must reflect on the roles that mental phenomena play in the explanation of human conduct, the contributions they make to the interpretation of the multifarious things that human agents do. To understand both mind and morality, one must consider the contributions that peculiarly moral mental phenomena—mental phenomena with specifically moral content—make to the interpretation of human agents.

Many would agree with Hume on these assumptions. Few can, however, be found to agree on just what it is Hume claims to discover when he turns his thoughts to mind and morality. That he assigns a crucial role to peculiarly moral sentiments is agreed on all hands, but there is no agreement on his views about the function and character of these sentiments, about their relations to sentiments that are not peculiarly moral ones, about their links to beliefs, whether moral or non-moral. For some, Hume is a subjectivist about morals. For others, despite his sentimentalism, he hankers after an arguably objectivist account of morality's claims. Some commentators find a moral cognitivist—a partisan not only of common-sense morality but also of moral beliefs and truths—lurking in the pages of the *Treatise* and the second *Enquiry*. Others discover in these pages a distanced theorist concerned to characterize the minds of moral critics, not—there being little room for this—the minds of specifically moral agents.

That Hume is at pains to understand the nature of justice, and that he introduces a notion of artifice when explicating obligations in that area, is obvious to all. But no agreement is to be found when one presses the question how, in Hume's view, matters of justice stand to matters of self-interest, or how they stand to matters of morality, or how they stand to other moral matters. Nor is any consensus to be found on the question whether for Hume morality is—or to what extent, or in what respects, morality is—a matter of convention.

Absence of agreement on the most fundamental questions concerning the interpretation of his views on mind and morality complements an utter absence of agreement as to the soundness of Hume's views, and as to the cogency—and even the aptness—of the arguments he musters in their support.

Part of the problem is that commentators have been insufficiently assiduous in seeking the foundations, in his philosophy of mind, on which Hume builds when constructing his theory of morality. Another part has been the practice of treating Hume's reflections on morality in a piecemeal way, the practice of taking his theory of morality as a patchwork of severally brilliant and provocative, but essentially unintegrated, parts.

This book will fasten on Hume's efforts to found a theory of morality on a theory of mind. I shall make, as methodologically sound, the assumption that Hume has a theory of mind and morality that, highly structured and systematic in character, is intended to be comprehensive in its scope. That assumption's soundness will be shown by the success of the interpretative project it supports.

My approach to the textual evidence is holistic, self-consciously seeking connections between what can seem to be isolated doctrines. I allow the parameters set by emerging theoretical design to play a substantive part in the interpretation of passages that have shown themselves resistant to ready reading. And I assign interpretative pride of place to the rendering of any arguments Hume deploys, including especially those he deploys in the pivotal *Treatise* Sections 'Of the influencing motives of the will', 'Moral distinctions not deriv'd from reason', and 'Justice, whether a natural or artificial virtue'. Scrutiny of his sustained arguments offers the surest route to the identification of what is central to Hume's thinking about the links between mind and morality.

Secure in our grasp of the most basic structural elements in Hume's thinking on these matters, we shall be better positioned for assessment. We shall find that Hume's chief arguments are much more potent and promising than they are typically taken to be. We shall discover reason to reject as inessential to the view of mind and morality that he forwards, and as obstacles in the way of his articulating that view, positions (about the passions, about the mechanisms of sympathy) that have a prominent place in Hume's actual presentation of that view. Especially when reflecting on the nature of evaluative language, we shall have occasion both to register, and to envisage remedy for, inadequacies in the constructive theory of evaluation that Hume sets out.

Though a highly systematic thinker, Hume does not spell everything out. Aspects of rhetorical strategy, as well as the jostling demands of at times divergent philosophical objectives, have shaped what he actually says. In attempting to interpret him, then, we must seek to make the in-explicit fully explicit, must try to bring into the open much that works in essentially subterranean fashion in his actual texts. Our efforts at excava-tion—of connections, of concepts, of theoretical configurations—may produce decidedly un-Humean representations of Humean doctrines. The abstractness and complexity of these representations will, however, help reveal the philosophical content of his own admirably elegant prose.

In setting out Hume's views on mind and morality I pay little explicit attention to those of his contemporaries and predecessors: a great many able commentators have already done much to make Hume's philosophical context available to modern readers. I also reserve comments on other Humean commentators, as well as on modern work on topics to which Hume attends, for footnotes where the interested reader will find some-thing of a modern setting for Hume's reflections. The resultant austerity of treatment will foster clarity in the presentation both of analysis and of assessment.

The project is an essentially philosophical one. In the attempt at ex-plicit articulation of Hume's systematic theory of mind and morality, I am concerned to make plain its claims on contemporary philosophical attention. There are grounds for criticism, to be sure, but the chief argu-ments Hume marshals in his theory's support suffice to scotch the claims of both its cognitivist and its conventionalist competitors. Hume's own demanding criteria for an adequate theory of mind and morality are ones his own finished theory meets—for the most part—effectively and eco-nomically. There are prospects for the extension of that finished theory to the treatment of a number of further topics that non-cognitivists have traditionally found intractable.

Hume's finished theory of mind and morality—his expanded moral conativism, as I shall call it—will emerge from reflection on the charac-ter of reasons for action (in Chapter 1), on the interrelations of the primi-tive notions of desire, volition, and affection (in Chapter 2), and on the inadequacies of moral cognitivism (in Chapter 3). Its key conception is that of specifically moral desires, desires whose careful characterization contributes to Hume's elaboration of a general theory of moral senti-ments (in Chapter 4), of a complex account of the connections between morality, justice, and convention (in Chapters 5 and 6), and of a theory of specifically moral agents (in Chapter 7).

I

Reasons and Actions

Treatise, II. iii. 3 ('Of the influencing motives of the will'), provides the central element in Hume's moral psychology, his analysis of the linked concepts of a reason for action and of the reason from which an agent acts. For Hume, these are explanatory concepts. One explains an agent's action by identifying the reason from which he acts. Knowing the reasons an agent has for acting in one way or another, one has a start on explaining what he actually does: one's task is simply to identify that reason, from amongst his reasons for acting, which is the reason that actually prompts the action. In developing and defending his views about their nature, then, Hume focuses on the role reasons play in the generation of actions.

Hume provides the ingredients for a *conativist* theory of reasons for action, a theory that assigns a distinctive and ineliminable motivational role to an agent's *desires*. He does so while attempting to subvert the claims of various *cognitivist* theories that, emphasizing an agent's *beliefs*, would dismiss, restrict, or dilute the conativist contention that desire is essential to the motivation of action. I shall begin by constructing, largely from ingredients Hume provides, a standard conativist theory of the sort that the arguments of *Treatise*, II. iii. 3, are designed to establish. With this conativist construction in place it will be a straightforward business to represent both a standard cognitivist theory and some of the many mutations that theory can undergo: a hard-edged sense of the possibilities here will prove invaluable as we turn to the task of setting out and assessing the arguments Hume deploys.

Hume offers two intricate arguments at *Treatise*, II. iii. 3. From the first, an argument that focuses attention on certain fairly obvious features of the practice of explaining actions, he draws three distinguishable conclusions: a constructive conclusion (the truth of conativism); a negative conclusion (the falsity of cognitivism); and a corollary of the negative conclusion (one having to do with competing reasons for action). For reasons that become obvious once one articulates it with care, Hume's first argument cannot secure any of his three conclusions: when the

argument is done cognitivism remains a clear option for at least some
cases; arguably it remains an option for all.

Hume's second argument has the same three conclusions as his first,
but it succeeds in a way the other does not. Turning on the notion of
truth-evaluability, it establishes a condition on action explanation that
calls for conativism, not cognitivism, in the construal of reasons for action. This is not to say that Hume's second argument constitutes a demonstration of his conativist claims: as we shall see, the would-be cognitivist
still has room to manoeuvre; and the conativist must undertake the daunting task of accommodating a number of seemingly resistant features that
some reasons for action, at least, would seem to possess. Hume's case for
conativism neither does nor can end with his second argument. That argument does, however, make a compelling case for a condition that, as
Hume's subsequent reflections show, the conativist can, and the cognitivist
cannot with any plausibility, meet.

In characterizing both conativism and cognitivism, and in setting out
Hume's two arguments (especially the second), I shall be regimenting,
supplementing, at times reconstructing, what is to be found in the pages
of *Treatise*, II. iii. 3. The reading that results will be an idealized one, a fact
that, for philosophical purposes, is all to the good. If an idealized reading,
it is none the less an idealized reading of Hume: in its attention to what
Hume says of the structures of his arguments, in its efforts to link characterizations of theory with actual argument, in its concern to sort the central from the peripheral, it transparently follows Hume's lead. It ignores,
or attempts to inoculate the reader against the distracting effects of, things
that must be mentioned if one's concern is to depict Hume warts and all.
In so doing, it aims to make maximally effective use of Hume's contributions to questions in moral psychology that concern both Hume and the
modern reader.[1]

1. REASONS AND ACTIONS: TWO THEORIES

When discussing the explanation of actions, Hume uses the terms 'motive' and 'reason' interchangeably. Discussing motivating obligations to

---

[1] Jonathan Harrison, in *Hume's Moral Epistemology* (Oxford, 1976), and Francis Snare, in
Morals, Motivation, and Convention: Hume's Influential Doctrines (Cambridge, 1991), provide extensive analyses and assessments of the arguments of *Treatise*, II. iii. 3 (as well as of the
arguments of *Treatise*, III. i. 1–2, that we shall examine in Chap. 3). Harrison pays much
attention to the warts; Snare is inclined to revise and reconstruct; each is much less san-
guine about the force of Hume's arguments than I am here. Briefer accounts are to be

honesty he poses the question 'What reason or motive have I to restore the money?' (*T* 479); in the second *Enquiry* he moves freely from talk of 'a reason why' (*E* 293) to talk of 'a motive to action' (*E* 294).² Standardly, he takes reasons or motives to be psychological states of an agent, states that are actual or potential causes of what the agent does. He argues explicitly, at *Treatise*, II. iii. 1–2, that the motive from which an agent acts is a cause of that action. Of course, in acting from one motive the agent may well be resisting the claims of competing motives. In any event, he will have other motives that, given their irrelevance to his circumstances at that time, will have no bearing on his conduct at that time. Motives or reasons for acting that the agent has but from which he does not act are potentially causes of action: they are psychological states that would cause him to act as they direct were certain further conditions to be met (including, trivially, the absence of stronger motives for some other action). The picture is a familiar one, and is elaborated in Hume's *Treatise* and *Enquiry* discussions of liberty and necessity.

As causes, reasons for action may be invoked to explain the actions they cause: action explanations that cite such reasons or motives are causal explanations. They are not merely causal explanations, however, for they possess explanatory features other causal explanations lack. When giving the reason for an agent's action one specifies what we may call (though Hume as it happens does not) a rational cause of that action. The twofold task of *Treatise*, II. iii. 3, is to characterize such rational causes of action and to elucidate their explanatory contribution. '[H]aving prov'd, that all actions of the will have particular causes, I proceed', Hume writes, 'to explain what these causes are, and how they operate' (*T* 412).

Hume contrasts two radically different kinds of causal theories of reasons for action. *Conativist* theories, while countenancing the contributions of the agent's beliefs, assign an essential role to desire. According to Hume, '[h]uman nature ... [is] compos'd of two principal parts, which are requisite in all its actions, the affections and understanding' (*T* 493). The ways in which the parts are requisite are displayed in an illustration from the second *Enquiry* (*E* 293) that makes plain Hume's intention, in the

found in: J. L. Mackie, *Hume's Moral Theory* (London, 1980), 44–75; Terence Penelhum, *Hume* (London, 1975), 131–50; Mark Platts, 'Hume and Morality as a Matter of Fact', *Mind*, 97 (1988), 189–204; and Barry Stroud, *Hume* (London, 1977), 154–92.
    ² All page references within parentheses in the text are to Hume's *A Treatise of Human Nature* [*T*], ed. L. A. Selby-Bigge; 2nd edn. with text revised by P. H. Nidditch (Oxford, 1978), or to his *Enquiries Concerning Human Understanding and Concerning the Principles of Morals* [*E*], ed. L. A. Selby-Bigge; 3rd edn. with text revised by P. H. Nidditch (Oxford, 1975). Unless otherwise noted, all italics within the quotations are Hume's.

context of reasons for action, to construe what he here terms affections more narrowly as desires. For Hume, a reason for action is a complex psychological state incorporating both a desire and a belief. Each constituent has a distinctive contribution to make. Having a desire, an agent is in a goal-setting or practical state: in having a desire he has a 'designed end or purpose', is not 'indifferent' to some or other actual or possible aspect of his situation, has a 'propensity' towards or an 'aversion' against some or other ways of behaving (*T* 414). In having a belief the agent is in a purportedly informational state: he represents, or purports to represent, the way things are. The belief and desire that jointly constitute a reason for action must, of course, be suitably related: the belief must present information pertinent to securing the goal set by desire. Specifically, the belief must represent the bearing of possible actions, or of the action to be explained, on the securing of what the agent desires. In Hume's example, the agent desires to keep his health and believes that exercising will contribute to his doing so: he has, then, a reason for exercising. (He may, of course, have reasons for not doing so as well.) If the reason thus constituted by his desire and belief causes the agent to exercise it is the reason from which he exercises and may be invoked to explain his doing so.[3]

Hume's model for the reasons from which an agent acts can be helpfully compared to the commonsensical model that Donald Davidson has developed with great care. 'Whenever', Davidson writes, 'someone does something for a reason . . . he can be characterized as (*a*) having some sort of pro attitude toward actions of a certain kind, and (*b*) believing (or knowing, perceiving, noticing, remembering) that his action is of that kind.'[4] Additionally, the pro-attitude and the related belief must have caused (in the right way, of course) the action they explain. On the face of it, Hume agrees with Davidson on the basic structure of a reason from which an agent acts, on much, at least, of what is required of the contents of the related belief and desire, and on the necessity of a causal connection. In practice (a point we shall return to in Chapter 2) he allows the term 'desire' to acquire the pantechnicon scope of Davidson's 'pro attitude'. Provided Davidson's pro-attitudes are, as Hume's desires clearly are, contrasted

---

[3] To constitute a reason from which the agent acted the desire and belief must, as many have noted, cause the action in the right way. Hume is silent both on this requirement and on the problems that so-called deviant causal chains pose for causal *analyses* of intentional action. See Donald Davidson, 'Freedom to Act', in *Essays on Actions and Events* (Oxford, 1980), 78–9, and D. M. Armstrong, 'Acting and Trying', in *The Nature of Mind and Other Essays* (Ithaca, NY, 1981).

[4] Donald Davidson, 'Actions, Reasons, and Causes', in *Essays on Actions and Events*, 3–4.

with beliefs and other cognitive states, Hume's and Davidson's theories are essentially the same.

In offering explanations of actions one may, of course, cut corners. There is no need to mention both desire and belief if mention of the one will enable an auditor to supply the other.[5] In explaining the agent's exercising it is enough to mention his belief that exercising will keep him healthy: that said, the rest is obvious. If obvious, of course, the rest is none the less essential. Hume adverts to the place of ellipsis, as also to the obvious fact that agents can offer explanations of their own actions, when he writes: 'Ask a man *why he uses exercise*; he will answer, *because he desires to keep his health*' (*E* 293).

An agent does something for a certain reason: he exercises in order to keep his health. His doing so is compatible with his having other reasons, not then efficacious, for doing that very thing: having promised his wife he would exercise he has that reason for exercising even though, let us assume, that is not in fact his reason for doing so. It is compatible with his having reasons, also inefficacious, for not doing what he does: disliking physical exertion he exercises none the less. He may also have further reasons for doing what he does. Our exercising agent may be seeking to avoid the pain consequent upon ill health. Or, in seeking health, he may be concerned to be fit for employment, thus able to earn his living, thus able to secure the pleasures he wants. Equivalently, he has reasons for (some of) the desires he has, these reasons being constituted by suitably related desires and beliefs: he wants to be fit for employment because he wants to earn his living and believes that being fit for employment is essential if he is to do so. A 'principal desire', Hume writes, 'may be attended with subordinate ones' (*T* 394).

The citation of further reasons for action, or of further reasons for desiring, must come to an end:

It is impossible there can be a progress *in infinitum*; and that one thing can always be a reason why another is desired. Something must be desirable on its own account, and because of its immediate accord or agreement with human sentiment and affection. (*E* 293)

No reason can be given for a desire for 'an ultimate end' (ibid.): no suitable belief/desire pair can be cited in explanation; nor can any belief be called upon to do so on its own. That beliefs alone are unavailing is the

---

[5] Indeed, one needn't actually mention either. Invoking an agent's patriotism as the motive of her action, one needn't mention the beliefs and desires that prompted that action; one none the less informs one's auditor of the sorts of desire and belief that did the job.

point of Hume's remark that 'the ultimate ends of human actions can never, in any case, be accounted for by *reason*, but recommend themselves entirely to the sentiments and affections of mankind, without any dependence on the intellectual faculties' (*E* 293). The rejected dependence on the intellectual faculties does not, we may take it, include dependence on the conceptual capacities that must be exercised if desires, whether principal or subordinate, are to have content.

An agent may explain her own action by explicit attribution of appropriate desires and beliefs. 'Why are you exercising?' 'I want to keep my health and I believe that exercising will enable me to do so.' She may also explain by giving voice, as we may say, or by giving expression to, those desires and beliefs. 'Why are you exercising?' 'Keeping healthy is desirable and exercising is a way to keep healthy.' In thus giving explicit expression to her reason for exercising she sketches an argument she takes to support her doing what she does: she offers a minimal justification for her action. To a first approximation, we may say that she gives voice, in effect, to a practical syllogism, the explicitly evaluative major premise of which expresses her desire, the descriptive minor premise her belief. To a first approximation, we may also say that the conclusion to the argument, in the setting envisaged, is an explicitly evaluative sentence expressing the exercising itself, an evaluative sentence suitably associated with the action that the agent's reason for action causes.[6]

This linking of explanation, expression, and argument goes beyond anything to be found quite explicitly in the *Treatise*, even if the picture it introduces seems to lie behind Hume's famous paragraph on the prospects for deriving 'ought' from 'is' (*T* 469–70). It does, however, help to highlight several important aspects of Hume's conativist theory of reasons for action: the notion that reasons rationalize the actions they cause; the structural relations amongst the differing elements that constitute the reason for action; the fundamental differences between desires and beliefs here marked by the presence or absence of explicitly evaluative terms in the sentences that express them. The linking also suggests a helpful bit of terminology. Noting the correspondence between argument and explanation we may say that the agent's desire, her desire to keep her health, is the *major* constituent in her reason for action and so plays the *major* role in that action's explanation; her belief that exercise is conducive to health is, correspondingly, the *minor* (but equally essential) constituent in that

---

[6] Better approximations will be attempted in Chap. 2, when volitions will be distinguished from desires. On the significance of distinguishing attribution and expression, see Donald Davidson, 'Intending', in *Essays on Actions and Events*, 86.

reason for acting. (An amended model can be developed for reasons for desire, with secondary desires taken as, or as expressed by, conclusions.)

Rejecting cognitivist theories of reasons for action and reasons for desire Hume writes that 'reason is perfectly inert and can never... produce any action or affection' (*T* 458). The phrase 'perfectly inert' must be handled with care. If read as 'causally inefficacious' (as the remainder of the passage suggests) it cannot represent Hume's considered view: within his conativist theory reason has a clear causal role, for beliefs are ineliminable constituents of an agent's reasons for doing and desiring. The phrase can only be an unhappy way of expressing the thought that beliefs cannot play a *particular* sort of causal role, the *major* role in reasons for action and desire that conativism assigns to desires. Hume elsewhere writes (the emphases are added): 'reason *alone* can never be a motive to any action of the will' (*T* 413), 'reason *alone* can never produce any action, or give rise to volition' (*T* 414), 'reason *alone*... can never have any such influence [on actions and the affections]' (*T* 457). Given Hume's conativist theory these claims are literally true, for desires are essential constituents in any reason for action or desire. The remarks can none the less mislead for it is also literally true, within Hume's conativist theory, that *desire* alone can never cause action or desire. Hume's claim, from which we started, that '[h]uman nature... [is] compos'd of two principal parts, which are requisite in all its actions, the affections and understanding' (*T* 493), while crucial to the interpretation of his views about motivation, can mislead by its use of 'affections'; it is also inexplicit on the respective roles of desire and belief. If succinct Humean summary is sought one must turn to one of the most notorious passages in the *Treatise*: 'Reason is, and ought only to be the slave of the passions, and can never pretend to any other office than to serve and obey them' (*T* 415). But one must read this, antiseptically, as the conativist thesis that reasons for action and desire are psychological complexes in which desire plays the major, belief the minor, role.

One gets a *cognitivist* theory of reasons for action (and of reasons for desire) by the simple expedient of substituting explicitly evaluative beliefs wherever Hume's conativist theory has or requires desires. An explicitly evaluative belief is one with explicitly evaluative content: a belief that it is desirable to keep one's health, for example, or that it would be good were poverty eradicated, or that one ought to improve the taste of the stew. On a *standard* cognitivist theory, as we may call it, the basic structure of reasons for action (as also of reasons for desire) mirrors the structure on which the conativist insists. Reasons for action are psychological complexes whose constituents have suitably related contents. One essential constituent plays a goal-setting or practical, the major, role; the other plays an informational, specifically the minor, role. As a cognitivist theory, however, it holds that beliefs play each of these essential roles. Explicitly evaluative beliefs play the major role and, unsurprisingly, are expressible by explicitly evaluative sentences providing (to a first approximation) the major premises of practical syllogisms: the belief that it is desirable to keep one's health is expressible using the sentence 'It is desirable to keep one's health'. Descriptive beliefs play just the minor role assigned them within a conativist theory: they are expressible in sentences (for example, the sentence 'Exercising is a way to keep one's health') that provide, within the model employed, the minor premises for practical syllogisms. In succinct parody of Hume, the standard cognitivist can claim that a descriptive belief is, and ought only to be, the slave of an explicitly evaluative one.

An austere theory, the standard cognitivist theory (as we are calling it) treats the conativist's desires as explicitly evaluative beliefs.[7] Its account of reasons for desire, then, is a theory of reasons for evaluative beliefs, one that introduces structures that mirror, once again, structures the conativist identifies. Its account of the concepts of competing, of alternative, and of further reasons, whether for action or desire, incorporates the all-important substitution of evaluative belief for desire. This substitution effects a dramatic philosophical transformation, for it introduces truth-evaluability for the psychological states that play the major role in explanations of action and desire.

Our austere standard theory provides a point of departure for the construction of a variety of alternative cognitivist accounts. A cognitivist can countenance desires distinct from evaluative beliefs, and with some (perhaps auxiliary) role to play in action explanation, while insisting that the presence of evaluative beliefs is in every instance essential. Another alternative approach allows cases in which desires distinct from evaluative beliefs play the major role in the generation of actions: in effect, it employs the standard cognitivist model for some cases of reasons for actions (for those involving an agent's moral evaluations, say), the conativist model for others. On this approach competition amongst reasons could be a matter of competition between desire and evaluative belief. Perhaps Hume has this alternative in mind when, attempting to represent traditional

[7] In parallel fashion, conativism treats some, at least, of the cognitivist's explicitly evaluative beliefs as desires. For a development of this thought, and an account of the qualification, see Chap. 4.

claims about 'the combat of passion and reason', he remarks the rational agent's alleged need to 'regulate his actions by reason' and so to resist when 'any other motive or principle challenge[s] the direction of conduct' (*T* 413).

Other clearly cognitivist departures from the standard theory can be, indeed have been, devised. A cognitivist theory of reasons for action, if wedded to a naturalistic theory of evaluation, can combine requiring the explanatory structures common to conativist and standard cognitivist theories with allowing essentially descriptive beliefs in the major position. A cognitivist theory can reject both the major/minor structure and the requirement of explicitly evaluative beliefs: explanation, it may be said, is merely a matter of the citation of descriptive beliefs of the sort to which other theories assign the so-called minor role. Such a theory can allow that we in fact cite explicitly evaluative beliefs, or desires, in the explanation of actions, but maintain that such citings introduce no genuinely explanatory entities other than the descriptive beliefs the theory takes to be sufficient for explanation.

Variant standard and non-standard cognitivist theories can be devised by the introduction of restrictions governing the epistemic or logical standing, or the provenance, or the structure of the content, of the theory's explanatory beliefs. Are they, can they be, beliefs in necessary truths? Are they products of ratiocination, deductive or otherwise? Could they have their source in intuition, or in perception? Must they be relational? The possibilities proliferate, and include specifically rationalist theories. What links each of the resultant cognitivist theories to each of the others, and distinguishes each from conativism as defined, is the thesis that an agent's beliefs *can* suffice for the generation of her actions. Common to each cognitivist proposal is the thought that truth-evaluable psychological states *can* suffice (and not merely in the way elliptical conativist explanations can suffice) for the explanation of what an individual does.

2. HUME'S FIRST CONATIVIST ARGUMENT

Hume's first conativist argument at *Treatise*, II. iii. 3, amounts to a reflection on actual explanatory practice, its point being to elicit recognition that, some appearances to the contrary notwithstanding, that practice is, indeed must be, as the conativist describes it. 'Reason', he concludes constructively, 'is, and ought only to be the slave of the passions, and can never pretend to any other office than to serve and obey them' (*T* 415). If conativism is true, cognitivism, in any of its forms, is false: 'reason alone', he concludes negatively, 'can never be a motive to any action of the will' (*T* 413). As a corollary of his negative, anti-cognitivist, claim it follows that 'reason alone . . . is . . . incapable of preventing volition, or of disputing the preference with any passion or emotion' (*T* 414–15): beliefs alone, that is to say, cannot constitute competing reasons for action.

Hume begins by focusing on the role theoretical reasoning—reasoning that involves transitions amongst beliefs—plays in the generation of action. Having earlier held that modes of mathematical and causal reasoning more or less exhaust the possibilities on the theoretical side (*T* 69–74), he here advances a number of complementary claims: that in action contexts agents engage in theoretical reasoning in order to determine how to secure their objectives; that the only bearing such reasoning has on action is through the contribution it makes to the determination of the means to antecedent goals; and that some at least of the products of theoretical reasoning, some of the beliefs to which it gives rise, have a bearing on the steps the agent takes towards securing his goals. A goal-setting psychological state, he writes, 'making us cast our view on every side, comprehends whatever objects are connected with its original one by the relation of cause and effect' and so 'reasoning takes place to discover this relation' (*T* 414). So much is obvious. Perhaps it is obvious that causal, or causal-cum-mathematical, reasoning—the modes of relevant theoretical reasoning that Hume allows—could make no other substantive contribution to the production of action. In any event, it is plain that beliefs produced by theoretical reasoning of this sort can be goal-relevant beliefs and so can contribute to the explanation of actions. Clearly some such beliefs can play the role assigned, both by conativist and by standard cognitivist theories, to beliefs expressible by the minor premise of a practical argument.

If theoretical reasoning is rightly restricted to the essentially causal and mathematical kinds Hume countenances, it may well be that it cannot, even if goal-relevant, set goals for action. It seems clear, at any rate, that it cannot generate beliefs that can play the *major* role in action explanations viewed along conativist or standard cognitivist lines. But is Hume right to restrict the scope of theoretical reasoning in this way? On the face of it, that restriction begs the question against a cognitivist who maintains that theoretical reasoning can be the source of explicitly evaluative beliefs. An additional difficulty is that, in focusing on theoretical *reasoning*, Hume fails to address a standard cognitivist who holds that explicitly evaluative beliefs can provide the major components in reasons for action even if they arise not from reasoning but in some other way: it is their content, such a cognitivist can say, not their provenance, that suits evaluative beliefs for their action-generating role.

The central issue must concern belief, not the contribution of theoretical reasoning. Let us reckon, then, with the possibility of beliefs that arise not from reasoning but in other ways that Hume recognizes: from 'intuition' (*T* 70), say, or from 'perception' (*T* 73). Let us reckon, as well, with beliefs other than causal and mathematical ones. At the very least, let us countenance beliefs concerned with any of the seven so-called philosophical relations that Hume catalogues: 'resemblance, identity, relations of time and place, proportion in quantity and number, degrees in any quality, contrariety, and causation' (*T* 69, italics omitted). Hume offers no comparable classification of non-relational properties, but recognizes, as he must, the existence of non-relational beliefs, including existential ones: let us countenance these as well. This more accommodating approach to beliefs and their contents puts obstacles in the way of Hume's begging the question.[8] Of course, if Hume is right, this more accommodating approach will not materially affect the decision between conativism and cognitivism: for Hume, *no* beliefs, not just no causal or mathematical beliefs, can function as major elements in action explanations. Since this more inclusive claim clearly escapes the reach of Hume's remarks about causal and mathematical reasoning, however, he has in fact offered no argument, thus far, in its support. Is there some other way in which reflection on explanatory practice can legitimate Hume's inclusive conclusion?

It is obvious, according to Hume, that someone with a reason for acting in a certain way is, at least in part, in what we have called a goal-directed, a practical, psychological state with respect to acting in that way. The individual is not 'indifferent' (*T* 414) to acting in the way in question, is 'in favour' (*E* 286) of so acting, has an 'inclination' (*T* 419) towards, a 'propensity' (*T* 414) towards, or 'appetite' (*T* 437) for, acting in that way, is subject to an 'impulse received from appetite or inclination' (*E* 294), is inclined to 'give preference' (*E* 286) to acting in that way. The individual has an 'end or purpose' (*T* 414) or a 'design' (*T* 475), finds the envisaged situation 'desirable' (*E* 293). Having a reason for acting, the individual is 'carry'd to . . . embrace' (*T* 414) some object, has a 'propensity, which unites . . . [him] to the object' (*T* 439), has a 'desire of approaching' (*T* 394–5) that object. The individual has, we may say, a

[8] It also introduces issues that bear importantly on the representation of Hume's arguments against moral cognitivism. See Chap. 3.

pro-attitude with respect to acting in the way in question. What could such a pro-attitude be but a desire?

Someone with a reason *not* to act in a certain way is in a similarly goal-directed, practical, state: Hume writes of 'aversion' (T 414), of 'averse motions of the mind' (T 574), of being 'carry'd to avoid' (T 414), of a 'propensity, which ... separates us from' (T 439) an object. The individual has a con-attitude with respect to acting in the way in question. For simplicity's sake we may take a con-attitude to be a pro-attitude with respect to not acting in a certain way. What could such a pro-attitude be but a desire with negative content, a desire not to act in a certain way?

This is not to say that someone with a desire necessarily does what he has a desire to do. In a given setting he may well have stronger desires directed towards other actions, other objects. He has a desire to eat an apple; he has a stronger desire for an orange; and he is presented with the choice of one or the other. She wants to continue windsurfing, but her publisher's deadline looms. He wants to leave; he also wants to stay. To have a desire is to be moved, other things equal, to act in a certain way. So moved, an agent has no more than prima facie reason for acting as she desires.[9]

It is obvious, Hume claims, that when someone acts for a reason her desires provide an essential ingredient in the explanation of what she does. It is equally obvious, he claims, that desire-relevant beliefs are also essential. He emphasizes causal beliefs about means to ends, writing of beliefs about 'certain actions as means of obtaining ... [a] desir'd good' (T 417), of beliefs about 'means . . . for the design'd end' (T 416). But he alludes to constitutive beliefs as well. Wanting to eat a fruit 'of an excellent relish', and believing that to eat the proffered apple would be to do just that, the agent eats (T 417). Whether constitutive or causal, however, belief is essential: granted that the agent's reason for eating the apple is that (putting the point elliptically, and in Hume's conativist way) he wants to eat a fruit 'of an excellent relish', he must believe that the apple is such a fruit. Granted that his reason for eating the apple is that (again putting the point elliptically) he believes it to be a fruit of excellent relish, it must also, of course, be true that he has a 'propensity' or 'inclination', in short a desire, to eat such a fruit.

Reflection on the practice of explanation reveals that the function of the practical element in reasons for action, the function of desire, is to set the agent's goals. That of the cognitive component, the agent's beliefs, is

---

[9] For Hume's handling of prima facie reasons, see Chap. 2.

to represent the world in ways relevant to the securing or the accomplishment of those goals. Given this distribution of functions the structure of a reason for action, and so the pattern of an action explanation, emerges. What beliefs bear on the agent's actions depend on what goals the agent has. Desire has, then, a certain structural priority over belief: it plays the major, belief the equally essential but minor, role. Conativism, Hume concludes, holds for the characterization of reasons for action.

He draws a corollary, a 'consequence' that is 'necessary' (*T* 415) in the sense of following from the conclusion (more precisely, from the negative component of the conclusion) just reached. Reason is 'incapable of . . . disputing the preference with any passion or emotion' and so is incapable of 'preventing volition' (*T* 414–15): beliefs cannot, by themselves, provide reasons for action that could compete with, perhaps dominate, reasons for action comprising, in the manner just described, linked desires and beliefs. Beliefs cannot prevent a volition, and so an action, that an agent has some reason to perform by providing her with a reason for not performing that action (perhaps a reason for performing some other, incompatible, action). Belief could provide a *competing* reason for action only if it could provide a reason for action *sans phrase*. It could prevent an action, in the sense intended, only if it could (by itself) motivate one. But this, by the main part of Hume's first argument, belief cannot do. 'Nothing can oppose or retard the impulse of passion', he writes, 'but a contrary impulse; and if this contrary impulse ever arises from reason, that latter faculty must have an original influence on the will, and must be able to cause, as well as hinder any act of volition' (*T* 415). But, given the main argument, 'reason has no original influence' (ibid.). Reason alone, which is to say belief alone, cannot, then, provide any reason for or against action at all.

To be sure, there is a clear sense in which reason *can* prevent volition or action. Change of belief, by changing one's reasons for action, can change what one does or is inclined to do. A change in constitutive beliefs can prevent one's doing what one otherwise would have done: were our agent who wants to eat a fruit 'of excellent relish' to come to believe that the proffered apple would not fit the bill, he would not do what he otherwise would have done. So can a change in one's causal beliefs: 'I may will the performance of certain actions as means of obtaining any desir'd good; but as my willing of these actions is only secondary, and founded on the supposition, that they are causes of the propos'd effect; as soon as I discover the falshood of that supposition, they must become indifferent to me' (*T* 417). That one ceases to have a given reason for action, simply in virtue of ceasing to have the requisite belief, is, of course, a quite different matter from having a reason for action simply in virtue of having a belief. The former possibility is a consequence of conativism; the latter is a possibility Hume's conativism rules out.

Given Hume's corollary, traditional talk of 'the combat of passion and reason' (*T* 413), interpreted as Hume interprets it, rests on a fundamental mistake in philosophical psychology, a mistake about the character of reasons for action. So, too, does the traditional doctrine that one ought to 'give the preference to reason' (ibid.), if construed as the requirement to act from reasons that belief alone provides. Taken 'strictly and philosophically' (*T* 415) these traditional views, as well as any that presuppose them, must, if conativism is correct, be rejected.

When, later, Hume refers back to the argument of *Treatise*, II. iii. 3, he claims to have there 'prov'd that reason is perfectly inert, and can never either prevent or produce any action or affection' (*T* 458). Assuming the 'affections' here in question to be 'desires', has he offered any such proof that *they* cannot be wholly based on belief? He has given an argument for conativism in the case of reasons for action. Has he given any such argument for a conativist account of reasons, not for actions, but for desires? Failing the provision of such an argument, it seems clear, he will have left room for the would-be cognitivist about reasons for action to press for cognitivism at a more fundamental level. Suppose conativism to be true of reasons for action. If cognitivism can be true of reasons for desire, then the desires that prompt action can themselves be based, not on belief and desire, but on belief alone.

Hume appears not to give the needed argument at *Treatise*, II. iii. 3. This surprising lacuna can be filled, however, by considerations akin to those he uses for the case of reasons for action. An agent exercises because he wants to preserve his health and believes that exercising will help him so do. Why does he want to preserve his health? Perhaps because he wants to earn his living and believes that continued good health is essential for that. The desire to earn his living would not by itself (save elliptically) explain his desire to preserve his health. Nor (save elliptically) would the belief that continuing in good health is essential to his earning his living. Counterfactual reflections prompt a recognition that suitably linked desires and beliefs are needed if desires are to be explained by giving the agent's reasons for having them. Reflection on the respective functions of the explanatory desires and beliefs suggests an explanatory structure paralleling that for the case of action: desire plays a major role, belief a minor role, and the resultant desire is, or corresponds to, the conclusion of a suitable argument. Giving voice to his desires and beliefs the agent can say: 'It is desirable that I earn my living; continuing in good health is essential to my doing so; it is desirable, then, that I continue in good health.' This account is compatible, of course, with recognition of (indeed, with the requirement of) ultimate desires, desires for which the agent has no reason, desires for which she can provide no argument. Conativism for desire complements conativism for action.

Does the argument for either amount, in Hume's expression, to a 'proof'? For the case of reasons for action Hume has provided, it seems, a nearly compelling case for several crucial theses: that action explanations require both major and minor psychological constituents in reasons for action; that these constituents must be suitably structured and suitably linked in terms of their contents; and that they must play the fundamental functional roles (respectively, the practical and the informational roles) that we have identified. The case is *nearly* compelling: there is *some* — if, as we shall see, not itself compelling — reason to wonder whether what has been assigned the major role must be taken as an independent causal factor.[10] Hume's first argument does, however, clearly place the burden of proof on those who would reject what is common to conativism and standard cognitivism.

The trouble, of course, lies precisely in the fact that the theses just listed are ones that conativist and standard cognitivist share. Where the theories differ is in their treatment of the major element, the element they agree has a practical, goal-setting, function. For the conativist this item is a desire; for the standard cognitivist it is an explicitly evaluative belief. According to the conativist, the agent expresses a desire when she says 'It is desirable to preserve one's health'; according to the standard cognitivist, she expresses a belief with explicitly evaluative content, the belief that it is desirable to preserve one's health. On the face of it, Hume simply assumes, contrary to the evidence of common practice, that practicality demands desire. In asking what else but desire could provide the practical component of a reason for action he ignores what seem to be clear cases of action-prompting beliefs. He ignores evidence that evaluative beliefs fall within the pantechnicon scope of pro-attitudes.

The standard cognitivist counters with a conception of practical, precisely because explicitly evaluative, beliefs. On the face of it, one *can* explain an agent's exercising by noting that she *thinks* — that is, she *believes* — it is desirable to preserve her health. (She must, of course, also believe that

---

[10] See the discussion of Nagel's views in Sect. 4 below.

exercise is health-preserving.) Explicitly evaluative beliefs *can* provide the practical component in a reason for action. Aping Hume's argument, the standard cognitivist asks what else could? Hume can insist that there are clear cases in which desire plays the major role: surely an agent can exercise because he wants to preserve his health, not because, say, he has the explicitly evaluative belief that he ought to. This conceded, Hume can insist that the objective of simplification for theories demands that what seem to be evaluative beliefs (for example, what seems to be a belief that one ought to preserve one's health) be construed as desires. In effect, he can use agreed criteria for theoretical adequacy to legitimate generalizing from common cases in which desires are invoked in the explanation of actions.

Unfortunately for Hume, the standard cognitivist can argue in isomorphic fashion. Since evaluative beliefs can obviously play the major role in action explanations, considerations of theoretical simplification demand that putative desires be read as explicitly evaluative beliefs. Moreover, that this, not Hume's, is the way to simplify is suggested by the fact that (as both theories agree) the practical, or goal-setting, states in question find expression in explicitly evaluative sentences ('It is desirable to preserve one's health'). One uses just such sentences in specifying the contents of explicitly evaluative beliefs ('She believes that it is desirable to preserve her health'); by contrast, one uses descriptive sentences, not explicitly evaluative ones, when identifying the contents of desires ('She desires that she preserve her health', *not* 'She desires that it is desirable to preserve her health'). The shared procedure for identifying the major constituent in a reason for action encourages the standard cognitivist's construal of desires as evaluative beliefs.

Cognitivism can compromise: it can countenance independent practical status for both evaluative beliefs and desires. We noted the possibility of such a cognitivist departure from *standard* cognitivism in Section 1. It suffices for the truth of cognitivism that beliefs *can* play the major role in an action explanation. Hume's conativism must be uncompromising: to allow the possibility of independent practical status for evaluative beliefs would resurrect the prospect of a 'combat of passion and reason'. To secure conativism, then, he must find a basis for generalizing, perhaps a way of effecting theoretical simplification, that is not open to a cognitivist theory.

Conativism for the distinguishable case of reasons for desire encounters similar obstacles. How is Hume to rule out the possibility that explicitly evaluative beliefs constitute the major constituents in reasons for desire? Granted an agent may want to preserve her health because she wants to earn her living. But what of an agent who thinks she ought to, or that it would be a good thing to, earn her living? Neither the presence of seemingly clear cases in which desires are cited in explanation of desires, nor recourse to the virtues of theoretical simplification, will suffice for Hume's purposes: here, as before, it seems the cognitivist can match his argument step for step.

For help Hume must turn to his second argument.

3. A SECOND CONATIVIST ARGUMENT

He requires an argument that will enable him to reject both the standard cognitivist's construal of action-explaining desires as evaluative beliefs and the compromise suggestion that both evaluative beliefs and desires can function as practical constituents in reasons for action. What he offers amounts to a more profound exploration of the conditions on giving the reasons for an action, an exploration that focuses on the concept of truth-evaluability. It is this, of the two arguments of *Treatise*, II. iii. 3, that Hume repeats when, in Book III, he turns to an analysis of specifically moral reasons for action. This intimation of the second argument's importance perhaps reveals his sense of the hobbling limitations to which the first argument is subject.

Much about his second argument is unclear, but on two structural points Hume is helpfully plain. (1) His second argument, while distinct from the first, has the very same conclusions as the first. Introducing his second argument at *Treatise*, II. iii. 3, he purports to 'confirm' the claim that '[r]eason is . . . the slave of the passions' (*T* 415): it is another argument, that is to say, for his constructive conativist conclusion. Repeating the argument at *Treatise*, III. i. 1, he identifies it as one of 'the arguments, by which I have prov'd, that reason . . . can never either prevent or produce any action' (*T* 457–8): it is another argument, in short, for his negative anti-cognitivist conclusion and its corollary. (2) The second argument contains a crucial premise that is itself viewed as the conclusion to an argument, and so may be called—at least for the nonce—an intermediate conclusion. It is in this intermediate conclusion that Hume focuses on the truth-evaluability of psychological states.

Having a firm sense of its function and structure encourages one to make something hard-edged of an argument that, it must be said, Hume has presented in an impressionistic, an insufficiently explicit, at places a seriously misleading fashion. It encourages one to suspect that insight has here outstripped execution, and so to attempt to set out, on Hume's behalf and with clearly Humean materials, an argument that will in fact serve the purposes his second argument is supposed to serve.[11] In constructing such an argument two conditions, in particular, will have to be met. First, the argument cannot assume that desires are essential elements in reasons for action: it cannot assume what it is designed to establish. Second, the argument's truth-evaluability premise (its intermediate conclusion) must contribute in a comprehensible way not only to the argument's negative, but also to its constructive, conclusion: it must contribute not only to non-cognitivism but also, specifically, to Hume's conativism.

Hume gives the argument for his intermediate conclusion, for the truth-evaluability premise of his second argument, twice. In the earlier version, at *Treatise*, II. iii. 3, he writes:

A passion is an original existence, or, if you will, modification of existence, and contains not any representative quality, which renders it a copy of any other existence or modification. When I am angry, I am actually possest with the passion, and in that emotion have no more a reference to any other object, than when I am thirsty, or sick, or more than five foot high. 'Tis impossible, therefore, that this passion can be oppos'd by, or be contradictory to truth and reason; since this contradiction consists in the disagreement of ideas, consider'd as copies, with those objects, which they represent. (*T* 415)

He gives the later version at *Treatise*, III. i. 1:

Reason is the discovery of truth and falshood. Truth or falshood consists in an agreement or disagreement either to the *real* relations of ideas, or to *real* existence and matter of fact. Whatever, therefore, is not susceptible of this agreement or disagreement is incapable of being true or false, and can never be an object of our reason. Now 'tis evident our passions . . . [and] volitions . . . are not susceptible of any such agreement or disagreement; being original facts and realities, compleat in themselves, and implying no reference to other . . . [facts and reali-

---

[11] It also encourages scepticism towards Annette Baier's dismissal of the paragraph in which the argument makes the first of its two appearances as a 'very silly paragraph that has perversely dominated the interpretation of his moral psychology', an 'unfortunate paragraph' in an 'unfortunately famous section' of the *Treatise*. See *A Progress of Sentiments: Reflections on Hume's Treatise* (Cambridge, Mass., 1991), 160, 164, 173. It should also make one reluctant too readily to endorse the first half of Terence Penelhum's judgement (addressed at least in part to this argument) that this is 'one of Hume's worst arguments, and unfortunately one of his most important'. See *David Hume: An Introduction to his Philosophical System* (West Lafayette, Ind., 1992), 143.

ties]. 'Tis impossible, therefore, they can be pronounced either true or false, and be either contrary or conformable to reason. (*T* 458)

Some preliminary clarifications are in order. First, the passions in question are desires. Hume's argument requires this reading and the illustration he uses—a passion, anger, that Hume classifies as a desire (*T* 367, 382, 591)—supports it.

Second, in characterizing desires and volitions as 'original existence[s], or . . . modification[s] of existence', or as 'original facts and realities', Hume's point is simply to deny that they are, in a sense to be explained, 'copies' or representations of items other than themselves.

Third, in writing, in the earlier version, of 'the disagreement of ideas' Hume is concerned not with so-called 'relations of [i.e. among] ideas' but with a relation that obtains between ideas, construed as copies, and what they (purport to) copy. Of course he does, in the later version, contrast '*real* relations of ideas' and '*real* existence and matter of fact'. In doing so, however, he merely contrasts alternative possible terms in the relation, just mentioned, between ideas, construed as copies, and what they (purport to) copy: he contrasts the case in which ideas copy, or purport to copy, relations of ideas with that in which they copy, or purport to copy, matters of fact.

Fourth, he uses phrases such as 'conformable to reason', on the one hand, 'contrary . . . to reason' or 'contradictory to truth and reason', on the other, as equivalent to 'true' and 'false', respectively.[12]

Fifth, in claiming that desires and volitions have 'no reference to other [facts and realities]', 'no . . . reference to any other object', he can have no concern to deny that they have objects or content. Such a denial would contribute in no way to securing Hume's negative, specifically his main anti-cognitivist, conclusion. How could the claim that neither desires nor volitions have content contribute to the conclusion that beliefs cannot, alone, constitute reasons for action? More importantly, such a denial would prove an insurmountable obstacle in the path of an argument for his conativism, for that theory requires appropriate relations amongst the contents of the desires and beliefs that constitute reasons for action. For all that, it may be said, Hume could have been confused about his argument's needs and so denied content to desires and volitions. In the absence of compelling reason to do so, however, charitable interpretation counsels against the attribution of confusion on a point of such central

---

[12] This conforms to his usage at *Treatise*, i. iv. 2 and 4, when discussing scepticism with respect to the external world. For an examination of that usage see my *Hume's Philosophy of Mind* (Edinburgh, 1980), 10–19.

importance to his philosophical psychology. It must be admitted that there are aspects of his explicit theories of desire and volition that on the face of it are incompatible with his granting them content. We shall attend to *this* problem of possible inconsistency in Chapter 2; meanwhile, we must let the needs of his central argument for conativism set the limits for reasonable interpretation. Is Hume too quick, then, and too inexplicit, in his remarks about the absence of 'reference' to facts and realities, or to objects? Of course. But that just counsels caution in interpretation, and a patient search for the thesis about desire and volition on which, even if it is imperfectly expressed in the brief paragraphs that contain his argument for his intermediate conclusion, Hume makes his second argument turn.

Taking these clarifications as read, the argument actually articulated in each of the two paragraphs cited runs, succinctly stated, as follows: It is evident that desires do not purport to represent or picture anything (any matter of fact, any relation of ideas); but to be truth-evaluable a psychological state must purport to represent or picture something; it follows that desires are not truth-evaluable. Surely Hume envisages, as a companion argument, the following: Beliefs purport to represent or picture something (some matter of fact, some relation of ideas); beliefs are, then, truth-evaluable. With his argument read this way, Hume's intermediate conclusion is the unsurprising, surely innocuous, claim: Beliefs are, desires are not, evaluable in terms of truth and falsity.

This rendering of Hume's apparent argument for his intermediate conclusion has the virtue of taking truth-evaluability as a property intelligibly attributed to a psychological state: it simply sets, as a condition on such attribution, the psychological state's possession of the prior property of purporting to represent or picture some situation (some matter of fact, some relation of ideas); and it takes beliefs to possess, desires not to possess, that property. But it raises many more questions than it answers. What need has Hume to argue for the innocuous claim that beliefs are, desires are not, truth-evaluable? Why argue that desires are not truth-evaluable while taking it to be evident that they do not purport to represent or picture anything? So far as the need for argument goes, the situation is surely just the reverse of this. And surely it is at least arguable that desires *do*, in virtue of their content, picture or represent the situations that desirers desire, situations that, were they to obtain, would satisfy those desires. Whatever be said in answer to these questions about his argument for his intermediate conclusion, what can Hume possibly have in mind when offering *that* conclusion as a *premise* in his wider (his second conativist) argument to his constructive and negative conclusions, and to his corollary? What bearing has the non-truth-evaluability of desires on the conclusion that only desires can provide the major constituent in a reason for action? How get from the intermediate conclusion that beliefs can be assessed in terms of truth and falsity to the anti-cognitivist conclusion that beliefs cannot, by themselves, constitute reasons for action? Hume nowhere says just how the argument *from* what we are calling his intermediate conclusion *to* his conativist conclusions is to proceed: he provides the argument just sketched for the intermediate conclusion, and leaves the rest to the reader. What is it, precisely, that the reader is to supply?

To make headway here we must seek a conception of representation that—if only insecurely Hume's—could conceivably do the job Hume clearly intends the notion of representation to do. Crucially, that conception must, by marking a fundamental difference between beliefs and desires, explain their difference with respect to truth-evaluability; and in doing so, it must point the way to Hume's conativism. For reasons adumbrated we must acknowledge—even as we seek this other conception of representation—that *both* beliefs and desires have representational content, and even that a given belief and a given desire (minor caveats registered) can have the very same representational content. (Jones believes that the picnic will finish by six o'clock and desires that the rain hold off until then: the differing 'that' clauses identify, we may say, the differing representational contents of the belief and the desire. He both desires and believes that the rain will hold off until six: his belief and his desire have the same representational content.) In seeking the needed conception of representation we must also see in Hume's ostensible *argument* for an innocuous intermediate conclusion the theoretically significant *explication* of an obvious fact.

Restricting ourselves to psychological states with representational content, let us distinguish amongst them in terms of what some modern writers have called 'direction of fit'.[13] Some such psychological states have the

---

[13] The terminology is John Searle's, *Intentionality: An Essay in the Philosophy of Mind* (Cambridge, 1983) and 'What is an Intentional State?', *Mind*, 88 (1979), 74–92; the basic conception is to be found in G. E. M. Anscombe, *Intention* (Oxford, 1963). I. L. Humberstone provides an exceptionally useful account in 'Direction of Fit', *Mind*, 101 (1992), 59–83. I have employed the notion of direction of fit in two essays concerned with Hume's theory of volitions: 'Hume's Volitions', in Vincent Hope (ed.), *Philosophers of the Scottish Enlightenment* (Edinburgh, 1984), 70–90; 'Locke, Hume and the Nature of Volitions', *Hume Studies* (1985 Suppl.), 15–51. On the question of its application to Hume's theory of desire see Michael Smith, 'The Humean Theory of Motivation', *Mind*, 96 (1987), 36–61, and Platts, 'Hume and Morality as a Matter of Fact', esp. 200–2.

mind-to-world direction of fit. It is incumbent on them to fit the world. Their role is to provide an accurate representation or picture of the way the world is. By way of its representational content, a given belief (or other *cognitive* state) represents the world in a given way: differing in its representational content, the belief that the picnic will be finished by six o'clock provides a quite different representation of the world from that provided by the belief that the world will be made safe for democracy. The belief that the picnic will end by six o'clock differs, in the way it represents the world to be, from the belief that it will not. Given its direction of fit, a belief succeeds if (or in so far as) it represents the world accurately, if the world is as it represents it to be. Given its direction of fit, a belief succeeds if in fact it fits the world. In short, it succeeds if it is *true*. A false belief fails by failing to fit the world. Remedy requires change of belief, not a change in the world. Specific conditions on a belief's truth, and so its success, are set by its representational content.

Other psychological states have the *world-to-mind* direction of fit. From the perspective of the subjects in such states, it is incumbent on the world to fit them. Their role is to provide a representation, not of how the world is, but of how the subject requires it to be. By way of its representational content a desire (or other *conative* state) requires the world to be in a certain way: the desire that it rain requires the world to be one way, the desire that it be sunny another. Given its direction of fit, a desire succeeds if (or in so far as) the world is as it requires it to be. It succeeds in so far as the world fits it. It succeeds not by being true but by being *satisfied*. It fails in so far as the world fails to fit the conditions the desire sets. From the subject's perspective, remedy requires change in the way the world is, not a change in what the subject wants.[14] The specific conditions on the success of a desire are set by that desire's representational content. While not conditions on the truth of the desire—for desires are not truth-evaluable—they are truth-conditions for corresponding beliefs, that is, for beliefs with corresponding content. Roughly, they are truth-conditions for beliefs that would be true were the desire satisfied.

Our division of psychological states in terms of direction of fit corresponds (at least to a first approximation) to a division based on a difference of truth-involving attitudes directed towards identical representational contents. An individual may *hold true* the proposition that it will rain before the week is out. Another individual may *want true* the proposition that it rains before the week is out. The former believes, the latter de-

[14] Here the story must be complicated to accommodate change of desire consequent upon recognition of the impossibility of satisfaction.

sires, that it will rain before the week is out. The latter's desire will be met just in case the former's belief is true: the belief's truth-conditions are the desire's satisfaction-conditions. The belief is, the desire is not, evaluable as true or false: the difference in attitude towards the truth of propositions explains the difference in the truth-evaluability of the attitudes themselves. We shall later have occasion to think more carefully about this conception of differing attitudes towards the truth of propositions.[15] For the present it is sufficient simply to have introduced the conception: its availability underlines the availability of the more-nearly-Humean notion of direction of fit.[16]

Our contrast of directions of fit provides a conception of representation that, while not being reducible to that of representational content, enables Hume to hold that beliefs do, whereas desires do not, in the requisite sense, represent or picture anything (some matter of fact, some relation of ideas). On this conception, beliefs represent and desires do not precisely because the former have, while the latter do not, the mind-to-world direction of fit. Our contrast allows Hume to insist on the narrowly representational character of some psychological states (beliefs), and the non-representational character of others (desires), despite their shared possession of representational content (including, at times, their shared possession of common representational content). It follows him in focusing on truth-evaluability and in linking talk of representation with talk of truth. It offers an explication of the obvious difference in truth-evaluability between desires and beliefs. And it provides a route from Hume's discussion of truth-evaluability to his anti-cognitivist, and to his conativist, conclusions.

It provides a route to his anti-cognitivist thesis that beliefs, alone, cannot constitute a reason for action. As cognitive states, beliefs have the mind-to-world direction of fit. Their function is accurately to represent the way the world is. That being so, how can they serve the practical or goal-setting task that, as conativist and standard cognitivist agree, the major constituent in a reason for action must perform?

That task calls for a psychological state with the world-to-mind direction of fit: it calls for a psychological state that, from the prospective agent's perspective, requires the world to be a certain way and so, in an appropriate setting, requires her to act in ways designed to ensure that the world fits the mind's requirements. It calls, that is to say, for a desire

[15] See Chap. 2.
[16] For the distinction of attitudes with respect to the truth of propositions see Donald Davidson, *Expressing Evaluations*, The Lindley Lecture (Lawrence, Kan., 1984), 8–9.

(in the extended sense in which we, with Hume, are using 'desire'). Of course in requiring actions that would ensure the mind's requirements being met, desire must be aided by relevant beliefs that, by meeting their own need to fit the causally relevant features of the world, enable the agent to act in ways apt to effect the satisfaction of desire.

Reflection on the conditions on acting for a reason, and of explaining an action by citing the agent's reason for acting, when deepened by reflection on the concept of direction of fit, leads directly to the conativist conception of reasons for action. (Perhaps that is why Hume neglected to spell out the steps.) It leads to the thought that beliefs, because truth-evaluable, are insufficient for the explanation of action. It leads, more constructively, to a recognition that only desires (in our, and Hume's, extended sense of 'desire') can play the major role in reasons for action even if desires alone cannot constitute such reasons. In effect, it leads to a recognition that an agent must both set requirements for the world (by having desires), and (by having suitably related beliefs) attempt to meet requirements set by the world, if she is to have reason for doing what she does. Reflection on direction of fit, that is to say, clears a path to Hume's conativism.

It warrants following Hume, not the standard cognitivist, in the reduction of psychological states that a concern for theoretical simplification recommends. The standard cognitivist reduces the putative desires that serve to explain actions (for example, the desire to preserve one's health) to explicitly evaluative beliefs (for example, the belief that it is desirable to preserve one's health). Hume's conativist theory, in striking contrast, reduces what appear to be explicitly evaluative beliefs to desires. Reflection on direction of fit demands reduction in the Humean, not the cognitivist, direction. Were they genuinely beliefs, the cognitivist's explicitly evaluative beliefs could not play the major role in reasons for action for they would have the mind-to-world direction of fit. On the other hand, if they can play the major role in action explanations—and it seems clear that they can—they cannot be beliefs, for, playing that major role, they must have the world-to-mind direction of fit. With the concept of direction of fit Hume can fill the crucial gap in his first conativist argument.

Having differing directions of fit, desires and beliefs cannot play one another's roles in the constitution of reasons for action. So Hume can write here, with a confidence his first conativist argument could not warrant, that 'an active principle can never be founded on an inactive' (*T* 457). And he can write that being 'inactive in itself', reason 'must remain so in all its shapes and appearances, whether it exerts itself in natural or moral subjects, whether it considers the powers of external bodies, or the actions of rational beings' (*T* 457).[17] Having the mind-to-world direction of fit, beliefs cannot have the world-to-mind direction of fit. Having the former, they have it no matter what their subject-matter. But this is to anticipate our later discussion of specifically moral reasons for action.

What of reasons for desire? On the assumption that reasons for desire must be, in part, practical or goal-setting states—an assumption common to the conativist and standard cognitivist—conativism holds for reasons for desire just as for reasons for action. In so far as they are goal-setting states they, just as the desires they help explain, must have the world-to-mind direction of fit.

Hume's second conativist argument, assuming it is sound, subverts not only standard cognitivism but also each of the non-standard forms of cognitivism identified earlier. It rules out the theory that descriptive beliefs of the sort to which the conativist and standard cognitivist assign the minor role can suffice (non-elliptically) for explanation, provided they have suitable descriptive content. Surely, the proponent of such a cognitivist theory claims, an agent's beliefs that an action would be in her interest, or that a situation would be a source of great pain, or that another is in need, provide her with reasons for acting? As beliefs, however, these have the mind-to-world direction of fit and so cannot set goals for action. For someone not concerned for the needs of others the belief that another is in need will provide no reason at all, not just no compelling reason, to take steps to help. Of course, there is no need to *say* that the agent wants to forward her interests or wants to avoid great pain: given the universality of those concerns it is, pragmatically speaking, enough to cite these beliefs when explaining the actions they help prompt.

If sound, Hume's second argument rules out cognitivist theories that insist that desires—the agent's own, those of others—can provide an agent with reasons for action, but only in a way quite different from the way Hume requires. On such a theory, desires, viewed not as forces but as data, and so as objects of belief, can help explain an agent's actions.[18] Recognizing that he will want to have money in the bank he has a reason for putting some aside now. Recognizing that someone will want to be able to call on her for help she has reason now to ensure that she will be in a

---

[17] This is not to deny that beliefs can, with no contribution from desire, be rational causes of other beliefs. The point is simply that, no matter what their subject-matter, beliefs cannot play the major role in a reason—not for belief, but—for action.

[18] The terminology is Gilbert Harman's, *The Nature of Morality: An Introduction to Ethics* (New York, 1977), 70–2; Thomas Nagel explores the role of desires as data in *The Possibility of Altruism* (Oxford, 1970).

position to provide it. But these beliefs, though they are about psychological states with the world-to-mind direction of fit, are themselves states with the mind-to-world direction of fit. They cannot, then, suffice for the explanation of action. Minimally, the agent must want to satisfy the wants she envisages herself or others having.

Hume's second argument blocks the cognitivist compromise that, while distinguishing desires from explicitly evaluative beliefs, allows either to serve as the major constituent in a reason for action. It rules out naturalistic forms of cognitivism that analyse explicitly evaluative beliefs as merely descriptive ones. It reveals as inefficaciously complex those essentially cognitivist theories that require desires to accompany evaluative beliefs if those beliefs are to prompt an agent to act.[19]

Given the character of Hume's argument from direction of fit, differences in cognitivist doctrine about the epistemic or logical standing of allegedly explanatory beliefs, or about their provenance, or about the logical structure of their content, will make no difference. From the vantage-point of his second argument any such theory fails by failing to provide for the practicality of the reasons from which agents act.

4. DIFFICULTIES AND DEFENCES

In articulating his conativist arguments, and in spelling out their consequences, we have largely let Hume do the running. It is time to consider what the cognitivist might say in response.

Some proponents of non-standard cognitivism may object that Hume's supposedly substantive thesis about the ineliminable role of desire only *seems* compelling because confused with a like-sounding thesis that, while true, is trivially so. 'The claim that a desire underlies every act is true', Thomas Nagel concedes, but 'only in the sense that *whatever* may be the motivation of someone's intentional pursuit of a goal, it becomes in virtue of his pursuit *ipso facto* appropriate to ascribe to him a desire for that goal.'[20] Perhaps the likelihood that an action will promote her future happiness—that is, the belief in that likelihood—motivates an agent to perform that action. It follows, says Nagel, that she has a desire for her future happiness. That desire is a necessary condition of—because a logical consequence of—her being thus motivated to act. But such 'merely consequential'

---

[19] Hints of such an inefficaciously complex cognitivist theory are to be found in W.D. Ross, *The Right and the Good* (Oxford, 1930), for example at 97–8 and 157–8. My 'Locke, Hume and the Nature of Volitions', 28–9, argues that Locke holds such a view.

[20] Nagel, *The Possibility of Altruism*, 29.

desires, as we may call them, are not the desires Hume's theory requires. They are not, in John McDowell's helpful phrase, 'independent extra components' in reasons for action, components that have an independent causal or explanatory role to play. [21] Once apprised of the distinction between Hume's and merely consequential desires, this non-standard cognitivist objection continues, one can recognize the possibility of combining the ineliminability of desire with a non-standard cognitivist account of reasons for action: merely consequential desires are ineliminable but reasons for action may none the less be exhaustively constituted by suitable descriptive beliefs. At the very least, this non-standard cognitivist objection claims, to recognize this possibility is to be inoculated against the seeming inevitability of the Humean theory.

Given Hume's second conativist argument, however, combining cognitivism with the ineliminability of merely consequential desire goes no way towards providing a satisfactory account of reasons for action. Merely consequential desires are not independent causal states with the world-to-mind direction of fit. They cannot, then, provide the requisite practical or goal-setting aspect of reasons for action and so cannot explain their motivating, and so their explanatory, role. Recognizing the possibility of combining cognitivism with the ineliminability of merely consequential desire provides no inoculation against the force of Hume's argument from direction of fit. The standing of the Humean theory derives not from its being confounded with Nagel's trivial truth but from the force of the conativist arguments that we have examined, including in particular that from direction of fit.

To be sure, Humean desires—desires that are not merely consequential but are 'independent extra components'—must be characterizable in a suitably independent way. But they are so characterizable. They are ineliminable elements, psychologically primitive elements, in an explanatory theory of human behaviour. As constituents in reasons for action they must be accompanied by relevant beliefs: in that sense they are not independent of belief. They have an ineliminable and independent role to play, however, a role for which they are equipped by their direction of fit.

It may be objected that the notion of direction of fit is mere metaphor, thus not a fit basis on which to found a substantive theory of motivation. [22]

---

[21] John McDowell, 'Are Moral Requirements Hypothetical Imperatives?', *Proceedings of the Aristotelian Society*, Suppl. Vol., 52 (1978), 15.

[22] See Platts, 'Hume and Morality as a Matter of Fact', 201. A more guarded intimation of the objection is to be found in his *Ways of Meaning: An Introduction to a Philosophy of Language* (London, 1979), 256–7.

That the metaphor captures a substantive distinction is clear, however, from its (approximate) correspondence, noted earlier, to the non-metaphorical contrast of the primitive psychological attitudes of holding a proposition true and of wanting a proposition (perhaps the very same proposition) to be true. That it captures a substantive distinction is clear, as well, from the ways in which the presence of states of each of the kinds it countenances will be displayed in an agent's behaviour in the face of his environment. The agent who believes that *p* but discovers that *not p* will, if rational, discard the belief that *p*: he will, that is to say, change his belief. The agent who desires that *p* but discovers that *not p* need not discard the desire that *p*: he will be disposed to change, not his desires, but the world.[23]

It may be objected that the notion of direction of fit, if taken literally, is no better placed than is the correspondence theory of truth—a theory with which it seems naturally to comport—to satisfy reasonable ontological scruples or to offer any but trivial explanations of what it is held to explain. We have no need of facts, it may be said. And if facts are identified as entities corresponding to true statements or sentences they can supply no explication of the truth of those sentences or statements.[24] The situation is the same, it may be said, when one shifts from statements to beliefs. We have no need of facts for beliefs to fit. And if facts are what true beliefs fit they can do nothing to explain the truth of such beliefs. Eschewing facts, we must eschew directions of fit as well.

It seems clear, however, that despite Hume's own casual allusions to facts they need play no essential role in a careful articulation of the notion of direction of fit. The belief that the world has been made safe for democracy is true if and only if the world has been made safe for democracy: in thus setting out conditions on the truth of the belief one does not, ineluctably, make an ontological commitment to facts that would render the belief true; the world itself, one could say, is the truth-maker. The desire that the world be made safe for democracy is satisfied if and only if the world is made safe for democracy. Simply by giving the desire's

[23] Compare Smith, 'The Humean Theory of Motivation', 54: 'the difference between beliefs and desires in terms of direction of fit comes down to a difference between the counterfactual dependence of a belief and a desire that *p*, on a perception that *not p*: roughly, a belief that *p* is a state that tends to go [out] of existence in the presence of a perception that *not p*, whereas a desire that *p* is a state that tends to endure, disposing the subject in that state to bring it about that *p*.'

[24] Donald Davidson develops these objections to a correspondence theory of truth in 'True to the Facts' in *Inquiries into Truth and Interpretation* (Oxford, 1984), 37–54. See, too, his 'The Structure and Content of Truth', *Journal of Philosophy*, 87 (1990), 279–328.

satisfaction-conditions one makes no commitment to facts as satisfiers. Avoiding facts (or situations, or states of affairs) one could hold that the world itself, were it made safe for democracy, would satisfy that desire. Whether a belief is true or a desire satisfied is a matter of the truth or falsity of their representational content: only if the contents of psychological states require structurally correspondent entities for their truth or falsity can the directions of fit of those states require such entities. There is, however, no reason to think contents have such requirements. At least, there is no more reason to think contents require facts than there is to think that such ontological commitments are demanded by the propositions to which we direct the asymmetrical attitudes of 'holding true' and 'wanting true'. There is evidence, even in the presentation of his second conativist argument, that Hume thinks of representation and truth in terms of correspondence to facts; there is, however, nothing in the doctrine of direction of fit that forces him to do so.[25]

Hume's argument from direction of fit assumes that a psychological state cannot have both the mind-to-world and the world-to-mind directions of fit. Equivalently, within his theory, a psychological state cannot be both cognitive and conative. Is the assumption sound? It *seems* a simple corollary of our characterization of direction of fit. In denying it one countenances a non-compound psychological state—a belief, say—that both is, and is not, truth-evaluable. One allows a non-compound psychological state—a belief, say—that represents both how the world is and how it is to be. On the face of it, neither suggestion makes any sense. Still, efforts have been made, at least for certain kinds of cases, to blur or blunt our sharp distinction between conative and cognitive states (and by implication our distinction of directions of fit). We shall consider cognitivist attempts to blunt the distinction when, in Chapter 3, we consider the case for allowing explicitly evaluative moral beliefs to play a major role in the explanation of action. We shall consider a conativist proposal to amend our representation of the distinction when, in Chapter 4, we turn our attention to moral language.

A variety of difficulties of quite a different sort can be raised concerning the adequacy of Hume's conativism, and of his doctrine of directions

[25] It should be noted that talk of differing attitudes towards the truth of propositions need entail no commitment to propositions. Davidson, who introduces the distinction of attitudes in 'Expressing Evaluations', argues against the need for propositions or other objects 'before the mind' in 'Knowing One's Own Mind', *Proceedings of the American Philosophical Association*, 60 (1986–7), 441–58, and in 'What is Present to the Mind?' in Johannes Brandl and Wolfgang Gombocz (eds.), *The Mind of Donald Davidson* (Amsterdam, 1989), 3–18. We shall return to the question of truth and direction of fit in Chap. 4, Sect. 4.

of fit. An agent can have a reason for acting in a certain way even if she hasn't beliefs of the sort that Hume's conativist theory pairs with desires: she has a reason not to mix the petrol into the tonic in her glass even though she wants a gin and tonic and believes, of the petrol, that it is gin.[26] What is Hume to make of this fact? Hume holds that volitions as well as desires have the world-to-mind direction of fit. Has he a way to make good this claim while keeping desire and volition distinct? Passions or sentiments other than desires can contribute to action explanations but Hume's conativist theory, as presented thus far, makes no place for them. Then, too, it seems these passions or sentiments possess neither of the directions of fit we have distinguished. How square Hume's conativism with these concessions?

We can accommodate the first of these points in a way to which Hume can have no serious objection. Extending the range of 'reason to act' we may say she has a reason not to mix the petrol into her drink provided both (1) she has a relevant desire (for example, a desire not to drink petrol) and (2) she would, were she aware that the petrol is petrol, be motivated not to mix it into her drink.[27] Of course, a reason an agent has only in this extended sense could not provide an explanation for what she actually does, but there is nothing puzzling in that.

We shall address the issues concerning volitions and concerning other passions or sentiments in Chapter 2, when we provide a taxonomy of desires, affections, and volitions. In that chapter we shall also take up an objection that strikes at the heart of the present *interpretative* project, the objection that, whatever the virtues of the doctrine of directions of fit, it cannot apply to desires (or to volitions) as Hume understands them.

---

[26] See Bernard Williams, 'Internal and External Reasons', in *Moral Luck* (Cambridge, 1981), 101–13.
[27] Compare Williams, 'Internal and External Reasons', 103.

2

Desires, Volitions, and Affections

As represented here, Hume's arguments for a conativist theory of reasons for action introduce a pantechnicon notion of *desires* with propositional content and the world-to-mind direction of fit. That notion has many philosophical merits, not the least of them being the contribution it makes to effective reflection on the nature of reasons for action. It will be objected, however, that whatever its philosophical merits this notion of desire cannot be Hume's. Hume's is a quite narrow notion of desire, it will be said, not one that allows desires to play the major role in *every* reason for action. His notion of desire cannot accommodate talk of a desire's content. As a consequence, it cannot countenance talk of a desire's possessing the world-to-mind direction of fit. *Hume's* desires can have no direction of fit at all: it is *this* fact about them that underpins the claim they can be neither true nor false.

We must weigh these interpretative objections before we proceed. In doing so, however, we must be prepared to allow due weight to the demands on theory that the ostensible objectives of Hume's conativist arguments impose. We must recognize that quite disparate theoretical drives— drives towards psychological atomism, towards associationism in psychology, towards a conativist theory of reasons for action, towards the subversion of psychological egoism, among others—may have made the formulation of a coherent all-in theory of desire an exceptionally difficult task. We must be open to the possibility that, for different purposes, or at different places, Hume adopted differing levels of abstraction in his characterization of psychological phenomena. And we must—here as elsewhere—be ready to regiment Hume's text. In pursuing this investigation we shall find reason to reject several well-entrenched elements in Hume's metaphysical model for desire. We shall also find occasion to examine his views on certain vexed questions—questions about egoism and hedonism, in particular—that any doctrine of the content of desire must address.

Attention to questions of content will aid the examination of Hume's doctrine of *volitions*. They, just as desires, have the world-to-mind direction of fit: the question, then, arises how they and desires differ. Volitions are implicated in actions: one must seek, then, to grasp their ties both to reasons for action and to the actions those reasons help explain. As we shall see, reflection on the role of volitions helps reinforce Hume's case for conativism. Reflection on their place in practical reasoning will also help us frame a Humean account of the functioning of competing reasons for action.

Volitions are ineliminable elements in the basic configurations of psychological phenomena that, for Hume, constitute actions for a reason. But there are more complex configurations still, configurations that have what, regimenting Hume, we shall call *affections*—the passions of pride, humility, love, hatred, joy, grief, hope, fear, among others—among their elements. We shall examine Hume's doctrine of affections, exploring, in particular, the pivotal questions of content and direction of fit. We shall attempt an explicit representation of the similarities and dissimilarities, and the dependencies, that obtain between affections, on the one hand, and either desires or volitions, on the other. Most importantly, we shall find Hume committed to the centrality of desire, to the thesis that the affections presuppose desires. Given that direction of dependency, affections can play only an indirect role in the generation, and so the explanation, of action. Given his commitment to the centrality of desire, it comes as no surprise that, both at *Treatise*, II. iii. 3, and at *Treatise*, III. i. 1, Hume attends to desires, not affections, when theorizing about the generation of action. He does, of course, lavish attention on the affections elsewhere in Book II, as well as in Book III. That he attends painstakingly to their description, however, is no indication that he assigns them doctrinal pride of place. Desire is theoretically central, a fact of some significance, as we shall see in Chapter 4, for the interpretation of Hume's views about moral evaluation.

I. DESIRES AND THEIR CONTENT

When introducing his category of the so-called 'direct passions' at *Treatise*, II. iii. 9, Hume lists 'desire and aversion, grief and joy, hope and fear' (*T* 438). The suggestion of a narrow notion of desire must not be allowed to mislead. Hume does consistently contrast desire and aversion: in virtue of desire '[t]he mind . . . tends to unite itself with the good', in virtue of aversion it tends 'to avoid the evil' (*T* 438). At a suitable level of abstraction, however, this contrast amounts to no more than a contrast between desires with positive, and those with negative, content: one wants her to win the race; or, being averse to her winning, one wants her not to win. This more inclusive sense of 'desire' comports readily with Hume's conativist arguments as we have represented them. For simplicity's sake, we shall, except when quoting Hume, ignore the desire/aversion contrast in what follows.

Hume contrasts desires with the other so-called 'direct passions', with grief and joy, with hope and fear. By implication he contrasts desires with certain of the so-called 'indirect passions', specifically with the passions he identifies as pride, humility, love, and hatred.[1] *These* contrasts are as they should be, for, as we shall see below, they constitute part of an unemphasized but quite fundamental contrast between conative states and affective ones.

His contrast between desires and the indirect passions just mentioned (pride, humility, love, hatred) must not, however, divert attention from a theoretically quite important array of desires that Hume introduces in the course of his discussion, in *Treatise*, II. ii., of passions consequent upon, or strongly analogous to passions consequent upon, the indirect affections of love and hatred. Benevolence, he writes, is 'a desire of the happiness of the person belov'd, and an aversion to his misery' (*T* 382; compare *T* 367, 591); anger is 'a desire of the misery of the person hated, and an aversion to his happiness' (*T* 382). Malice he characterizes as 'the unprovok'd desire of producing evil to another, in order to reap a pleasure from the comparison' (*T* 377). Pity (this is not a full account) is 'a desire of happiness to another, and aversion to his misery' (*T* 382). Unquestionably Hume's is, quite explicitly, a much more inclusive conception of desire than a glance at *Treatise*, II. iii. 9, would suggest. In examining his doctrine of desire it is this more inclusive conception—one that ignores the contrast of desire and aversion, one that is designed to accommodate such desires as benevolence, anger, pity, and malice as well as desires more narrowly construed—to which we shall direct our attention.

When writing as a psychological atomist with associationist objectives Hume characterizes desires in ways that make no satisfactory provision

[1] Hume's terms for the several affections often do not comport very happily with contemporary usage. It is best to think of these as technical terms intended to be unusually comprehensive in scope. '*Terror, consternation, astonishment, anxiety,* and other passions of that kind', Hume writes, 'are nothing but different species and degrees of fear' (*T* 447). Referring to the 'sub-divisions of the other affections' he illustrates his practice by writing: 'Love may shew itself in the shape of *tenderness, friendship, intimacy, esteem, good-will,* and in many other appearances; which at the bottom are the same affections, and arise from the same causes, tho' with a small variation, which it is not necessary to give any particular account of' (*T* 448).

for those of their properties—their practicality, their possession of content, their world-to-mind direction of fit—on which his conativist arguments pivot. When articulating what, for ease of reference, we may call his official theory, he represents desires as psychological simples, as *sui generis* psychological items with no propositional content. He assigns them qualitative or phenomenological content, but of a wholly non-representational sort. Their content—just as that of the bodily pains and pleasures to which they are analogous—is, more narrowly, hedonic: desires, taken strictly, are unstructured pleasant or painful feelings.

In Hume's official theory differences between one type of desire and another, or between desires and other psychological states, are differences arising from the possession of, or from the precise character of, qualitative content. Desires of one type differ from those of another—benevolence, for example, differs from pity—as states with intrinsically different qualitative content. Desires differ from bodily pains and pleasures (which Hume takes to be 'impressions of sensation', not 'impressions of reflection'), and from what we have called affections (passions that, together with conative states, exhaust the class of 'impressions of reflection'), in virtue of their intrinsically different, albeit similarly hedonic, qualitative contents. They differ from still other psychological states (other impressions of sensation, all ideas) in that they have no representational content, whether of a qualitative or a propositional sort.[2]

Hume emphasizes his atomistic approach to desire when, in the 'Appendix' to the *Treatise*, he contrasts the very different ways in which feeling enters into desire and belief. In the case of belief, feeling is not a matter of an isolable psychological atom: rather, feeling 'modif[ies] the conception [of what is believed], and render[s] it [the conception] more present and intense' (*T* 625). Very differently, desire is an 'impression or feeling, distinguishable from the conception' of what is desired, a feeling 'annex'd to' some thought or conception, a feeling associated with, but not a modification of, a 'particular conception of good and pleasure' (*T* 625).

To be sure, Hume takes purported differences in qualitative content between desires, or between desires and either bodily pains and pleasures or affections, to be tightly linked to differences both in associated thoughts (in 'ideas', to use Hume's term) and in behavioural bearing. But these relational differences amongst states with intrinsically different

---

[2] For a sketch of the division between qualitative and propositional content, as well as that between representational and non-representational content, see Colin McGinn, *The Character of Mind* (Oxford, 1982), 8.

hedonic contents are not ones that, when setting out his official theory, Hume allows to affect his elucidation of the concepts in question.

He makes frequent reference to objects of desire. He writes of 'an object either of desire or aversion' (*T* 440), of a 'proper object' of a desire (*T* 459), of the 'distinct object[s]' (*T* 396) of the passions, including the desires, that constitute 'the amorous passion' (*T* 394). As his descriptions, cited earlier, of the differences between benevolence, anger, pity, and malice make plain, he is cognizant of the differences in thought-content that mark differences in desire. When articulating his official theory, however, the picture he employs is that of a conceptually isolable desire, with no propositional or other representational content of its own, a desire that is linked to a thought whose content specifies what, proleptically, he terms the object of that desire. When endorsing his official theory it seems clear he is committed to denying the intentionality of desire.[3]

He writes, of course, of the role desire plays in the generation of behaviour, distinguishing that role from the one he assigns to belief: recognition of that role lies at the heart of his central conativist arguments. On the face of it, however, he inclines towards representing the link between desire and behaviour as conceptually inessential, perhaps precisely because it is causal. He views himself as departing from his preferred atomistic picture when, discussing the desire he terms 'pity', he finds himself compelled to say 'that 'tis not the present sensation alone or momentary pain or pleasure, which determines the character of any passion, but the whole bent or tendency of it from the beginning to the end' (*T* 381). Whatever his settled view of the conceptual status of the tie between desire and behaviour, he clearly thinks that it is specifically its hedonic quality that explains a desire's practicality: it is precisely because they have pleasurable or painful qualitative content that desires prompt the behaviours they do.[4]

One can appreciate the appeal of this radically atomistic conception. It has—or at least appears to have—a certain no-nonsense concreteness to it: it views desires as isolable and introspectible elements in the stream of consciousness; it sees their motivational capacity as a natural product of their being pleasures or pains. It appears to further Hume's efforts to establish an associationist psychology of the life of the emotions. As pleasant or

[3] Compare Anthony Kenny, *Action, Emotion, and Will* (London, 1963), 25n.

[4] Locke's account, while focusing on the hedonic qualitative content of desire, none the less differs from Hume's. For Locke, desire is 'an *uneasiness* of the Mind for want of some absent good'. John Locke, *An Essay Concerning Human Understanding*, ed. P. H. Nidditch (Oxford, 1975), II. xxi. 31.

painful psychological states desires are associated, through what Hume terms a resemblance of impressions, to other passions, to other states with pleasant or painful qualitative content. They are linked to thoughts that are themselves associated, through some or other of the three laws governing the association of ideas, to other thoughts. A desire has, that is to say, a place both as *explanans* and as *explanandum* in an associationist framework employing what Hume calls a 'double relation of impressions and ideas' (*T* 381).

Hume's atomistic official account provides, too, compelling reason to deny the truth-evaluability of desires, a denial that plays, as we have seen, a crucial role in his second conativist argument concerning reasons for action. With no propositional content they can have no direction of fit and so cannot coherently be viewed as true or as false.

Whatever its initial appeal, Hume's official theory must be rejected.[5] Its supposed virtues are merely illusory. Its seeming concreteness is a product of confounding the quasi-bodily feelings sometimes prompted by the presence, the satisfaction, or the disappointment of desire with desire itself. Its proposed conjunction of hedonic qualitative content and motivational capacity represents a too crudely mechanistic model of the action-generating role of desire. As Hume himself becomes aware, it can be combined with a promising associationist theory of conative and affective states only if relations of phenomenological resemblance give way, within the theory, to relations based upon similarity of contribution to behaviour.[6]

Most importantly, given our present concerns, its way of ensuring the non-truth-evaluability of desire would make it impossible for Hume to secure his constructive conativist conclusions. By compromising the thought of a desire's content it subverts Hume's first conativist argument, that focusing on the conditions on the explanation of action: without content desires cannot play the major role in reasons for action, they cannot find expression in practical premises, they cannot be suitably related to

---

[5] For an extended examination of the atomistic elements in Hume's general theory of the passions see my 'Emotion and Thought in Hume's *Treatise*', *Canadian Journal of Philosophy*, Suppl. Vol. 1 (1974), 53–71.

[6] The need to accommodate pity and malice within his associationist theory prompts Hume to write (*T* 381): 'that we may understand the full force of this double relation, we must consider, that 'tis not the present sensation alone or momentary pain or pleasure, which determines the character of any passion, but the whole bent or tendency of it from the beginning to the end. One impression may be related to another, not only when their sensations are resembling, as we have all along suppos'd in the preceding cases; but also when their impulses or directions are similar and correspondent.'

beliefs that play the ineliminable minor role. By reducing a desire's content to qualitative content it undercuts the crucial claim that desires and beliefs differ in their direction of fit and, for that reason, their truth-evaluability. It thereby scotches the second conativist argument's attempt to locate the action-explanatory capacity of desire in its possession of the world-to-mind direction of fit. Given his conativist objectives, Hume's atomistic official theory of desire must be given up. He must withdraw the attribution of atomistic properties incompatible with the properties that, in the course of his conativist arguments, he himself assigns to desires.

A modest revision in his official theory would enable Hume to deal with some, at least, of his difficulties concerning the content of desire. Suppose a modestly revised theory to identify a desire not with the impression that the official theory takes to be the desire but with a psychological complex comprising both that impression and the linked thought that, within the official theory, and proleptically, Hume represents as the thought of the desire's object. Jack desires that Jill win the race. His desire is not, as the official theory has it, just a distinctive pleasurable feeling; it is rather the complex comprising that feeling plus the thought of her winning the race. With this modest revision, an essentially Humean theory can countenance the propositional—more generally, the representational—content of desires.[7] Countenancing propositional content it has a way—the obvious way—of distinguishing one desire from another in terms not of putative differences of qualitative content but of the thoughts the desires implicate. It has a ready way of distinguishing desires from bodily pains and pleasures. And it has a plausible start, at least, on the project of differentiating desires and affections. It offers what can seem a more promising basis for distinguishing desires from beliefs. Countenancing propositional content the theory also, of course, can allow desires to be linked, in the ways required, to the beliefs to which, in his conativist arguments, Hume assigns the minor role in reasons for actions.

While accommodating desire's propositional content, and so freeing Hume from many of the intolerable constraints imposed by his official theory, our modestly revised account remains subject to all the difficulties surrounding its dubious doctrine of isolable, introspectible, qualitative elements in the stream of consciousness. More pressingly, it provides no assistance towards the characterization of the peculiar practicality of desire, no help with the thought that desires have the world-to-mind

---

[7] Compare Davidson's treatment of Hume on the content of propositional pride in 'Hume's Cognitive Theory of Pride', *Essays on Actions and Events*, 278.

direction of fit. Despite appearances, ingredient feelings of pleasure or pain provide no theoretical assistance here. Bodily pains can prompt a behavioural response in a quite direct, quite automatic way: one automatically withdraws one's hand from the hot stove. But the practicality of desire is, quite differently, that of the major element in a reason for action, an element expressible in an explicitly evaluative sentence that can provide the major premise to a practical argument. Pains, having no propositional content, have no direction of fit. The practicality of desire, however, is essentially a matter of its world-to-mind direction of fit. Something other than its content, it may be said, must explain a thought's possession of that direction of fit, but it is utterly unclear how the presence of an isolable hedonic element can provide the needed explanation. (Is the *absence* of such an hedonic element sufficient for a thought to have the opposite, the mind-to-world, direction of fit?) And why—to anticipate— do the feelings ingredient in desires generate the world-to-mind direction of fit while those involved in the affections generate no direction of fit at all? Why— again to anticipate—are affections *non*-motivational *despite* their hedonic character? To be forced to invoke intrinsic differences amongst pleasant and painful feelings, in this case differences that in turn explain differences between desires and affections in the matters of motivational role and direction of fit, is to compound the theoretical demands on antecedently doubtful doctrine.[8]

The point of these objections is not that the modestly revised Humean theory, with its doctrine of ingredient feelings, is incompatible with Hume's descriptions of desire's practicality and direction of fit. The problem is rather that these feelings appear to do none of the theoretical work that a full-dress conativist theory requires. Given the independent difficulties that the doctrine of ingredient feelings faces, Hume—and we— must look elsewhere for illumination about the metaphysics of desire.

Alternative metaphysical models for desire can be imagined, albeit markedly un-Humean ones. One model, designed to accommodate the notion of direction of fit, construes the difference between desire and belief—adverbially, as it were—in terms of differing ways in which thoughts

---

[8] Are we wrong to require, for the case of desire, that the purported motivational contribution of pleasure and pain be somehow linked to possession of the world-to-mind direction of fit? Should we, interpreting Hume, make do with pleasure and pain and eschew the doctrine of direction of fit? To do so would be to eschew making sense of his centrally important second conativist argument, with its focus on representation and truth-evaluability, and its three conclusions. (It should be noted that when setting out his second argument— in the long passages quoted at the start of Chap. 1, Sect. 3, above—Hume makes no mention of the hedonic character of desire.)

are conceived, differing modes of conception. The desire that poverty be eradicated and the belief that poverty is eradicated involve (minor caveats here omitted) the very same thought: the thought of poverty's being eradicated. The desire and the belief differ, however, in that in desiring that poverty be eradicated one has the thought in the world-to-mind way, in believing that poverty is eradicated one has it in the mind-to-world way. Having a thought in the world-to-mind way one has a practical thought, a thought suited to serve as the major element in a reason for action. Having a thought in the mind-to-world way one has a thought suitable, other things equal, for serving as the minor element.

The model eschews isolable ingredient feelings. It neglects the deliverances of introspection, and adopts instead a more fruitful vantage-point from which desires and beliefs are viewed in terms of their explanatory roles, and in particular their roles in the explanation of action. In setting out the model the practicality or non-practicality of psychological states— more accurately, the possession of one or the other of the two directions of fit – are taken as primitive features of those states: features that are not explicable by reference to more basic features; features that are definitive of the states in question, given the explanatory status the states themselves have. The model of modes of conception is made to order for capturing all and only the features that desires must, given their explanatory role, be taken to possess. It clearly complements the conativist theory of reasons for action for which, as we have seen, Hume argues.[9]

Another metaphysical model substitutes a contrast of relations for the contrast of modes of conception. It contrasts two fundamentally different attitudes towards the truth of propositions. One may *want true* a proposition. Very differently, one may *hold true* or *believe true* that very same proposition. Desiring that poverty be eradicated, one wants true the proposition that poverty is eradicated. Believing that poverty is eradicated one holds true, or believes true, that very proposition. Wanting true a proposition, one is in a psychological state suited to play the major role in a reason for action. This psychological state is so suited because it possesses the world-to-mind direction of fit. Holding a proposition true one is in a state of the sort required for the minor role, a state that can serve that role in virtue of its mind-to-world direction of fit. Each of the two attitudes is a psychological

---

[9] In sketching this model I have been influenced by Kenny's so-called 'Theory of Volition', in *Action, Emotion, and Will*, 212–39. A more careful sketch would require recognition that belief is only one of several types of psychological state possessing the mind-to-world direction of fit. Hume writes, of course, that in the case of belief feeling 'modif[ies] the conception' (*T* 625), but his point in claiming this is to *contrast* belief with desire and volition.

primitive: each plays an ineliminable role in explanations of action; neither can take the explanatory place of the other. In representing the contrast of desire and belief as one of fundamentally different attitudes towards the truth of propositions one fastens on the roles of belief and desire in explanatory theories of human behaviour: one adopts the perspective of the explanatory theorist, not that of the introspective observer of the stream of consciousness. In effect, one devises a theory that accords with the characterizations of desire and belief that constrain the conativist arguments Hume deploys in *Treatise*, II. iii. 3.[10]

Neither alternative metaphysical model of desire is Hume's. Neither is just a modest revision of his atomistic official theory. Neither incorporates—this is part of the point—dubious Humean doctrines about the explanatory centrality of isolable items possessing hedonic content. Of course, it goes without saying, neither has here been furnished with the more careful analyses and arguments that full-dress defence would demand. Their availability as alternatives is, however, sufficient to show that the fate of Hume's conativist arguments of *Treatise*, II. iii. 3, is not ineluctably joined to that of his atomistic official theory of desire. Hume's conativist arguments are compatible with, indeed are clearly much better served by, non-atomistic theories of either of the two sorts we have just sketched. One may follow Hume's conativist lead without following him into the atomist cul-de-sac.

Hume mishandles the concept of a desire's content. Despite that, his critiques of psychological egoism and psychological hedonism constitute a substantive contribution to the theory of desire that his conativism requires.

Consistently, through the *Treatise* and the second *Enquiry*, Hume rejects the doctrine of psychological egoism, the doctrine that an agent's desires are in all instances directed to the securing of his or her own interests rather than those of others. Many desires are, of course, directed to one's own interests: one desires one's own fame or fortune, food and shelter for oneself, revenge on one's enemies. But many, to all appearances,

<hr/>

[10] In sketching this model I am influenced by Davidson's representation of attitudes with respect to the truth of propositions in *Expressing Evaluations*, 8–9. As noted earlier, a commitment to attitudes towards the truth of propositions entails no residual commitment to propositions. Snare, at several places in *Morals, Motivation, and Convention*, remarks on the attractions of pursuing Humean themes not in Hume's officially introspectionist way but with a view to the characterization of common-sense psychology. Attention to either of the non-atomist models for desire that we have introduced reflects just such a shift of perspective. In doing so it accords with Hume's actual practice in the construction of his conativist arguments.

are not. Benevolence, as Hume represents it, is a desire directed to securing the interests of some other person, a person one loves. In pitying
another one desires that person's happiness, or at least the ending of her
misery.

Hume argues explicitly against proponents of the doctrine of 'universal ... selfishness' (*E* 297), urging that attempts to depict benevolent
appearances as selfish reality have proved unconvincing efforts proceeding 'entirely from that love of *simplicity* which has been the source of
much false reasoning in philosophy' (*E* 298). He describes cases in which,
it seems clear, an agent cannot, without trivializing the claim, be said to
be acting out of a '*real* interest' of the agent's own: 'What interest can a
fond mother have in view, who loses her health in assiduous attendance
on her sick child, and afterwards languishes and dies of grief, when freed,
by its death, from the slavery of that attendance' (*E* 300). And he insists
that 'an *imaginary* interest known and avowed for such' (ibid.) cannot plausibly serve in the absent real interest's explanatory stead.

This is not to deny that individuals—the agent herself, presumably
others as well—may be subject on occasion to delusions about the presence of self-interested motives: 'Our predominant motive or intention
is ... frequently concealed from ourselves when it is mingled and confounded with other motives which the mind, from vanity or self-conceit,
is desirous of supposing more prevalent' (*E* 299). Nor is it to deny that
genuinely other-directed desires may be seconded, or confirmed, in their
motivational force by self-interested desires. In particular, it is not to deny
that an other-directed desire may be seconded by a self-interested desire
for the pleasures consequent upon the satisfaction of that other-directed
desire; or that experiencing the pleasures of such satisfactions may confirm one in one's other-directed desires. As Hume sees it, when pursuing
a 'speculative science of human nature' (*E* 297) one discovers that 'a natural unforced interpretation of the phenomena of human life' (*E* 244) requires acknowledgement of non-reducible other-directed or altruistic
desires.

These non-reducible altruistic desires are *non-instrumental* ones. One
may desire that others secure their interests, indeed may take steps to
help them do so, because one believes one's own interests will thereby be
served. As we shall see such instrumental altruism plays a role in Hume's
analysis of the formation of conventions. But one may also be moved,
non-instrumentally, by a concern for interests other than one's own. One's
desires, despite being non-instrumentally and non-reducibly altruistic,
may be *partial*. Though altruistic they may be desires directed specifically to

the interests of individuals standing in some or other special relationship to oneself. One's benevolence may be directed to a friend, a relation, a benefactor: if non-instrumental, one's benevolence is an altruistic, not a self-interested, desire none the less. We may reserve consideration of *impartial* altruistic desires for Chapter 4.

The existence of altruistic desires is one thing, the extent of their role in the explanation of conduct quite another. Hume raises the latter, essentially empirical, question when he alludes to 'that vulgar [i.e. common] dispute concerning the *degrees* of benevolence or self-love, which prevail in human nature' (*E* 270). If essentially empirical, the question appears to resist hard-edged answers: 'the phenomena, which can be produced on either side, are so dispersed, so uncertain, and subject to so many interpretations, that it is scarcely possible accurately to compare them, or draw from them any determinate inference or conclusion' (*E* 271). As Hume reads the evidence, however, it is clear that altruistic motives do sometimes dominate in the determination of action. Both in the *Treatise* and the second *Enquiry* he hazards rough estimates of the situation. He takes an utterly minimal claim to be clearly secure: 'Let these generous sentiments be supposed ever so weak; let them be insufficient to move even a hand or finger of our body, they must still direct the determinations of our mind, and where everything else is equal, produce a cool preference of what is useful and serviceable to mankind, above what is pernicious and dangerous' (*E* 271). If still cautious, he is elsewhere a bit bolder: 'So far from thinking, that men have no affection for any thing beyond themselves, I am of opinion, that tho' it be rare to meet with one, who loves any single person better than himself; yet 'tis as rare to meet with one, in whom all the kind affections, taken together, do not overbalance all the selfish' (*T* 487). To a revisable first approximation, the limits of partiality mark the limits of altruism's influence: 'Nothing is more certain, than that men are, in a great measure, govern'd by interest, and that even when they extend their concern beyond themselves, 'tis not to any great distance; nor is it usual for them, in common life, to look farther than their nearest friends and acquaintance' (*T* 534). The point, now, is not to assess the seemingly commonsensical estimates Hume hazards, but just to note how unequivocally he commits himself to desires with other-directed content.

Hume connects his refutation of psychological hedonism to his rejection of psychological egoism. Attacking the latter doctrine he argues explicitly against the suggestion, often urged in its support, that seeming benevolence is really a concern for 'self-enjoyment' (*E* 302), that it is

really not a concern for the interests of others but a desire for the pleasures consequent upon benevolence. If the suggestion were merely that a
desire for such pleasures can second the motivational force of benevolence Hume would have no objection: he acknowledges that, for an individual who has experienced the pleasures of satisfied benevolence, 'another's
happiness or good' can 'afterwards [be] pursued, from the combined
motives of benevolence and self-enjoyment' (*E* 302). He insists, however,
that experience of those pleasures presupposes genuine benevolence, a
genuine concern for the interests of others.

In this respect the case of benevolence is no different from the non-
altruistic cases of 'bodily wants or appetites' or of desires (Hume writes
of 'mental passions') for 'fame or power ... or vengeance' (*E* 301). In each
case these *primary* desires,[11] whether self-interested or altruistic, have
objects other than pleasure, and it is the securing of these non-hedonic
objects that, by generating pleasure, generates the possibility of a 'secondary' desire with explicitly hedonic content. 'In all these cases', Hume
writes, 'there is a passion which points immediately to the object, and
constitutes it our good or happiness; as there are other secondary passions which afterwards arise and pursue it as a part of our happiness,
when once it is constituted such by our original affections' (*E* 301). A condition on one's experiencing, and so coming to desire, the pleasures of
benevolence or revenge is that one have those non-hedonic desires themselves.

Hume, as noted earlier, criticizes psychological egoism for misusing
the criterion of theoretical simplicity in its efforts at reducing apparently
altruistic to really self-interested motivation. Here, however, he claims
to secure an appropriate simplicity of theory by his introduction of primary desires. Their introduction, together with the denial of psychological hedonism their introduction entails, provides a unified account of the
complex motivational role both of self-interested and of altruistic desires.

Hume's anti-hedonist doctrine of primary desires plays a role not only
in the second *Enquiry* but in the *Treatise* as well. Hume there writes:

Beside good and evil, or in other words, pain and pleasure, the direct passions
frequently arise from a natural impulse or instinct, which is perfectly unaccountable. Of this kind is the desire of punishment to our enemies, and of happiness to
our friends; hunger, lust, and a few other bodily appetites. These passions, properly

---

[11] Compare Norman Kemp Smith, *The Philosophy of David Hume* (London, 1941), 168, and
Páll S. Árdal, *Passion and Value in Hume's Treatise* (Edinburgh, 1966), 10.

speaking, produce good and evil, and proceed not from them, like the other affections. (*T* 439; compare *E* 201)[12]

Hume misleads when claiming these desires are unaccountable; indeed he elsewhere offers his own associationist explanations of anger ('the desire of punishment to our enemies') and benevolence ('the desire … of happiness to our friends'). His point, as the last sentence in the passage makes plain, is not that they cannot be accounted for but that they cannot coherently be understood as prompted by the prospect of one's own pleasure. Despite the casual suggestion that benevolence is directed specifically to the happiness of others there is no reason to think that Hume, while rejecting psychological hedonism for self-interested cases, would commit himself to some form of altruistic hedonism. There is no reason to think him committed to the odd doctrine that, so far as one is concerned with others, one is concerned, exclusively, with their pleasures and pains.

Hume writes, elsewhere in the *Treatise*: 'The chief spring or actuating principle of the human mind is pleasure or pain; and when these sensations are remov'd, both from our thought and feeling, we are, in a great measure, incapable of passion or action, of desire or volition' (*T* 574). Of course, were the combination of Hume's conativism and his official theory of desire correct, it would follow that pleasure or pain would in *every* case be required for action done for a reason: given the combination of doctrines in question every such action would be caused by desire and desire would be a *feeling* with hedonic qualitative content. The passage concerns not this role for pleasure and pain but the very different role they play in the *propositional content* of desire. Read this way, the qualifications Hume enters are in order. Pleasure and pain are (with emphasis added) 'the *chief* spring or actuating principle'; one is '*in a great measure*, incapable of passion or action, of desire or volition' in their absence. In many instances, Hume holds, but not possibly in all, one desires (one's own) pleasure and the reduction of (one's own) pain. Why not in all? Some of one's desires must, he maintains, be primary desires. Others, as he insists, are altruistic. The rejection of psychological hedonism (as also that of psychological egoism) remains in place. As a doctrine about content this rejection is, of course, compatible with a further thesis that would surely tempt Hume, the thesis that *pleasures consequent* upon the satisfac-

---

[12] In *The Natural History of Religion*, ed. A. Wayne Colver (Oxford, 1976), 25, Hume refers to 'an original instinct or primary impression of nature, such as gives rise to self-love, affection betwixt the sexes, love of progeny, gratitude, resentment'.

tion of desires can *confirm* the motivational capacity of desires for objects other than pleasure.[13]

2. VOLITIONS

'[H]aving prov'd, that all actions of the will have particular causes, I proceed', Hume writes, 'to explain what these causes are, and how they operate' (*T* 412). With these words as preface, he proceeds, in *Treatise*, II. iii. 3, to the presentation of his two arguments for a conativist theory of reasons for action. In presenting these arguments he explicates the structure of a fundamental configuration of psychological phenomena, a configuration of three elements—desire, belief, and action—present in every case of action for a reason. As the phrase 'actions of the will' intimates, however, Hume takes this configuration to be more complex than it at first appears. Talk of 'actions of the will' introduces a notion not just of 'voluntary action[s]' (*T* 406) but of 'operations of the will' (*E* 93), of 'willing[s]' (*T* 417), of 'act[s] of volition' (*T* 415), of (in Hume's preferred expression) 'volition[s]' (*T* 415). For Hume, volitions are psychologically primitive elements implicated in an agent's voluntary actions. As such they are amongst the *explananda* when so-called reasons for action are invoked to explain an agent's actions. Alternatively, they must be invoked in addition to reasons for action, if actions are to be explained.[14]

Hume writes: 'by the *will*, I mean nothing but *the internal impression we feel and are conscious of, when we knowingly give rise to any new motion of our body, or new perception of our mind*' (*T* 399). Agents may act in bodily or merely mental ways: they may raise their hands or tie their shoes; they may rehearse proofs in their heads or turn their thoughts to other things. In either case, in Hume's view, volitions—the 'internal impressions' he mentions—have an essential part to play. He offers an atomistic official

---

[13] Richard Brandt, in *Ethical Theory: The Problems of Normative and Critical Ethics* (Englewood Cliffs, N J, 1959), 307–14, makes a here-pertinent distinction between three theses: the Pleasure Theory of Goals; Motivation by Pleasant Thoughts; Conditioning by Pleasant Experiences. Harman, in *The Nature of Morality*, 140–50, expresses methodological misgivings about, in effect, the way in which Hume approaches the issue of psychological egoism. In *Understanding Hume*, ed. Peter Lewis and Geoffrey Madell (Edinburgh, 1992), 162–71, John Jenkins expresses scepticism about each of the anti-egoist arguments Hume deploys in the second *Enquiry*.

[14] The present discussion of Hume's doctrine of volitions derives from more extensive accounts in my essays 'Hume's Volitions' and 'Locke, Hume and the Nature of Volitions'. For other treatments of the topic, see Árdal, *Passion and Value in Hume's Treatise*, 80–5; Bruce Aune, *Reason and Action* (Dordrecht, 1975), 50–3; Jonathan Bennett, *Locke, Berkeley, Hume: Central Themes* (Oxford, 1971), 206–9; and Penelhum, *Hume*, III–17.

theory that parallels his official theory of desire. Volitions are indefinable internal impressions. They are impressions or feelings, not ideas or thoughts. As internal impressions they are akin to passions, including desires, or to bodily pleasures and pains, rather than to sensations: they have qualitative rather than propositional content, and that content is hedonic rather than representational. They are indefinable: having asserted their presence in every case of bodily or mental action Hume claims they are 'impossible to define, and needless to describe any farther' (*T* 399). Though 'simple' (*E* 69) and indefinable, however, they can take causal descriptions. In this they are 'like ... pride and humility, love and hatred' (*T* 399) about which Hume elsewhere writes:

'tis impossible we can ever, by a multitude of words, give a just definition of them, or indeed of any of the passions. The utmost we can pretend to is a description of them, by an enumeration of such circumstances, as attend them. (*T* 277; compare *T* 329)

While having no propositional content themselves they are linked to thoughts with propositional content, thoughts whose contents specify the so-called 'immediate object[s] of volition' (*E* 66). They have an intimate, if non-conceptual, bearing on the agent's behaviour: like desires they are 'propense and averse motions of the mind' (*T* 574) in virtue, presumably, of their hedonic qualitative content. They are not evaluable in terms of truth and falsity: because they are not capable of 'an agreement or disagreement either to *real* relations of ideas, or to *real* existence and matter of fact' it is 'impossible ... they can be pronounced either true or false' (*T* 458).

A psychological atom in the sense in which, in Hume's official theory, a desire is, a volition is a 'distinct impression' (*T* 625) quite unlike the feeling that in part constitutes a belief or judgement. As remarked earlier, a feeling of the latter sort 'modif[ies] the conception' of what is believed; it is not 'only [i.e. merely] annex'd to it [the conception of what is believed], after the same manner that *will* and *desire* are annex'd to particular conceptions of good and pleasure' (*T* 625). A belief or judgement is a thought modified in a certain way; the thought's modification is incapable of independent existence. As distinct impressions Hume's volitions, just like desires in his official theory, are logically capable of occurring without the accompanying thoughts of what Hume characterizes, proleptically, as their objects.

Hume's psychological atomism is no better placed to illuminate volitions than it is to illuminate desires. If volitions are indeed to play a part in an all-in conativist theory of reasons for action they must be construed, not in the atomistic fashion of his official theory, but paralleling the way in which Hume treats desires when constructing his two conativist arguments. Construed this way, volitions have propositional content, have a peculiar practicality that needs to be specified but that derives in part from their possessing the world-to-mind direction of fit, and are for *that* reason unassessable in terms of truth and falsity. To capture the fact that they have content, mild revision of Hume's official theory is perhaps sufficient. To capture their practicality and direction of fit, however, it is necessary to leave Hume's atomism behind and think along lines sketched earlier for the case of desire. One possibility is to take volitions to involve a distinctive primitive—a volitional—mode of conception. Another is to view them in terms of a distinctive primitive attitude—that of willing true, say—with respect to propositions. As earlier in the case of desires, the availability of these alternative metaphysical models insulates Hume's doctrine of volitions against objections directed to an unacceptable psychological atomism. Adopting this revisionist vantage-point requires, as earlier, that one focus—as Hume does in conativist contexts—on the role assigned to volitions within the framework of action explanations. Given the properties Hume assigns to volitions when thinking of that framework—their content-possession, practicality, non-truth-evaluability, and world-to-mind direction of fit—it requires attention, as well, to the respects in which desires and volitions are alike and, as importantly, to the respects in which they differ.

If alike in direction of fit, desires and volitions differ in their functional or causal roles. Consider the case of a bodily action such as an agent's raising her hand to catch the speaker's attention. The desire to catch the speaker's attention, together with the belief that by raising her hand she will do so, causes her volition to raise her hand; that volition, in turn, causes the rising of her hand. Both the desire and the volition have propositional content, and the contents of each are suitably linked to the other, and to the content of the belief. Neither the desire nor the volition are truth-evaluable, for each has the world-to-mind, not the mind-to-world, direction of fit. Each has satisfaction- rather than truth-conditions. The desire is satisfied if and only if the agent catches the speaker's attention; the volition is satisfied just in case the agent raises her hand. Desire, we may say, sets the agent's goal in acting; volition seeks to effect that goal. Hume uses the metaphor of command to mark this peculiar practicality of volition. An 'act of volition', he writes, 'produces motion in our limbs': 'by the simple command of our will, we can move the organs of our body'

(*E* 64). In a similar vein he writes that we 'have command over our mind to a certain degree, but beyond *that* lose all empire over it' (*T* 632), writes of the will 'governing our thought'[15] and of the will's 'authority' (*T* 633).

Desires and volitions differ not only in functional location but also (if connectedly) in their contents. Hume takes no pains to spell out the differences, or to indicate why they are necessary, but he does write:

DESIRE arises from good consider'd simply, and AVERSION is deriv'd from evil. The WILL exerts itself, when either the good or the absence of the evil may be attain'd by any action of the mind or body. (*T* 439)[16]

His practice suggests that in his view desires may, but needn't, be directed to one's own actions: one may want to make the world safe for democracy; one may want, with no view to one's own doings, just that it be so. Volitions, however, have the agent's own actions as their target. Hume writes of one's 'willing of these actions' and that one 'may will the performance of certain actions' (*T* 417). Of course the contents of volitions, just as the contents of desires, must be non-evaluative in character: one wills that one raise one's arm, not that it be a good thing that one raises one's arm. Hume says nothing of this, but perhaps he would also hold that, as with desires, the linguistic expression of volitions, despite the descriptive contents of the volitions themselves, must be explicitly evaluative in character.

Though he does not do so uniformly, Hume tends to distinguish intention or resolution from volition. (He appears to identify them at *E* 66 and 88, but to distinguish them at *E* 100 when he writes of 'volitions and intentions'.) When distinguishing them he appeals to temporal elements in their contents: resolution and intention pertain to the future; volition concerns the present. '[T]he will', he writes, 'has an influence only on present actions' and does not 'regard ... some future time' (*T* 516); in the case of 'intentions and resolutions' there is a temporal 'distance from the final determination' (*T* 536), thus room for the notion that one might attempt to 'fortify that resolution' (*T* 382). Despite this difference, intention and volition each concern particular actions on the agent's part: my intention concerns, for example, an 'action, which I am to perform a twelve-month hence' (*T* 536); my 'willing' pertains to my 'present actions' (*T* 516). Hume could simplify matters by taking volitions to be a

[15] David Hume, *Abstract of a Treatise of Human Nature*, ed. J.M. Keynes and P. Sraffa (Cambridge, 1938), 21.
[16] Hume is silent on the qualifications needed if this passage is to comport with his rejection of psychological hedonism.

species of intentions, the here-and-now ones.[17] There is no need for two practical primitives in addition to desire. Reckoning volitions as intentions would also circumvent objections to volitions that stem from unease about the introduction of what is clearly a term of philosophical art.

What reason is there to take volition (or intention, for that matter) as an ineliminable primitive? Why not view volition (or intention) as somehow definable in terms of the primitives of desire, belief, and action? Hume takes the presence of volitions to be obvious to introspection: one is immediately aware of them in one's every voluntary action; one is aware, by introspection, of their phenomenologically distinctive character. There is little to this line of thought, especially if one distinguishes, as Hume does, volitions from the feelings that at times accompany their formation.[18]

One requires *explananda* for reasons for action, of course, but why items other than the actions themselves? Perhaps one requires a psychological element expressible linguistically by an evaluative sentence that can serve as the conclusion to a practical argument, but what bars actions themselves from being thus expressible? Perhaps the psychological item thus expressible must have propositional content, something that volitions, but not actions, have?[19]

If surely suggestive, this last consideration is not, perhaps, compelling. What does contribute to a compelling case for the primitiveness of volitions, however, is the possibility that they may be unfulfilled or unsatisfied. An agent has a reason to act in a certain way, forms a volition to act in that way, yet fails, perhaps unwittingly, so to act. Having reason to raise his hand he wills to do so, yet his hand does not rise. Hume remarks that a 'man, suddenly struck with palsy [i.e. paralysis] in the leg or arm, or who had newly lost those members, frequently endeavours, at first to move them, and employ them in their usual offices' (*E* 66). He imagines the individual, unaware of his inability to move the limb in question, to form volitions of the arm-moving or leg-moving kind, 'to command such limbs' (ibid.). Though the would-be agent forms such volitions, however, he fails, for obvious reasons, to raise his arm or move his leg. It is clear the would-

[17] For here-and-now intentions see Wilfrid Sellars, 'Thought and Action', in Keith Lehrer (ed.), *Freedom and Determinism* (New York, 1966), 105–39.
[18] Hume refers to a feeling of '*nisus*, or strong endeavour' (*E* 67 n.) but distinguishes it from volition; it is only felt when we 'exert our force' in the face of resistance, whereas 'in common thinking and motion ... the effect follows immediately upon the will, without any exertion or summoning up of force' (ibid.). Such feelings are best viewed as effects of volitions, or of volitions in the face of difficulty.
[19] On the assumption, here appropriate, that actions do not incorporate volitions.

be agent does something here, something identical, save for *its* effects, to what he does when, in the normal case, he voluntarily moves his arm or leg. It is clear that he forms a volition. If ineliminable volitions must be invoked for abnormal cases, however, simplification of theory recommends their introduction for otherwise similar normal cases as well. Does the very abnormality of the imagined cases call into question the introduction of volitions? If volitions are viewed (as suggested above) as here-and-now intentions, the prospect of unsatisfied volitions is no more problematic, at bottom, than that of unfulfilled intentions. And *they*, it is clear, can be used to argue the primitiveness of intention.[20]

Hume says too little about volitions and the events they cause to have provided, in any serious sense, an analysis of action. Perhaps he identifies actions with complexes comprising volitions and (certain of) their effects? Perhaps he identifies actions with volitions, or at least with volitions that have (certain sorts of) effects? Perhaps he takes actions to be certain behavioural or other events that have volitions as their causes? There is, it seems, no saying.[21] When defending the causal character of the tie between a volition and those of its effects that are implicated in the action the agent performs, however, he does shed some light on the connections between content and conduct.[22]

Focusing on the case of bodily actions he writes:

---

[20] The argument from unfulfilled intentions to the primitiveness of intention is to be found in Davidson, 'Intending', 83–102. Gilbert Harman defends the primitiveness of intention in 'Practical Reasoning', *Review of Metaphysics*, 29 (1975–6), 431–63, writing (at 441): 'it seems quite obvious that actions cannot be explained in terms of beliefs and desires alone; these attitudes must be translated into intentions before one can act.'

Anticipations of Hume can be found in Locke. In the *Essay*, ii. xxi. 71, he alludes to the particularly interesting case of 'sudden Palsy'. In a letter to the Dutch theologian Philippus von Limborch he writes: 'I readily recognize ineffective volition, as when a paralytic wills to move his palsied hand; I grant that that volition is ineffective and without result.' See *The Correspondence of John Locke*, ed. E. S. de Beer, vii (Oxford, 1982), 404.

In *Philosophical Investigations*, transl. G. E. M. Anscombe (New York, 1958), i. 621, Wittgenstein poses the famous question: 'what is left over if I subtract the fact that my arm goes up from the fact that I raise my arm?' For Hume, the answer would be obvious: arm raising minus arm rising equals volition. Compare G. N. A. Vesey, 'Volition', in Donald F. Gustafson (ed.), *Essays in Philosophical Psychology* (Garden City, NY, 1964), 55.

[21] For an examination of some of the alternatives, but with the concept of trying substituting for that of volition, see McGinn, *The Character of Mind*, 86–90.

[22] Hume emphasizes characteristic themes when he writes that 'the will being here consider'd as a cause, has no more a discoverable connexion with its effects, than any material cause has with its proper effect' (*T* 632) and that '[w]hen we consider our will or volition *a priori*, abstracting from experience, we should never be able to infer any effect from it' (*Abstract*, 23). At *E* 65–9 he offers arguments for these claims, first for the case of bodily actions, then for merely mental ones.

the immediate object of power in voluntary motion, is not the member itself which is moved, but certain muscles, and nerves, and animal spirits, and, perhaps, something still more minute and more unknown, through which the motion is successively propagated, ere it reach the member itself whose motion is the immediate object of volition ... Here the mind wills a certain event: Immediately another event, unknown to ourselves, and totally different from the one intended, is produced: This event produces another, equally unknown: Till at last, through a long succession, the desired event is produced. (*E* 66)

Of the volition's many effects only those whose description maps, in appropriate ways, onto the content of the volition are implicated, we may say, in the action the agent wills to perform. The agent does, in the palmary sense, only what, through the content of his volition, he represents himself as doing. Despite their undeniable causal role, intervening physiological events—not represented in the content of the agent's volitions at least in part because unknown to the agent—are not amongst the events to be mentioned in a specification of what the agent does. Hume emphasizes what is epistemically available to the agent. He might equally have emphasized what is jointly available to the agent and to someone, an interpreter, who would explain the agent's doings: for the case of bodily actions, at any rate, what the agent does is something of a sort accessible both to agent and interpreter. Content and explanation concern normally observable distal, not proximal, effects of the agent's volitions. Its distal, not its physiologically proximate, effects contribute to the conditions on a volition's satisfaction.

Hume has a conception of acting, as we may say, in the normal, simple way.[23] '[N]ature', he writes, 'has taught us the use of our limbs, without giving us the knowledge of the muscles and nerves, by which they are actuated' (*E* 55). In his example the agent moves his arm while knowing nothing about *how* he does it. Better, he moves his arm without there being any means by which he does it. His moving his arm is 'the *immediate* object of volition' (*E* 66, emphasis added): he moves his arm but not by doing something else that is itself an object of volition. By implication Hume must countenance non-immediate objects of volition and so actions done by the doing of something else. He writes, of course, of deeds 'perform'd with a certain design and intention' (*T* 475), or 'from a particular fore-thought and design' (*T* 349); he writes that one 'will[s] the performance of certain actions as a means of obtaining any desir'd good' (*T* 417). He offers no explicit analysis of non-immediate objects of volition,

---

[23] The helpful phrase is Harman's, 'Practical Reasoning', 443.

however, and says nothing of the questions of individuation that their introduction raises. Reckoning with the fact that an agent's actions may themselves have effects Hume does, however, remark that in so far as these are unknown to the agent the agent acts 'ignorantly and casually' (*T* 412). Such effects of the agent's volitions are 'involuntary and accidental' (*T* 350).

We explain an agent's action—explain, more narrowly, his volition—by citing his reason for that action. In citing that reason we invoke, explicitly or implicitly, the suitably linked desire and belief that caused his action. Such explanation is a matter, in Hume's words, of 'the interpretation of ... [his] actions from our knowledge of ... [his] motives and inclinations' (*E* 85). Of course, the agent may have had other, even other causally efficacious, reasons for performing that very action. As noted earlier, Hume acknowledges the possibility of 'combined motives' (*E* 302) for a given action. He even envisages a motive's capacity to recruit additional motives for a projected action: 'A man, who from any motives has entertain'd a resolution of performing an action, naturally runs into every other view or motive, which may fortify that resolution, and give it authority and influence on the mind' (*T* 382). Of course, the agent may well have been subject to competing motivations, to 'contrary passions' (*T* 441), with respect to that very action, may well have had reason not only to do, but also to refrain from doing, it. Trivially, one of his competing motives—or some set of compatible motives—was the 'more powerful' (*T* 314) and so 'prevailed' (*E* 291): it was the motive, or the set of motives, that caused, and whose citation correctly explains, what the agent did.

Somehow the agent moved from the set of competing motives to the formation of the volition implicated in his action; somehow he proceeded to a 'choice' (*E* 226) amongst his alternatives. Hume doesn't comment on the fact that we do not need to know how that transition took place in order to explain his action correctly.[24] But, cognizant of the motivational complexities lurking behind most volitions, he is of course aware of the difficulties both in identifying the agent's actual reason for his action and in the predictive activity of forming an '*inference* from motive to voluntary actions' (*E* 90). There is 'great difficulty', he points out, in 'deciding concerning the actions and resolutions of men, where there is any contrariety of motives and passions' (*T* 418).[25] He attends to these difficulties when exploring, both in the *Treatise* (*T* 399–407) and in the first *Enquiry* (*E*

---

[24] Compare Davidson, 'Psychology as Philosophy', in *Essays on Actions and Events*, 233.

[25] *T* 440 displays an awareness of the contribution that the agent's probability assessments makes to these complexities.

80–96), the prospects for discovering strict causal laws linking reasons for action and the actions they explain.[26]

The competing motives that make the explanation and prediction of voluntary action so difficult for the interpreter provide the agent himself with a set of competing considerations that bear on his choice of what to do. These considerations set the agent's task when he 'deliberates concerning his own conduct' (*E* 289). Deliberation incorporates, of course, straightforwardly theoretical reflection pertinent to the constitution or achievement of the agent's several goals. It involves, too, the weighing of his competing concerns.

Hume makes no serious effort to provide a model for practical reasoning as it moves from competing reasons for action to the formation of volition. At least in the second *Enquiry*, however, he seems to think that the desires ingredient in such reasonings are in some way conditional in character. He writes of certain altruistic desires: 'Let these generous sentiments be supposed ever so weak; let them be insufficient to move even a hand or finger of our body, they must still direct the determinations of our mind, and *where everything else is equal*, produce a cool preference of what is useful and serviceable to mankind, above what is pernicious and dangerous' (*E* 271, emphasis added). In a similar vein: 'Let us suppose such a person ever so selfish; let private interest have ingrossed ever so much his attention; yet in instances, where that is not concerned, he must unavoidably feel *some* propensity to the good of mankind, and make it an object of choice, *if everything else be equal*' (*E* 226, emphasis added for the condition). He writes, too, of 'a plain foundation of preference, *where everything else is equal*' (*E* 235, emphasis added).

Perhaps, unexcitingly, Hume's point is merely that a reason for action prompts volition, and so action, on condition that some stronger reason for action does not hold sway. Perhaps, however, he here intimates the significant thought that desires for the performance of particular actions are conditional on the envisaged properties of those actions. An agent desires to perform a particular action in so far as that action has a certain feature F: he wants to swim at noon in so far as doing so will be refreshing. In so far as it has some other feature, G, however, he may well want not to perform that action: he wants not to swim at noon in so far as doing so will take time from his work. Linguistic expression of these desires demands explicitly evaluative sentences that display their conditionality. Perhaps the sentence 'Other things being equal, my swimming at

---

[26] See Chap. 7.

noon is desirable' would serve for the first of the two desires. Perhaps 'In so far as it would be refreshing my swimming at noon is desirable' or 'The fact that it would be refreshing makes my swimming at noon prima facie desirable', by being more explicit, would be better. Were the agent to choose to swim, linguistic expression for his volition would require an explicitly evaluative sentence that eschews the conditionalization of desire. Perhaps in context 'My swimming at noon is desirable' would do. With conditionalization absent, this sentence would express the all-out or unconditional character of the agent's decision, made in the light of the several competing considerations, to swim. The similarities and differences in the sentences that, on this rendering, express desire and volition respectively correspond to those, already noted, in their respective functional or causal roles.[27]

An adequate model for the structure of practical reasoning must make room for the agent's summing of the pros and cons with respect to acting in a given way. Here Locke sees more clearly than Hume. Locke distinguishes what he terms the 'last judgement of the understanding' from the volition that follows it, taking the former to be a judgement of comparative value with respect to options currently available to the agent.[28] '[A]n action of willing this or that', he writes, 'always follows a judgement of the understanding by which a man judges this to be better for here and now';[29] in forming this last judgement the agent makes a 'judgement of the understanding about the thing to be done',[30] judges 'what is best for him to do',[31] judges 'which is best, *viz.* to do, or forbear'.[32] Hume notes no need for something summary prior to volition.

He sees more clearly than Locke, however, in recognizing that the practicality of volitions (a feature of volitions on which Locke himself insists) requires the practicality, and so the conativity, of reasons for action. Where Locke has last judgements *of the understanding* Hume must require, were he to take the point about the need for summing comparative assessment, intervening states of *desire*. He must construe summing comparative assessments in ways consonant with his conativist, not Locke's

---

[27] This sketch derives from Davidson's account of practical reasoning in 'How is Weakness of the Will Possible?' in *Essays on Actions and Events*, especially 36–9. Here, and elsewhere, I follow Ross, Davidson, and others in the use of the expression 'prima facie'. For an argument that *pro tanto* considerations, rather than prima facie ones, are in question in reasons for action see Susan Hurley, *Natural Reasons: Personality and Polity* (Oxford, 1989), 125–35, and 'Conflict, Akrasia and Cognitivism', *Proceedings of the Aristotelian Society*, 86 (1985–6), 23–49.

[28] Locke, *Correspondence*, vii. 411.   [29] Ibid. 410.   [30] Ibid. 411.

[31] Locke, *Essay*, II. xxi. 48.   [32] Ibid. 71.

cognitivist, theory of reasons for action. Presumably our noontime swim-mer could express this intervening state of desire by saying 'The consid-erations pro and con make my swimming at noon prima facie desirable'.[33]

It may be objected that seeking a Humean model for practical reason-ing is quite misguided. After all, Hume denies, in a notorious passage from the *Treatise*, that choice can be 'contrary to reason'. But if the tran-sition from reasons for action to volition can neither conform to, nor be contrary to, reason how can it coherently be construed as a case of rea-soning? His words are undeniably provocative:

'Tis not contrary to reason to prefer the destruction of the whole world to the scratching of my finger. 'Tis not contrary to reason for me to chuse my total ruin, to prevent the least uneasiness to an *Indian* or person wholly unknown to me. 'Tis as little contrary to reason to prefer even my own acknowledg'd lesser good to my greater, and have a more ardent affection for the former than the latter. (*T* 416)

If attention-getting, however, the passage is terminologically unfortu-nate. Hume's point is not that the preferences described are not irra-tional but that they are not properly modelled within a *cognitivist* theory of reasons for action. In saying the preferences are not 'contrary to rea-son' his contention is, narrowly, that they are not evaluable as true or as false. On the face of it, this leaves open the question of their evaluability as rational or irrational, and so the possibility that Hume does indeed have, as he clearly seems to have, a conception of practical reasoning. Can a *conativist* conception of practical reasoning in fact accommodate claims of rationality or irrationality in preference? Can it provide a model for the formation of an irrational preference? We shall consider some questions concerning irrationality and weakness of will when, in Chap-ters 4 and 6, we examine what Hume says about moral sentiment, and about convention. We shall return, if only briefly, to the question of ra-tionality in Chapter 7.

---

[33] Davidson, in 'How is Weakness of the Will Possible?' and 'Intending', sees more clearly than either. On his analysis, practical reasoning requires a summary prima facie judgement of comparative value before one moves to an unconditional or all-out evaluative judgement. The requirement—if in linguistic terms—resembles Locke's. But he takes both the sum-mary and the unconditional judgements—as also the prima facie evaluative judgements the summary one presupposes—to express psychological states that 'belong to the same genus of pro attitudes' ('Intending', 102). Roughly, prima facie evaluative judgements, sum-mary or otherwise, express wants; again roughly, unconditional judgements express inten-tions. Here, he resembles—if, again, in linguistic terms—the conativist Hume rather than the cognitivist Locke. (For Hume's *non*-linguistic use of 'judgment', see below, Chap. 3, n. 1.)

3. AFFECTIONS AND THEIR DEPENDENCE
ON DESIRES

Issues of so-called official theory to one side, Hume's desires and volitions are alike in being conative states with descriptive propositional content, alike in possessing the world-to-mind direction of fit. Both have
satisfaction-conditions, not truth-conditions. Both are expressible in explicitly evaluative sentences. They differ, however, in their causal or functional role: his desires set an agent's goals; his volitions initiate efforts at
implementing those goals. Connectedly, they differ in their determinate
contents: volitions represent particular actions of the agent's own; desires
are not thus restricted in what they represent. Presumably they differ,
too, in the evaluative sentences that provide their expression. Sentences
that serve to express desires must have the properties—perhaps, in particular, the prima facie character—required of major premises in practical arguments; those expressing volitions must have the properties—in
particular the all-out character—required in conclusions to such arguments.

Despite their similarities, Hume's desires and volitions differ in another respect as well, for desires are, volitions are not, what he calls 'passions'. '[P]roperly speaking', at least, 'the WILL ... [is] not comprehended
among the passions' (*T* 399).[34] In Hume's taxonomy, the passions comprise desires and what, regimenting his terminology, we shall call *affections*.

Construed narrowly, desires are 'direct passions', passions that 'arise
immediately from good or evil, from pain or pleasure' (*T* 276).[35] Construed broadly, as Hume's conativism requires, desires include the passions
of benevolence, anger, pity, and malice, passions that Hume assembles—
along with a number of others—under the heading of so-called 'indirect
passions'. As indirect passions these 'proceed ... [from good or evil, from
pain or pleasure], but by the conjunction of other qualities' (*T* 276). What
other qualities? We shall return to the question shortly.

Affections, too, are either direct or indirect. Hume writes at one place
of 'the direct affections' (*T* 439), including under that heading the passions—not themselves desires—of joy, grief, hope, and fear. At another,
identifying the chief indirect passions—in this case, indirect passions that
are not themselves desires—he writes of 'the affections of pride or humility,

---

[34] On this point compare Penelhum, *Hume*, 114.
[35] Anti-hedonist caveats must be taken as read.

love or hatred' (*T* 334).[36] It is time to examine Hume's doctrine of the affections, both direct and indirect. What, in his view, is their nature? How do they differ from desires (whether direct or indirect) and volitions? In what relations do they stand to desires and volitions? What role, if any, have they in the explanation of action?

Hume offers an atomistic official theory of the affections. They are simple, isolable, introspectible feelings with hedonic qualitative content. Possessing no propositional or other representational content, they are not evaluable as true or false. They are none the less associated with thoughts characterizable, proleptically, as thoughts of their objects. As 'impressions of reflection' they have other psychological states amongst their causes; they have, many of them, psychological states of specific types amongst their effects. Hume extends what we have seen him say of pride and humility to the other affections as well: 'being simple and uniform impressions, 'tis impossible we can ever, by a multitude of words, give a just definition of them' (*T* 277); '[t]he utmost we can pretend to is a description of them, by an enumeration of such circumstances, as attend them' (ibid.). It is 'their sensations, or the peculiar emotions they excite in the soul ... which constitute their very being and essence' (*T* 286).

The task of enumerating, in systematic fashion, the attendant circumstances of these 'simple impressions' is, for Hume, the task of identifying the causal laws that would constitute an associationist psychology of the affections. For the case of the indirect affections of pride, humility, love, and hatred, at least, it is the task of articulating the associationist laws that govern a 'double relation of ideas and impressions' (*T* 286). Within the associationist framework for these indirect affections the affection resembles a prior affection in virtue of its hedonic quality: each is pleasant or each is painful. The thought of the later affection's object is linked, by some relation (from among the associative relations of resemblance, causality or contiguity) among their contents, to a thought that accompanies the prior affection. Pleased by Brown's generosity to Green one feels pleasure directed towards (feels love for) Brown. Displeased by Smith's surliness one feels displeasure (hatred) towards Smith. Pleased by one's performance in the title role of *Hamlet* one has the pleasant feeling of pride directed towards oneself. Displeased by one's ineptitude on the golf course one has the painful feeling of humility (or shame) with oneself, again, as its object. 'Those principles, which forward the transition of ideas', Hume writes, 'here concur with those, which operate on the passions;

---

[36] As we shall see below, there are other indirect affections as well.

and both uniting in one action, bestow on the mind a double impulse' (*T* 284).[37]

As earlier in the cases of desire and volition, there is no point in following Hume down the atomist's blind alley. But what else, his atomism aside, does or can Hume say of the affections? Mildly amending his official theory he can, of course, allow them to have propositional, or other representational, content. He can, then, offer as comments on their distinctive contents such claims as:

When good is certain or probable, it produces JOY. When evil is in the same situation there arises GRIEF or SORROW.

When either good or evil is uncertain, it gives rise to FEAR or HOPE, according to the degrees of uncertainty on the one side or the other. (*T* 439)

Even with propositional, or other representational, content, however, affections are not truth-evaluable: one's joy or grief, love or hatred, is neither true nor false. Affections haven't the mind-to-world direction of fit, thus clearly differing from beliefs and other cognitive states. As clearly, however, they haven't the world-to-mind direction of fit either, and thus they differ, quite fundamentally, from both desires and volitions.[38] My delight in my son's achievements rests on the belief, evaluable as true or false, that he has had them, but my delight is not similarly evaluable. My delight presupposes, as we shall see, a desire that he have achievements, a desire with satisfaction-conditions and the world-to-mind direction of fit. But that delight does not itself set goals for action, does not itself have satisfaction-conditions.

Not having the world-to-mind direction of fit, affections cannot have the practicality of desires, or that of volitions. My delight in my son's achievements cannot play the major role in a reason for action; its linguistic expression cannot provide the major premise in a practical argument. Nor can it constitute the choice of a course of action. Affections play none of the functional roles identifiable—for desires, for beliefs, for

---

[37] I emphasize the difficulties in Hume's official theory of the affections in 'Emotion and Thought in Hume's *Treatise*'. In 'Hume's Associationist Psychology', *Journal of the History of the Behavioral Sciences*, 8 (1974), 397–409, I examine his associationist accounts both of thinking and of the passions.

[38] Affections have, in Searle's terminology, the null direction of fit. In *Intentionality*, 8, Searle writes: 'there are ... Intentional states that have the null direction of fit. If I am sorry that I insulted you or pleased that you won the prize, then, though my sorrow contains a belief that I insulted you and a wish that I hadn't insulted you and my pleasure contains a belief that you won the prize and a wish that you won the prize, my sorrow and pleasure can't be true or false in the way that my beliefs can, nor fulfilled in the way my desires can.'

volitions—in the basic psychological configuration that constitutes action for a reason. They can play, then, no central role in the explanation of actions. It is utterly unsurprising that Hume ignores them when, at *Treatise*, II. iii. 3, he constructs his two arguments for a specifically conativist account of reasons for action.

To understand affections one must—following Hume's terminological lead—call upon a distinctive concept of *satisfaction*. 'A relation', Hume writes, 'is requisite to joy, in order to approach the object to us, and make it give us any satisfaction'; for 'joy as well as pride' our tendency to compare one object with others affects the 'satisfaction' we feel (*T* 291). In feeling joy we are 'satisfy'd with the thing [the object] itself' (*T* 293). The prior affection that, within Hume's associationist theory, prompts love involves 'a separate satisfaction' (*T* 336). Individuals can be 'satisfy'd with their own character, or genius, or fortune' (*T* 331); a suitable 'mental quality in ourselves or others gives us a satisfaction' (*T* 574–5). Hume writes of '[t]he *satisfaction* we take in the riches of others' (*T* 357), of 'the satisfaction, which we sometimes receive from the discovery of truth' (*T* 449), of the 'very sensible satisfaction' arising from '[h]ealth, when it returns after a long absence' (*T* 292). Contrasting satisfaction with its complement—with dissatisfaction, as we may say—Hume typically writes of 'satisfaction and uneasiness' (*T* 312, 471, 475).

Intimating a more specialized notion of satisfaction that is peculiarly suited (for reasons we shall consider below) to the characterization of certain indirect affections Hume writes (for the case of pride) of 'self-satisfaction' (*T* 293), of being 'satisfy'd with ourselves' (*T* 297), of 'pride or self-satisfaction' (*T* 320). Humility (shame) is a form of dissatisfaction with ourselves. Love and hatred are forms of satisfaction and dissatisfaction, respectively, that are directed towards others.

A pun points up a deep connection between desires and affections. Desires have satisfaction-conditions but are not themselves forms of satisfaction. Propositional affections (affections with propositional content), not having the world-to-mind direction of fit, do not have satisfaction-conditions. They are, however, forms of satisfaction or dissatisfaction prompted by beliefs, of the satisfaction-conditions for desires, that those conditions have, or have not, been met. Contrasting desire with the other direct passions Hume contrasts 'the propensity or aversion, with the consequent emotions' (*T* 438): the latter are forms of satisfaction or uneasiness consequent upon one's possessing or securing, or failing to possess or secure, what one wants. They may be consequent, as well, upon estimates that one is likely or unlikely to acquire what one wants: 'An object, whose existence we desire, gives satisfaction, when we reflect on those causes, which produce it; and for the same reason excites grief or uneasiness from the opposite consideration' (*T* 440). There are 'mental passions', as we saw when discussing egoism, 'by which we are impelled immediately to seek particular objects, such as fame or power, or vengeance' (*E* 301): one desires that one be famous or powerful, or that one has revenge. On securing these objects of desire we have affections that constitute our sense of satisfaction: 'when these objects are attained a pleasing enjoyment ensues, as the consequence of our indulged affections' (*E* 301).[39] One is pleased that, one is satisfied by the fact that, one is famous or powerful, or that one has secured one's revenge. Once acquainted with these satisfactions we can, of course, have them as objects of 'secondary' desires. Having these satisfactions as objects of desire 'we feel a[n] ... emotion of aversion or propensity, and are carry'd to avoid or embrace what will give us this uneasiness or satisfaction' (*T* 414).

How, non-atomistically, shall we model propositional affections as satisfactions or dissatisfactions? One possibility, familiar in outline from our discussions of desire and volition, is to view them as special modes of conception. An individual thinks—in a satisfied manner—that her luck has turned, that her daughter has made a name for herself, that a co-worker has been uncommonly generous. She thinks—in a dissatisfied fashion— that the sheriff is at the door, that she is quite without talent, that an acquaintance has been condescending. A thought thus modified has neither the mind-to-world nor the world-to-mind direction of fit. Nevertheless its occurrence requires, as causal conditions, both an appropriate desire and a belief, of the satisfaction-conditions for that desire, that they obtain. One thinks, in a satisfied manner, that one's luck has turned: one must both want it to turn and believe that it has. How characterize the satisfied and dissatisfied modes of conception the model introduces? Presumably here, as in the cases of desire and volition, the phenomenological approach that Hume would naturally favour had better give way to the interpreter's emphasis on causal role or functional location. Officially an atomist about the affections, Hume at least nods in the direction of modes of conception when writing, in 'A Dissertation on the Passions', that 'it is essential to pride to turn our view on ourselves with complacency and satisfaction'.[40]

---

[39] The 'affections' Hume mentions here must be understood as desires. Recall that, in referring to his doctrine of affections, we are regimenting Hume's terminology.

[40] David Hume, 'A Dissertation on the Passions', in *Essays Moral, Political, and Literary*, ed. T. H. Green and T. H. Grose, ii (London, 1889), 144.

An alternative non-atomist model recognizes a fourth primitive attitude (actually, a complementary pair of attitudes) towards the truth of propositions. One can believe a proposition to be true, want a proposition to be true, will (or intend) a proposition to be true: we have encountered these primitive attitudes when reflecting on the basic configuration constitutive of action for a reason. One can also be satisfied or dissatisfied by the truth of a proposition. One stands in one or other of these affective attitudes towards a proposition *p* only if one both wants *p* to be true and either believes it true (thus feeling satisfied) or believes it false (thus feeling dissatisfied). One wants true the proposition that one's luck turns; and one believes true the proposition that it turns—or the proposition that it does not. In consequence, one is satisfied by the truth of the proposition that one's luck turns—or dissatisfied by the truth of the proposition that it does not.

We have yet to explicate Hume's distinction between direct and indirect passions, whether affections or desires. Nor have we explored the more specialized notions of satisfaction and dissatisfaction that, in Hume's usage, take persons, not propositions, as their objects. While noting the associationist structure of Hume's account of the indirect passions of pride, humility, love, and hatred, we have not pressed for clarification of the principal elements in that structure. We must complicate the picture of desire and affection that we have sketched thus far. Interpreting—and regimenting—Hume we must, in particular, make two partly overlapping distinctions: that between *person-directed* and *propositional* affections; and that between propositional passions, whether desires or affections, that are *person-implicating*, and those that are *not*.

Humean joy and grief are the most basic affections.[41] Joy arises when the securing of what one desires is certain or probable; grief is a consequence of the belief that the evil one desires not to occur will in fact, or is likely to, occur. Hope and fear, Hume holds, are complex products of joy and grief: they 'arise from the different mixture of these opposite passions of grief and joy, and from their imperfect union and conjunction' (*T* 443); provided a good or evil is uncertain one experiences fear, alternatively hope, 'according to the degrees of uncertainty on the one side or the other' (*T* 439). Joy and grief, hope and fear, are propositional affections.

Hume typically represents them as *direct*—and so, as not indirect— affections. As with desires, however, he has a conception of joy and grief

---

[41] Recall that Hume's terms for the passions must be taken as technical, explicitly generic, terms.

(thus of hope and fear) that crosses his direct/indirect divide. Joy and grief are *indirect* propositional affections if and only if—in Hume's insufficiently explicit formulation—their contents incorporate reference to 'good or evil . . . pain or pleasure' but only as conditioned by 'the conjunction of other qualities' (*T* 276). They are indirect propositional affections if and only if, that is to say, they are *person-implicating* ones. They are person-implicating if and only if, in their contents, they make appropriate reference to—in that sense implicate—persons. Wanting a sunny day one is pleased that the day is sunny: the joy one experiences, making no reference of the requisite sort to some person or other, is a direct affection. Wanting someone to give a helping hand one is pleased that Tom is doing so: one's joy, with its essential reference to the person Tom, is an indirect affection. In effect, joy and grief are person-implicating if and only if they could constitute the *prior* affections that Hume cites as the causes of the (also indirect, but non-propositional) *person-directed* affections of pride, humility, love, and hatred. (Pleased that Tom is giving a helping hand, one loves Tom.) As propositional affections, joy and grief are forms of satisfaction or dissatisfaction consequent upon the securing, or the failure to secure, what one *desires*. Given that they are person-implicating affections, the desires they presuppose must likewise be *person-implicating* ones. The 'other qualities' Hume refers to when marking the direct/indirect division are, in effect, *appropriate* relations to *persons*, relations that, when incorporated in the contents of desires and propositional affections, fit those desires and affections for their special place in the generation of the several person-directed affections.

　　What relations to persons are the appropriate ones? From Hume's side, the task of specifying these is precisely that of setting out, within his associationist theory, the causal conditions on the occurrence of pride, humility, love, and hatred. It is the task of identifying just those elements in the contents of propositional affections that lead a person to be proud or ashamed of herself, to love or hate another. It requires identifying the peculiar relations in which the goods or evils in question must stand to the person who has the propositional affection in question if that person is to feel a consequent person-directed affection. 'We may feel joy', Hume writes, 'upon being present at a feast, where our senses are regal'd with delicacies of every kind: But 'tis only the master of the feast, who beside the same joy, has the additional passion of self-applause and vanity' (*T* 290). All those present are pleased, perhaps, but only the master is proud. In what peculiar relation must the feast stand to the master of the feast, and not to the others present, if he, but not the others, is to have a person-implicating satisfaction (a person-implicating, thus indirect, joy) and so feel the person-directed affection of pride? An answer to this question, and many others like it, would together constitute a determinate specification of the 'other qualities' Hume has in mind.[42]

It is no part of our present concern to set out in detail these 'other qualities'. It is sufficient, here, to fasten on the structure that, abstractly considered, Hume's associationist theory of the person-directed affections (pride, humility, love, hatred) reveals. The person-directed affections require prior propositional affections that have two essential characteristics. First, they resemble the person-directed affections they cause by being instances of satisfaction (for the cases of pride and love) or of dissatisfaction (for the cases of humility and hatred). Second, they are person-implicating affections and their propositional contents are linked to the contents of the person-directed affections they cause by incorporating suitable reference to the very individuals who are the objects of these person-directed affections. The pianist is satisfied with himself (pride) because he is satisfied with his performance of the sonata (joy). The judge is dissatisfied with herself (humility or shame) because dissatisfied with her conduct of the trial (grief). The listener is pleased (displeased) with the soprano (love or, alternatively, hate) because pleased (displeased) with the quality of her voice (joy or, alternatively, grief). The person-implicating affections in their turn require person-implicating desires whose satisfaction-conditions set the conditions on affective satisfaction or dissatisfaction. The pianist is satisfied with his performance of the sonata (joy): he wanted himself to play it as he did (desire). The judge is dissatisfied with her conduct of the trial (grief): she wanted not to conduct it as she did (desire). Hume traces much of this causal route from person-implicating desire, through person-implicating affection of joy or grief, to person-directed affection of pride or humility, love or hatred, when he writes:

The most immediate effects of pleasure and pain are the propense and averse motions of the mind; which are diversified into volition, into desire and aversion, grief and joy, hope and fear ... But when along with this, the objects, that cause pleasure or pain, acquire a relation to ourselves or others; they still continue to excite desire and aversion, grief and joy: But cause, at the same time, the indirect passions of pride or humility, love or hatred, which in this case have a double relation of impressions and ideas to the pain or pleasure. (*T* 574; compare *T* 438–9)

---

[42] Obviously, the presence of pronominal self-reference would not be sufficient to make a desire or affection person-implicating. A man desires that *he* eat a muffin; in eating it he experiences a consequent satisfaction in *his* doing so. There is pronominal self-reference but the desire and affection are direct.

Person-implicating forms of joy and grief give rise to the *person-directed* affections of pride or humility, love or hatred. Affections of the latter sort, on whose characterization Hume lavishes some ninety pages of the *Treatise*, have persons—the individual herself who has the affection, someone other than the individual herself—as their objects. Experiencing pride or humility a person has herself as object: in their cases 'the immediate *object* is self or that identical person, of whose thoughts, actions, and sensations we are intimately conscious' (*T* 329). For the affections of love and hatred 'the *object* . . . is some other person, of whose thoughts, actions, and sensations we are not conscious' (ibid.). One may be satisfied or dissatisfied with oneself or with some other.

On the assumption that they are not themselves propositional, how, non-atomistically, are person-directed affections to be modelled? As modes of non-propositional conceptions of oneself or of some other person? In terms of yet another primitive attitude (or complementary pair of primitive attitudes), but one directed not to propositions but to persons? If they are modelled in terms of modes of conception, the peculiarities of the particular modes will need spelling out, presumably in terms of functional location or causal role. If primitive attitudes are preferred, it would seem essential not to confound an attitude such as that of x being satisfied with y with the attitude, appropriate for propositional affections, of x being satisfied with the truth of proposition p. To construe person-directed affections as, despite Humean appearances, propositional would be to reduce them to the person-implicating propositional affections that, for Hume, are their causes.[43]

Some person-directed affections in their turn prompt desires for the well-being or ill-being (as the case may be) of the persons who are their objects. 'The passions of love and hatred', Hume writes, 'are always followed by, or rather conjoin'd with benevolence and anger' (*T* 367): 'Love is always follow'd by a desire of the happiness of the person belov'd, and an aversion to his misery: As hatred produces a desire of the misery and an aversion to the happiness of the person hated' (ibid.). He denies such a link between affection and consequent desire for the cases of pride and

[43] Annette Baier argues, 'Hume's Analysis of Pride', *Journal of Philosophy*, 75 (1978), 27–40, the inadequacy of efforts to read Hume's theory of the passions as a theory of *propositional* passions. Perhaps her conception of 'complex-term attitudes' (40) would help in the modelling of person-directed affections. Davidson, in 'Hume's Cognitive Theory of Pride', concentrates on what he calls '*propositional pride*' (277). Propositional pride is, I take it, equivalent to what I have identified as the person-implicating affection that gives rise to the person-directed affection of pride. Davidson elaborates on the causal conditions of propositional pride but does not place desire among them.

humility, describing these as 'pure emotions in the soul, unattended with any desire, and not immediately exciting us to action' (ibid.).[44]

The complex Humean picture of the intersection of desire, belief, volition, and affection that has now emerged, if obviously an idealization, is a theoretically satisfying and illuminating one. While eschewing his psychological atomism, and while emphasizing some things he does not himself emphasize, it depicts a structure clearly present in the passions as Hume describes them. Building on the basic configuration of desire, belief, and volition that constitutes action for a reason it introduces the concept of affections, the concept of states of satisfaction or dissatisfaction consequent on the realization, or the failure to realize, the satisfaction-conditions on desire. Introducing special classes of person-implicating desires and affections, as well as person-directed passions, it introduces a yet more complicated configuration. Person-implicating desires (perhaps through the volitions to which they give rise) prompt the person-implicating affections of joy or grief that in turn prompt the person-directed affections of pride or humility, love or hatred. The person-directed affections of love or hatred in their turn generate the desires Hume calls benevolence or anger. These desires, it goes without saying, prompt volitions, affections, and desires in their own turn.

Attention to this more comprehensive configuration of psychological elements reveals the functional or causal position of the affections, and how that position contrasts with those of desires and volitions. It thus makes plain both why affections cannot have the central role to play in the explanation of actions and how they can be action-explanatory none the less. Precisely because of their ties to desires, and thus to volitions, affections can serve effectively in elliptical explanations of what a person does. Being cognizant of the comprehensive configuration one can understand an agent's action when told that she acted from love, or because she was afraid, or because she was pleased with how he had behaved, even though these explanations cite affections rather than desires.

Commitment to the comprehensive configuration appears to commit Hume to an unqualified thesis of the *centrality of desire*: the satisfactions or dissatisfactions that constitute the affections, whether person-directed or propositional, whether person-implicating or not, presuppose desires and the conditions on their satisfaction. Is the thesis, thus stated, too strong? Though committed, in the main, to the centrality of desire, does Hume perhaps admit cases of person-directed affections that do not presuppose

---

[44] Hume claims not that pride and humility do not have person-implicating desires amongst their *causes* but, very differently, that they do not have desires amongst their *effects*.

prior propositional affections, or cases of propositional affections that presuppose no desires? Can the prior pain or pleasure that a person-directed affection requires, within Hume's associationist framework, not be a *bodily* pain or pleasure, thus not an affection? After all, '[b]odily pains and pleasures are', as Hume writes, 'the source of many passions' (*T* 276). It hardly follows, however, from their being the source of many passions, that they cause, without the intervention of propositional affections, person-directed ones. 'A fit of gout', Hume writes, 'produces a long train of passions, as grief, hope, fear' (*T* 276). It produces, that is to say, a train of propositional (albeit not person-implicating) affections. Perhaps he would say, similarly, that the bodily pain caused by someone's stepping on one's gouty toes prompts the person-directed affection of hatred towards that person by first prompting the person-implicating affection of dissatisfaction (grief) at that person's having caused the pain.

What, more fundamentally, of the unqualified claim that *propositional affections* depend on *desires*? Does Hume perhaps allow that propositional affections consequent upon *bodily* pains or pleasures do not presuppose desires pertinent to those pains and pleasures? Does he perhaps allow that the grief consequent upon the pains of gout does not require a prior desire not to feel pain, or at least not to feel those pains? To be sure, the bodily pain itself requires no prior desire, but then that pain is a sensation (an 'impression of sensation'), not an affection. From the special standing of pleasant and painful sensations, however, nothing follows for the aetiology of the propositional affections—the joy or grief—they prompt. Hume might very well hold that such an affection presupposes a desire, perhaps the desire he identifies as 'the general appetite to good, and aversion to evil, consider'd merely as such' (*T* 417). The sufferer hasn't in the requisite sense a reason for feeling the pain but, not wanting to feel pain, he may none the less have a reason for his grief.

Hume has a conception of 'reasons for . . . passions' (*T* 278), including, as the context makes clear, reasons for affections. He has a complementary conception both of combined and of competing reasons for affections, employing the latter when writing that 'where any person can excite . . . [certain] sentiments, he soon acquires our esteem; unless other circumstances of his character render him odious and disagreeable' (*T* 614). Persons, as he is well aware, have both attractive and unattractive qualities; actions and situations can have both desirable and undesirable aspects. Person-implicating affections, it seems, are conditional on the properties of the persons whom they concern. In so far as a man is witty he prompts a propositional form of satisfaction; in so far as he is grasping he prompts dissatisfaction. In forming their affections others 'consider ... him as' the one thing and 'as' the other (*T* 357). On the face of it, desires, providing reasons for such conditionalized affections, must themselves (as we suggested earlier) be conditionalized. 'In so far as a man is witty he is a desirable sort of man; Jones is witty; in so far as he is witty, then, Jones is a desirable sort of man. Unfortunately, he is also grasping.' The imagined speaker expresses the conditionalized desire that, together with the belief expressed, provides a reason for the conditionalized affection that he then expresses. He goes on to express a belief pertinent to a competing desire and a competing affection. The fact that the desire here provides (part of) a reason for a propositional affection rather than for a more determinate desire is to be explained, presumably, by the character of the mediating belief.

Must one reach unconditional person-implicating affections in the face of such competing considerations? Must one reach unconditional person-directed ones? What, too, of competing direct affections? Hume offers no explicit answers to these specific questions. Writing more broadly about the affections, however, he envisages a variety of upshots in situations where reasons for affections are in competition: 'where the objects of contrary passions are presented at once, beside the encrease of the predominant passion ... it sometimes happens, that both the passions exist successively, and by short intervals; sometimes, that they destroy each other, and neither of them takes place; and sometimes that both of them remain united in the mind' (*T* 441). He *seems* not to think that competition amongst reasons for the affections must be resolved in the way in which, in forming volitions, one resolves competition amongst desires. In seeming not to think this he seems to be right.

Attending austerely to the structure of Hume's comprehensive configuration of desire, belief, affection, and volition we have ignored much that is of extraordinary interest in his detailed explorations of the several affections. We have represented only the bare bones of the theory of the affections that Hume elaborates in Book II of the *Treatise*.[45] By concentrating on questions of structure, however, and by coming to recognize

---

[45] Árdal, in *Passion and Value in Hume's Treatise*, provides an extensive and detailed account of Hume's theory of the passions, with special emphasis on what we have called affections. Penelhum, *Hume*, 89–110, is economical but quite helpful. Baier, *A Progress of Sentiments*, especially 129–51, is illuminating in many ways. Jenkins, *Understanding Hume*, 126–48, concentrates on criticism of Hume's account of the person-directed affections. Together, Davidson, 'Hume's Cognitive Theory of Pride' and Baier, 'Hume's Analysis of Pride' constitute an exceptionally stimulating, philosophically fruitful, discussion of Hume's theory of pride.

Hume's commitment—whether in unqualified form, or in a form per-haps qualified so as to accommodate the peculiarities of bodily pains and pleasures—to the structural centrality of desire, we have made discoveries that will prove quite invaluable when it comes time, in Chapter 4, to examine his views on the nature of moral passions or sentiments. Before attending to his theory of the moral sentiments, however, we must exam-ine his proposed refutation of the doctrine of moral belief. We must turn, that is to say, to his arguments against cognitivist theories of specifically moral reasons for action.

3

Against Moral Cognitivism

Having argued at *Treatise*, II. iii. 3, for his conativist theory of reasons for action Hume turns, at *Treatise*, III. i. 1 ('Moral distinctions not deriv'd from reason'), to the question of specifically moral reasons for action. Among the reasons an agent can have for action, among the reasons that can be cited in the explanation of an individual's actions, are specifically moral reasons. She came to the rescue because she believed herself to be morally obliged to do so. He kept his promise because he thought it would be wrong to break it. Considering it a morally desirable thing to do, she volunteered to assist with the care of elderly patients. Moved by a recognition of the injustice of doing otherwise, he repaid the loan. Writing of such reasons Hume remarks that among the 'operation[s] of the mind' are 'those judgments, by which we distinguish moral good and evil', judgements by which we 'distinguish betwixt vice and virtue, and pronounce an action blameable or praise-worthy' (*T* 456, italics omitted). He writes, too, of 'motives drawn from ... duty' (*T* 382), of motives provided by 'the sense of morality or duty' (*T* 479). '[M]en are often', he says, 'govern'd by their duties, and are deter'd from some actions by the opinion of injustice, and impell'd to others by that of obligation' (*T* 457).[1]

Taking such explanations at face value, the typical *moral cognitivist* holds that specifically *moral beliefs*—beliefs with explicitly evaluative moral content—can, and often in fact do, play an essential explanatory role. While admitting that specifically moral reasons have a place in the explanation of actions, the *moral conativist* refuses to allow seemingly cognitivist appearances to settle the question of their character: for the moral conativist, what may seem to be practical moral beliefs are in fact specifically *moral desires*, desires whose contents distinguish them from other desires. The moral cognitivist claims to catch moral reasons within the net of his cognitivist theory of reasons for action, whether it be the standard cognitivist

---

[1] As understood here, Hume's 'judgments' are not essentially linguistic occurrences. They are psychological states or occurrences that are expressible linguistically but that are not to be identified with the linguistic occurrences in which they find expression. We shall consider the linguistic expression of moral judgements in Chap. 4, Sect. 4.

theory or one of the several variants we encountered in Chapter 1. For the moral conativist, specifically moral reasons can be understood only within the framework of a conativist theory of reasons for action.

At *Treatise*, III. i. i, Hume presents two arguments designed to support moral conativism and to subvert moral cognitivism in any of its forms. The first, his *direct* argument, simply applies the conclusions of his *prior* conativist arguments (in particular, the argument from direction of fit) to the case of specifically moral reasons for action. His second, or *indirect* argument, elaborates the case for moral conativism and against moral cognitivism by attacking the moral cognitivist's crucial claims about the distinctive content—the explicitly evaluative content—of purported moral beliefs. As Hume sets it out this indirect argument is sufficient, assuming it is successful, to scotch the cognitivist's conception of explicitly evaluative belief for the general case, not just for that of specifically moral belief. It thus enables Hume to allay lingering misgivings—misgivings that originate with the thought of psychological states with a double direction of fit—about the efficacy of his centrally important prior argument from direction of fit.

In attributing two arguments for moral conativism to Hume we are regimenting the text. Hume does explicitly contrast a direct and an indirect argument, but in his hands the actual conclusion, in each case, is a denial that the moral features of particular actions are a function of their conforming, or failing to conform, to moral truths. Getting clear about the structure and objectives of Hume's direct and indirect arguments for *that* conclusion will prove essential to grasping his direct and indirect arguments for *moral conativism*.

Here, as earlier with Hume's prior arguments for conativism, revision and idealization are in order. There are places at which Hume mishandles the presentation of his argument, thus misleading the reader. There are places where he lavishes attention on the peripheral at the expense of the central. Intent on the difficulties besetting a quite concrete proposal, he neglects, at times, to display needed links to more abstract issues. Helped by close attention to what he says of the structures and objectives of his direct and indirect arguments, however, we shall be in a position to clear what is clearly a Humean path to moral conativism.

1. THE CHARACTER OF MORAL COGNITIVISM

However they are to be distinguished from their non-moral but none the less evaluative cousins, the moral 'judgments' or 'opinions' (to use Hume's just-quoted words) that concern us here have explicitly evaluative content. The moral cognitivist takes such judgements or opinions, when they serve as constituents in reasons for action, as explicitly evaluative beliefs. Incorporating this construal of such moral judgements within one or other of the variant cognitivist theories we distinguished earlier, he produces a fleshed-out form of moral cognitivism, a determinate theory purportedly able to elucidate the bearing of moral judgement on the explanation of action.[2]

In what, recalling our earlier taxonomy of cognitivist theories of reasons for action, we may call its *standard* form, moral cognitivism holds that all moral reasons for action are psychological complexes comprising explicitly evaluative beliefs (whose function is to play the major role) and suitably linked descriptive beliefs (serving the equally essential, but so-called minor, role).[3] It identifies specifically moral reasons for action as those in which specifically moral beliefs—beliefs whose explicitly evaluative content is more narrowly moral in character—play the major role. It thus assigns the requisite practical or goal-setting role in moral reasons for action to moral beliefs, thus to psychological states it takes to be evaluable in terms of truth and falsity. It countenances competition of several sorts amongst reasons for action: competition involving non-moral reasons alone, or specifically moral reasons alone, or both moral and non-moral reasons. It countenances further moral reasons for at least some of the moral reasons one has. And it takes the moral beliefs in question to be expressible in explicitly evaluative sentences that—at least to a first approximation—could provide the major premises in practical arguments (or in arguments in justification of some more determinate moral beliefs).

The standard version of moral cognitivism takes the moral beliefs in question—beliefs about what is morally good, desirable, obligatory, to be done—to be both practical and truth-evaluable. In assigning particular moral features to actions, agents, and arrangements of various kinds, moral beliefs set out moral requirements of several sorts. In setting out such requirements they dispose the agent to act in a suitable way. In Hume's phrase they 'impose an obligation' (*T* 456) in the sense that, having such beliefs, the agent is thus far moved to behave as the beliefs direct.

Insisting on the truth-evaluability of moral beliefs, standard moral cognitivism takes the ostensibly realist commitments of these beliefs quite

---

[2] Again, Humean moral judgements are psychological states or occurrences, but not essentially linguistic ones.

[3] Here, and throughout, a *moral* reason is to be contrasted, not with an immoral reason, but with a *non-moral* reason.

seriously. It takes the specifically evaluative, more narrowly moral, features invoked by way of the contents of moral beliefs—the obligatoriness, desirability, fittingness, virtuousness, and the like, of actions, agents, and situations of various kinds—to be genuine features of items of the kinds to which they are assigned. When attending to what have come to be called *non-natural* properties[4] one attends, despite terminological appearances, to the 'natural fitness and unfitness of things' (*T* 465), to 'what exists in the nature of things' (*E* 171), to 'the nature of things' (*E* 294), to 'objects as they really stand in nature' (ibid.). Cognitively encountering the distinctively moral features of actions and other things one comes into contact with features analogous to the so-called primary qualities of things, their shape, say, or their mass. These strongly objective moral features are analogous to primary qualities at least in this sense: they are aspects of the fabric of the world, not features partly a product of the 'fabric and formation of the human mind' (*E* 172; compare *E* 170, 294). They resemble other strongly objective aspects of the world's fabric in that it is their presence or absence that determines, for beliefs with the relevant contents, the issue of truth or falsity. But they differ from those other strongly objective features of the world in that beliefs in their presence are practical or goal-setting beliefs, beliefs that can play the major role in a reason for action. Registering their presence disposes an agent to act in an appropriate way.

As Hume is well aware, equally standard forms of moral cognitivism may differ from one another in the structures they countenance for the contents of moral beliefs, in the logical or epistemic standing they assign to the implicated moral truths, in the accounts they offer of the believer's access to the moral truths in question, and in other ways as well.[5] Hume emphasizes theories that assign a relational structure to the content of moral beliefs, theories that postulate special 'moral relations' (*E* 288); but he at least alludes to theories that invoke non-relational, albeit peculiarly moral, properties for moral beliefs to be about. He concentrates his descriptive attentions on cognitivist theories—specifically rationalist

---

[4] The term is associated particularly with a view of moral properties developed in G. E. Moore, *Principia Ethica* (Cambridge, 1903). See, in addition: Ross's *The Right and the Good*, and *Foundations of Ethics* (Oxford, 1939); H. A. Prichard, *Moral Obligation: Essays and Lectures* (Oxford, 1949); and A. C. Ewing, *Ethics* (London, 1953).

[5] They may differ in the primitive moral properties they recognize, in their views about the dependence of one moral property on another, in their views about the dependence of moral properties on non-moral ones, and so on. See the differences between Moore, Ross, Prichard, Ewing, and Platts, to stick just to modern representatives of moral cognitivism. For Platts, see not only *Ways of Meaning*, but also 'Moral Reality and the End of Desire', in Mark Platts (ed.), *Reference, Truth, and Reality* (London, 1980), 69–82.

theories, we might say—that view moral truths as necessary truths: he represents them, perhaps tendentiously, in terms of his own doctrine of so-called 'relations of ideas' (*E* 25; compare *T* 458). He acknowledges, however, the possibility of cognitivist theories that assign a contingent status to fundamental moral truths. Having argued that 'morality consists not in any relations, that are the objects of science' he claims the same argument can show that morality 'consists not in any *matter of fact*, which can be discover'd by the understanding' (*T* 468; compare *E* 287). He tends to focus on theories that emphasize the role of inference, especially that of demonstrative inference, in the acquisition of purported moral truths. Having contrasted two 'species of reasoning', one in which the understanding 'judges from demonstration' and one in which it 'judges from . . . probability' (*T* 413), he employs the contrast to help structure the presentation of his anti-cognitivist arguments of *Treatise*, III. i. 1. As for the case of cognitivism generally, however, he can have no reason to discount the possibility of moral cognitivist theories postulating 'intuition' (*T* 70) or even 'perception' (*T* 73) as the route to moral truth.

Historically prominent forms of moral cognitivism have proliferated the properties they assign to the moral truths or standards to which, as cognitivist theories, they are committed. Moral standards are 'immutable' (*T* 496), are 'inflexible, even by the will of the Supreme Being' (*E* 294). Moral truths are 'eternal' truths (*T* 496; *E* 294). They are impersonal: as with 'all sound judgement of truth and falshood' sound moral beliefs are 'the same to every rational intelligent being' (*E* 170); the 'eternal fitnesses and unfitnesses of things . . . are the same to every rational being that considers them' (*T* 456). Perhaps in consequence of their impersonal status, moral standards are 'universally obligatory' (*T* 496): 'the immutable measures of right and wrong impose an obligation, not only on human creatures, but also on the Deity himself' (*T* 456). Stripped of theological accoutrement, these descriptions constitute an historically prominent emphasis on the strongly objective status of morality: moral standards are independent of the minds of those who must recognize their truth.

A distinction must be made here, one introducing a departure, on the point of strong objectivity, from what we have called standard moral cognitivism. A moral cognitivist *can* hold that moral features, while being real features of the items that possess them, are not utterly mind-independent, are not wholly independent of the 'fabric and formation of the human mind' (*E* 172). She can hold that they are real features of the actions or other items which are recognized to possess them, but in a way analogous to that in which mind-dependent secondary qualities such as colour are genuine features of coloured objects.[6] If mind-dependent in this way, however, they—just like secondary qualities—are mind-*in*dependent in another, more deeply important, way. Their presence or absence, it may be said, is prior to, is not somehow a function of, the proclivities or preferences—the conative attitudes—of those who, in forming correct moral beliefs, come to recognize their presence. A weaker form of objectivity, this is objectivity none the less. A moral cognitivist theory that makes do with it takes moral beliefs as genuine beliefs, and so as truth-evaluable. The belief that promises ought to be kept is no less truth-evaluable than the belief that canaries are yellow. The obligatoriness of promise-keeping is no less independent of the believer's conative attitudes than is the colour of a canary. If thus independent of the believer's desires, however, special moral features have a fundamental property that so-called secondary qualities do not: they are such that, when recognized to be present, they dispose the believer to act in the way indicated. It is this that explains the fact that, despite being truth-evaluable, moral beliefs are practical or goal-setting psychological states as well. Thus it is, the theory says, that moral beliefs are suited to serve as major constituents in reasons for action.[7]

One can remain a moral cognitivist while departing from the standard theory in other ways as well. Adopting a compromise theory, one can allow desires that, while not construable as explicitly evaluative beliefs (whether moral or non-moral), can compete with moral beliefs for the governance of action. One can, that is to say, countenance a possible 'combat of passion and reason' (*T* 413) viewed as a combat of desire and (moral) belief. One can require that moral beliefs be accompanied by desires if those beliefs are to govern action. Perhaps one requires an overarching desire to act morally; perhaps one thinks instead of more determinate

---

[6] In envisaging this version of moral cognitivism we do not assume that so-called secondary qualities *are* mind-dependent. The point is simply that theorists for whom secondary qualities are mind-dependent in the sense intended can take them, none the less, to be objective determinants of the truth values of beliefs attributing them to objects.

[7] Hume, of course, must himself distinguish beliefs concerning secondary qualities from desires, even if he thinks of secondary qualities as mind-dependent. Such beliefs have the mind-to-world direction of fit, while desires have the world-to-mind direction of fit. Sentences expressing beliefs concerning secondary qualities are evaluable as true or false; explicitly evaluative sentences expressing desires are (or so Hume might argue) not truth-evaluable at all. Desires can play the major role in action explanations; beliefs concerning secondary qualities can play only the minor role. Clearly Hume can no more accept a moral cognitivist theory that takes distinctive moral properties to be mind-dependent than he can accept more strongly objective versions of the theory.

desires such as the desire, consequent upon recognition of a moral obligation to keep one's promises, to keep one's promises.[8]

In naturalistic forms of moral cognitivism the purportedly non-natural properties of the standard theory give way, upon analysis, to straightforwardly empirical ones. A given naturalistic form will be defined by the property or properties it claims provide the reductive analysis. Perhaps it fastens on the properties of causing or preventing pain, or the properties of satisfying or frustrating desire. Perhaps it invokes the property of maximizing the satisfactions of all concerned, or that of prompting responses of certain sorts on the part of the agent himself, or of members of the agent's community, or of members of some other actual or ideal community. Where the standard theory sees a belief that an action possesses some non-natural evaluative property, the naturalistically inclined moral cognitivist sees an empirical belief that—to mention just one possibility—the action will maximize the pleasure of the sentient individuals involved. Naturalistic proposals for the analysis of the content of moral beliefs can, of course, be combined with one or other of widely differing views about the roles of moral beliefs, and of moral and non-moral desires, in the generation of action. What might be thought of as a *standard* naturalistic theory will mirror the standard form of moral cognitivism in all respects save its treatment of the content of moral belief.

Hume argues that *no* form of moral cognitivism, standard or non-standard, non-naturalist or naturalist, can be correct. He argues that one must substitute for moral cognitivism a moral conativist theory that, by identifying putative moral beliefs with specifically moral desires, accommodates the cognitivist appearances within the straitened framework of a conativist theory of reasons for action. We shall look to his constructive moral conativism in Chapter 4. First, however, we must examine the case he makes against its many cognitivist competitors.

2. HUME'S DIRECT ARGUMENT

Moral cognitivism is a doctrine in moral psychology, a doctrine, specifically, about the character of specifically moral reasons for action.[9] Properly

---

[8] The position here envisaged takes the postulated desires as 'independent extra components'. No substantive departure results from requiring desires if one construes them in the 'merely consequential' way that Nagel has introduced, as we saw in Chap. 1, Sect. 4.

[9] An *expanded* moral cognitivism is a theory designed to accommodate moral beliefs in addition to those involved in moral reasons for action. As we shall see in Chap. 4, Hume's moral conativism is part of an *expanded* moral conativism, a theory designed to accommodate moral affections (as we shall call them) as well as moral desires.

elaborated, however, it imports two non-psychological conceptions: that of moral truths; and that of conformity to a moral truth. An agent with correct moral beliefs is cognizant of moral rules that must be reckoned as moral truths. Characterizing moral cognitivism Hume writes of an agent's access to 'the rule of right' (*E* 288), to 'the . . . measures of right and wrong' (*T* 456). Granted a conception of moral truths to which correct beliefs provide cognitive access, the moral character of a particular action is a function of that action's conforming to, or failing to conform to, a moral rule, a moral truth. Actions, it may be said, 'are denominated good or ill, according as they agree or disagree with' (*E* 288) moral truths, with 'the rule of right', with 'the . . . measures of right and wrong'. '[V]irtue', on this view, 'is nothing but a conformity to reason' (*T* 456); 'men are only so far virtuous as they conform themselves to . . . [reason's] dictates' (*T* 413). Morally correct action is a matter of conformity to moral truth; equivalently, it is a matter of correspondence with correct moral belief.[10]

To understand the arguments of *Treatise*, III. i. 1, it is essential to distinguish (1) the psychological thesis that is moral cognitivism proper, from the non-psychological theses (2) that there are moral truths, and (3) that the moral character of a particular action is a matter of its conforming or failing to conform to such a truth. Hume offers two quite elaborate arguments. Each pays particular attention, in ways that must be spelled out, to the moral cognitivist's third claim, the claim about conformity. In their structurally differing ways, each may be counted an argument for the rejection of that third claim. The first of the two arguments has three stages. (1) Applying the conclusions of his two prior arguments (his conativist arguments from the character of action explanation, and from direction of fit, that we examined in Chapter 1) to the case of explicitly evaluative moral reasons for action, Hume arrives at the psychological thesis of moral conativism and the rejection of moral cognitivism. (2) He moves from that to the rejection of moral truths. (3) From that, he concludes that the moral character of an action cannot derive from its conforming to, or its failing to conform to, a moral truth. In the second of his two arguments Hume attacks the moral cognitivist's third, or conformity, claim head-on. He draws no further conclusions—at least he draws none explicitly—from his rejection of the doctrine of conformity. As will become readily apparent, however, the considerations that constitute this attack on the moral cognitivist's third claim subvert his second claim, the

---

[10] Here we ignore complexities introduced by the possibility of having, while not being cognizant that one has, mistaken moral beliefs.

doctrine of moral truths, as well. And—the crucial point for present purposes—they enable Hume to drive home the conclusion that moral cognitivism's first, or psychological, claim must be rejected, and moral conativism endorsed, if one is to understand the tie between morality and action. In effect, Hume's second argument (if completed in the way sketched out) reverses the order of his first.

That Hume has two principal arguments at *Treatise*, III. i. 1, and that he attends in each to the moral cognitivist's third, or conformity, claim, is plain enough. Against the moral cognitivist's claim that 'virtue is nothing but a conformity to reason' (*T* 456) he purports to prove 'that actions do not derive their merit from a conformity to reason' (*T* 458), that '[l]audable or blameable ... are not the same with reasonable or unreasonable' (ibid.). And he purports to prove what he calls 'the same truth' both by a circuitous and by a quite straightforward route.[11] That he is concerned to reject the moral cognitivist's second claim on behalf of moral truths is also plain: in the course of his first argument he draws the interim conclusion that '[t]he rules of morality ... are not conclusions of our reason' (*T* 457). That his rejection of the moral cognitivist's second and third claims is linked, in the differing ways just suggested, to his rejection of the first— the central psychological—claim will become apparent as we proceed.

Regimenting in a modest way, let us fix attention on the bearing of each of the three-stage arguments just described on the central psychological question, the question of conativism versus cognitivism as a theory of specifically moral reasons for action. With attention thus fixed, let us distinguish Hume's *direct* argument for moral conativism from his *indirect* argument for the same psychological thesis. In his *direct* argument for moral conativism (an argument constituting just the first stage in the first of the three-stage arguments just described) Hume applies the conclusions of his prior conativist arguments (the arguments from *Treatise*, II. iii. 3, that we examined in Chapter 1) to the case of specifically moral reasons for action and concludes that putative moral beliefs are in fact moral desires. In his *indirect* argument for moral conativism (an argument that results when one formally completes the second of the three-stage arguments in the way sketched above) Hume deploys his reflections on the

---

[11] Hume claims to prove 'the same truth' both '*directly*' (his emphasis) and 'more indirectly' (*T* 458). *This* contrast of 'direct' and 'indirect' arguments must not be confounded with the contrast of direct and indirect arguments for moral conativism that we develop in the body of the text. What in the text we term Hume's *direct* argument for moral conativism constitutes the first of three stages through which Hume proceeds when arguing 'more indirectly'; what we term his *indirect* argument for moral conativism may be thought of as the terminus of the proceedings when Hume argues 'directly'.

question of conformity to moral truth in order to subvert the moral cognitivist's central psychological claim about the explanatory role of beliefs with explicitly evaluative content. Let us begin with the direct argument for moral conativism.

Eschewing needed qualifications for the moment, we may say that moral conativism follows from the conjunction of conativism and the practicality of putative moral beliefs. Assume conativism to be true. Assume, that is to say, that reasons for action are psychological complexes comprising desires and suitably related descriptive beliefs, the desires playing the major or practical role, the descriptive beliefs playing the minor or informational one. Assume, further, that what appear to be explicitly evaluative moral beliefs play the major role in reasons for action. It would follow (given needed qualifications) that what appear to be explicitly evaluative moral beliefs are in fact desires of some special, specifically moral, sort. It would follow, that is to say, that moral conativism is true.

Of course, Hume has argued that conativism is true: we examined the two arguments in Chapter 1. Introducing his direct argument for moral conativism he alludes to these prior arguments when he writes that 'reason alone, *as we have already prov'd*, can never have an influence on the actions and affections' (*T* 457, emphasis added). Lest he be 'tedious' he repeats only the second of the two prior arguments '*by which I have prov'd*, that reason [better: reason alone] is perfectly inert, and can never either prevent or produce any action or affection' (*T* 457–8, enphasis added). The argument he repeats is that from direction of fit, the more promising, by far, of the two prior arguments.

Hume assembles three sets of considerations to support his claims that putative moral beliefs are practical and—more specifically—that they play the major role in action explanations.

It is 'common experience', he says, 'that men are often govern'd by their duties, and are deter'd from some actions by the opinion of injustice, and impell'd to others by that of obligation' (*T* 457). It is common practice, we may say, to explain an agent's actions by citing his moral beliefs, opinions, or judgements and by assigning them the so-called major position in such explanations. Why is the agent acting as he is? He believes that to do otherwise would be to break a promise and he believes it is wrong to break promises. She believes it would be good were poverty eradicated and is persuaded that contributing to Oxfam will help. More generally, she acts as she does because she judges actions of a certain type to be right (obligatory, morally required, morally desirable, what virtue demands) and thinks of her present action as of that type. Some—perhaps those who deny 'the reality of moral distinctions' (*E* 169), perhaps some proponents of 'the selfish hypothesis' (*E* 298)—would treat putative moral reasons, and so action explanations that invoke them, as illusory. But Hume is one with his cognitivist opponents in thinking moral reasons are, so far at least as the explanation of action goes, the real thing.[12]

Again, the practice of moral training or instruction presupposes that putative moral beliefs provide reasons for actions. We educate or instruct others (our children, say) in the making of moral distinctions so that they will be disposed to behave accordingly. 'If morality had naturally no influence on human passions and actions', Hume writes, ''twere in vain to take such pains to inculcate it; and nothing would be more fruitless than the multitude of rules and precepts, with which all moralists abound' (*T* 457).

Finally, traditional philosophical practice, including that of most moral cognitivists, squares with these common practices and their presuppositions. 'Philosophy is commonly divided into *speculative* and *practical*; and as morality is always comprehended under the latter division, 'tis supposed to influence our passions and actions, and to go beyond the calm and indolent judgments of the understanding' (*T* 457). Provided proper stress is placed on the words 'calm and indolent' this begs no question against the moral cognitivist.[13]

Since ostensible moral beliefs are practical[14] they must, when viewed strictly and philosophically, be reckoned as desires of a peculiar, specifically

[12] This is not to say the appearances are never illusory. Nor, of course, is it to say that real moral reasons must, in competition with other reasons, always win the day. It is *obviously* not to concede that, in thinking of putative moral beliefs *as* beliefs, one is free of illusion. If Hume is right the moral cognitivist is subject to illusion on just this point. For a modern writer who appears to deny that moral reasons are, in the sense intended, the real thing, see P. H. Nowell-Smith, *Ethics* (Harmondsworth, 1954).

[13] Commenting on the passage in which Hume lists the three considerations just examined, Platts remarks on Hume's '(uncharacteristic) repetitiveness and vagueness in his assertions about the practical nature of morality' ('Hume and Morality as a Matter of Fact', 193 n.). A close reading reveals neither vagueness nor repetitiveness. Given common misreadings of Hume, however, it is helpful to note just how careful he is here to emphasize the practicality of morals when constructing his direct argument against moral cognitivism. Referring to Hume's 'strange and muddled-looking argument', Penelhum claims, in *David Hume*, 141–2, that in moving from *Treatise*, II. iii. 3, to *Treatise*, III. i. 1, Hume shifts from the topic of reasons for action to that of moral discriminations, where the latter are viewed as matters of approbation not of motivation. On the present evidence, however, there is no such shift. Rather, Hume elaborates the account of reasons for action devised at *Treatise*, II. iii. 3 by extending it at *Treatise*, III. i. 1, to cases in which agents are moved to act by moral rather than other considerations.

[14] Some modern moral cognitivists would, it must be noted, deny this.

moral, sort. They must, that is to say, be construed as the moral conativist construes them.[15]

There is an easy Humean route—although Hume himself makes no effort to mark one out—from his conativist moral psychology to his further conclusions rejecting cognitivist conceptions both of moral truths and of a relation of conformity (or of failure to conform) between particular actions and such truths. Given moral conativism one has no need of candidate moral truths corresponding to the contents of putative moral beliefs, no need for moral truths expressible by the explicitly evaluative sentences that serve to express the practical psychological states in question. Indeed, given the moral conativist's identification of putative moral beliefs as peculiarly moral desires, there remain within the regimented framework of his theory no explicitly evaluative *contents* to which candidate moral truths might be thought to correspond. Moral conativism reconfigures the putative moral belief that lying is wrong as a specifically moral desire that lying not occur: the explicitly evaluative content of the one gives way to the wholly descriptive content of the other. It renders the putative moral belief that it would be good to share the wealth as the peculiarly moral desire that the wealth be shared: in doing so it makes do with psychological content that is unexceptionably non-evaluative in character. On the assumption that metaphysics must follow where philosophical psychology leads—an assumption Hume shares with many moderns—moral truths must go the way of moral beliefs.[16] Completing the second stage of his first three-stage argument, Hume states: 'The rules of morality . . . are not conclusions of our reason' (*T* 457).

If there are no moral truths an action's moral character cannot be a function of its conforming, or its failing to conform, to a moral truth. Completing the third of the three stages of his overall argument Hume writes: 'actions do not derive their merit from a conformity to reason, nor their blame from a contrariety to it' (*T* 458). Morally correct action is a matter of correspondence, not with correct moral belief, but with moral desire.

Of course, everything here depends on the strength of Hume's earlier

[15] Emphasizing its negative side, Hume provides a succinct rendering of this argument when he writes: 'Since morals . . . have an influence on actions and affections, it follows, that they cannot be deriv'd from reason; and that because reason alone, as we have already prov'd, can never have such influence' (*T* 457; compare *T* 458).

[16] Platts writes, 'Hume and Morality as a Matter of Fact', 193, that Hume 'can . . . be seen to have shared a strategy with a number of contemporary philosophers, that of approaching "metaphysical" questions of fact and value through considerations of philosophical psychology'. He mentions Thomas Nagel, John McDowell, and himself.

case for conativism as a general theory of reasons for action. Without conativism, his argument from the practicality of putative moral beliefs to moral conativism would collapse; with its collapse would go his case against moral truths and against the moral cognitivist's account of the moral character of particular actions.

As we saw in Chapter 1, Hume's first conativist argument secures a number of important claims that the conativist shares with the standard cognitivist: reasons for action are psychological complexes comprising suitably linked psychological states that play, respectively, the so-called major and minor roles. By itself, however, that argument fails to secure the conativist's all-important thesis about the explanatory role of desire because it fails to rule out the possibility that explicitly evaluative beliefs can play just that role.

On the face of it, however, Hume's earlier conativist argument from direction of fit is quite compelling. It introduces a requirement that psychological states, if they play the major role in reasons for action, be states with the world-to-mind direction of fit. If truth-evaluable, then, a psychological state, no matter its content, cannot be the major constituent in a reason for action: if truth-evaluable it must possess the mind-to-world direction of fit. If follows that beliefs, whatever their content, cannot serve as major constituents in reasons for action. On the assumption that what appear to be explicitly evaluative beliefs *can* function as major constituents in reasons for action, it follows that such states must, despite appearances, be desires, not beliefs. On the face of it, this second argument succeeds where Hume's first conativist argument fails: it encompasses (what appear to be) explicitly evaluative beliefs within its scope. That being so, it is made to measure as an argument for *moral* conativism. What appear to be explicitly evaluative *moral* beliefs *can* perform the major role in explanations of action: putative moral beliefs *can*, as Hume argues, be practical. They must, then, despite appearances, be desires. It comes as no surprise that Hume repeats his argument from direction of fit, not his first conativist argument, when he turns in Book III to the ties between morality and action.

As we have seen, attempts to undercut the underlying doctrine of directions of fit, or the use of that doctrine in the characterization of practical psychological states, are ultimately unsuccessful. As we have also seen, however, Hume's use of that doctrine to secure a conativist theory rests on the assumption that a given psychological state cannot have *both* the world-to-mind and the mind-to-world directions of fit, cannot (as construed within the confines of the theory) be *both* conative and cognitive.

We have taken the assumption to be sound. It seems a simple corollary of our characterization of direction of fit. To discard it would be to countenance non-compound psychological states—beliefs, say—that both are, and are not, truth-evaluable. To give it up would be to allow non-compound psychological states—beliefs, say—that represent both how the world is and how it is to be. More might be said on its behalf but, on the face of it, its denial makes no sense. With the assumption in place, Hume's direct argument for moral conativism goes through.[17]

The would-be moral cognitivist has, however, the makings of a reply. Whatever its surface plausibility, it may be said, our interdict against double direction of fit fails for the special case of explicitly evaluative, and so for the case of moral, beliefs. Only inattention to the striking peculiarities of evaluative content could persuade us the interdict is compelling. Once these peculiarities are taken seriously the burden falls on the would-be moral conativist to sustain—not on the would-be moral cognitivist to accede to—a denial of double direction of fit. Moral beliefs *are* peculiar in that they represent both how the world is (morally speaking) and how it is to be. It is precisely because they have explicitly evaluative content that moral (and other such) beliefs have both directions of fit and so are, as on the surface they seem to be, beliefs that are at once practical and truth-evaluable.

The envisaged counter is unavailing. Before showing that this is so, however, let us look at Hume's *indirect* argument for moral conativism, an argument that focuses on the peculiarities of the contents of explicitly evaluative moral beliefs.

3. HUME'S INDIRECT ARGUMENT

Just how Hume's *indirect* argument for moral conativism is designed to support that doctrine is not immediately apparent as one reads the text of *Treatise*, III. i. I. He takes few pains to explain why he starts the argument just where he does. His presentation of the argument is prolix and laconic by turns. He fails, at least in so many words, to actually draw the conativist conclusion. Much to which he assigns a weight-bearing function seems to merit the very cool reception it has had even from commentators claiming sympathy with his overall anti-cognitivist project. His

---

[17] For further discussion of the question of double direction of fit, see Sect. 4, below, and Chap. 4, Sect. 4.

discussion of William Wollaston seems to display an inability to see, or a willingness to misrepresent, the point of moral cognitivism. His handling of examples (that of parricide, that of incest) occasions the dismissive thought that theoretical myopia has been induced by his suspect doctrine of philosophical relations.

If one attends to the state of play as his indirect argument gets underway, however, and if, with a firm sense of Hume's conativist objectives, one is prepared to fill in some blanks, the structure of his indirect argument is not far to seek and its force is fairly readily apparent. The argument begins with close scrutiny of the moral cognitivist's contention that the moral features of an action are a function of that action's conforming to, or failing to conform to, some moral truth. (For brevity's sake we may call this the Conformity Thesis.) Sorting through a number of candidate renderings of the Conformity Thesis, and finding all but one of these transparently unavailing, it focuses sustained critical scrutiny on that (morally realistic) survivor. It questions that survivor's capacity to meet three conditions on an adequate moral cognitivism: (1) that moral cognitivism supply metaphysical underpinnings for the explicitly evaluative content of what it takes to be moral beliefs; (2) that it provide an acceptable account of an agent's epistemic access to putative moral truths; and (3) that it explicate the practicality of putative moral beliefs in terms of the peculiarities of their content. In showing, in particular, that a morally realistic moral cognitivism cannot meet the third condition, it blocks the moral cognitivist's envisaged counter, described just above, to Hume's *direct* argument for moral conativism. That counter blocked, the direct argument for moral conativism does indeed go through.

What precisely is the Conformity Thesis, scrutiny of which provides the starting-point for Hume's indirect argument? Hume articulates it in a variety of ways. '[A]ctions ... derive their merit from a conformity to reason, [and] ... their blame from a contrariety to it' (*T* 458). '[V]irtue is nothing but a conformity to reason' (*T* 456); wrong actions are 'actions contrary to truth and reason' (*T* 461). 'The very essence of morality', he writes, 'is suppos'd to consist in an agreement or disagreement to reason' (*T* 460). The thesis concerns 'the source of morals' (*T* 459), 'the origin of immorality' (*T* 461 n.), 'the first spring or original source of all immorality' (*T* 461), 'the foundation of all guilt and moral deformity' (*T* 461 n.). It concerns what 'bestow[s] on any action the character of virtuous or vicious, or deprive[s] it of that character' (*T* 460).

To get our footing here, let us state the Conformity Thesis (CT) in a preliminary way as follows:

CT1 An action is right (wrong) if and only if it conforms to (fails to conform to) a moral truth.

The actions in question are actual or prospective particular actions, not action types.[18] Selection of 'right' and 'wrong' as the explicitly evaluative predicates is a matter of convenience: they may be viewed as standing in, respectively, for disjunctions of appropriate positive, and disjunctions of appropriate negative, moral predicates. For present purposes the thesis makes no commitment on a question of some importance in the full development of a moral cognitivist theory, the question whether general moral truths are perhaps prima facie in character.[19] It incorporates a by now familiar shift from reason to truth: following Hume, it construes 'contrary to reason' as 'false', 'in conformity to reason' as 'true'. It invokes specifically moral truths but that, in the statement of the Conformity Thesis, is uncontroversial.

On the face of it, moral cognitivism must subscribe to CT1. It must (for some suitable reading) deny that an action can be right (wrong) yet not conform to (fail to conform to) a moral truth. It must deny that an action can conform to (fail to conform to) a moral truth and yet not be right (wrong).[20] On the face of it, to reject CT1 would be to sever moral cognitivism's putative moral truths from the characterization of particular actions and so to deny those truths any theoretical or practical point.

Presumably CT1 must be taken not as a substantive moral truth but as a truth *about* morality, a meta-ethical or metaphysical truth about the status of the rightness or wrongness of a particular action. But how is its central notion of conformity to be understood? Any number of formally satisfactory alternatives could, of course, be constructed. From our present vantage-point, however, it is clear that a satisfactory specification of CT1 must meet two substantive conditions: it must credibly count as complementing moral cognitivism as a theory of moral reasons for action; and it must hold out at least some promise of helping moral cognitivism get around Hume's argument from direction of fit. When enmeshed in Hume's

[18] Issues of universalizability, while not irrelevant to a satisfactory formulation of CT, may be ignored here. A variant of CT1 making appropriate reference to types might take the following form: An action is right (wrong) if and only if it is of a type all the tokens of which conform to (fail to conform to) a moral truth.

[19] Ross introduces the notion of prima facie duties as part of a moral cognitivist theory in *The Right and the Good*, 18–36. For Davidson's seminal examination of the logical form of prima facie evaluative principles, see 'How is Weakness of the Will Possible?', especially 36 ff.

[20] Here, allowance must be made for complications that would be introduced were general moral truths construed as prima facie truths.

critique of William Wollaston's several variants of CT1, one must not lose sight of these, clearly fundamental, conditions.[21]

Responding to Wollaston, Hume considers several readings of CT1 that agree in construing 'conforms to (fails to conform to) a truth' as 'is true (false)'. Consider, first, the following:

CT2 An action is right (wrong) if and only if that action is true (false).[22]

In Hume's words, 'moral distinctions' are here 'deriv'd from the truth or falsity of' the items to be assessed, the actions themselves (*T* 460). An unprepossessing doctrine, CT2 must be rejected because its unrestricted assumption that actions have the mind-to-world direction of fit and so can be either true or false is unacceptable. '[A]ctions', Hume writes, 'are not susceptible of any such agreement or disagreement' as truth and falsity require; it is 'impossible, therefore, they can be pronounced either true or false, and be either contrary or conformable to reason' (*T* 458). Hitting someone on the head hasn't a direction of fit and so isn't truth-evaluable; but a particular hitting *can* be morally assessable. CT2 must, then, be rejected as a specification of CT1.[23]

Whatever be true of actions generally, some actions—acts of assertion—invite assessment in terms of truth and falsity. Let us, then, replace CT2 with the duly cautious principle:

CT2.1 An action is right (wrong) if and only if (a) that action is an assertion and (b) what it asserts is true (false).

While avoiding Hume's objection to CT2, however, the replacement is no better at providing a satisfactory reading of CT1: actions other than acts of assertion can be right or wrong.

Neither CT2 nor CT2.1 assigns any special role to specifically moral truths. To remedy this defect let us substitute:

CT2.2 An action is right (wrong) if and only if (a) that action is a moral assertion and (b) what it asserts is true (false).

---

[21] Selections from Wollaston's *The Religion of Nature Delineated* (1724) can be found in D. D. Raphael (ed.), *British Moralists: 1650–1800*, i (Oxford, 1969), 237–58. We are not here concerned with the accuracy of Hume's interpretation of Wollaston, but for some helpful material on that question, see Mackie, *Hume's Moral Theory*, 20–3, 52, 55–6, 82–3, 139.

[22] This rendering of CT fits naturally, it should be noted, with Hume's own practice, noted earlier, of using 'conformable to reason', on the one hand, 'contrary to reason' or 'contradictory to reason', on the other, as equivalent to 'true' and 'false', respectively.

[23] To be sure, volitions—implicated in actions—have a direction of fit, but it runs in the world-to-mind, not the mind-to-world, direction.

This principle is no more compatible than its predecessor with the fact that actions other than assertions can be right or wrong. It suffers, as well, from a quite fatal flaw of its own. To the suggestion that a 'mistake of *right*' is often 'criminal' Hume responds: ''tis impossible such a mistake can ever be the original source of immorality, since it supposes a real right and wrong; that is, a real distinction in morals, independent of these judgments' (*T* 460). The immorality of such mistakes (conceded for the sake of argument) is 'only a secondary one, and is founded on some other, antecedent to it' (ibid.). The point is simple and devastating. If CT2.2 is right about the moral evaluability of moral assertions CT2.2 cannot be true; so CT2.2 cannot be true. If moral assertions are right (wrong) if and only if what they assert is true (false) then actions other than moral assertions must also be morally evaluable (contrary to condition (a)) and moral evaluability cannot be tied in the requisite way to truth and falsity (contrary to condition (b)). To see this, let us suppose that the moral assertion that promise-keeping is right is itself a right action. Given CT2.2 it follows that promise-keeping is right. But this (on the assumption that keeping a promise is not identical with making a moral assertion) is incompatible with CT2.2's claims that only moral assertions are morally evaluable and that actions are morally evaluable only if they assert something evaluable in terms of truth and falsity. Since CT2.2 must, to be true, be right about the moral evaluability of moral assertions, CT2.2 must be rejected.[24]

Hume considers the suggestion that morally relevant actions be viewed as, or identified with, moral assertions. 'A person who takes possession of *another's* goods, and uses them as his *own*, in a way declares them to be his own' (*T* 462 n.). 'A man that is ungrateful to his benefactor, in a manner affirms, that he never received any favours from him' (ibid.). The first in effect falsely declares that he has no obligation to refrain from using the items in question; the second in effect falsely declares that he is not obliged to treat the other person with any special kindness. A moral cognitivist might think to get around the difficulty of the previous paragraph by blocking, in this way, the assumption on which it turns. In doing so she might also hope to turn the objection that actions other than moral assertions can be right or wrong. But as Hume insists, what (if anything) legitimates taking the instanced actions *as* moral assertions is the supposition of 'some antecedent rule of duty and morals' (*T* 462 n.). One can make moral assertions by one's actions (if one can) only if actions of the type in question are independently evaluable as right or wrong. Neither moral asser-

---

[24] The argument assumes that moral assertions can concern the morality of actions.

tions, nor actions that count as such, can alone be evaluable in moral terms.[25]

It is easy to grow impatient with the excessive attention Hume lavishes on CT2 and its kin: one is just not tempted to tie moral evaluability, quite generally, to the truth-evaluability of actions; and one rightly recognizes that the specific objections he levels against Wollaston do little to advance Hume's case for moral conativism. Despite one's impatience, however, it is essential to fasten on just what his discussion of Wollaston reveals about the overall structure of Hume's indirect argument. As that discussion makes plain, the indirect argument, abstractly considered, requires moral cognitivism to produce *some* satisfactory version of CT1. And it requires, in particular, a version that both complements moral cognitivism's account of explicitly moral reasons for action and explains their practicality. With Wollaston's proposal so obviously wanting, some other specification of CT1 must be sought. Perhaps CT3 is more promising:

CT3 An action is right (wrong) if and only if it is true that the action is right (wrong).

Moral cognitivism must hold CT3 to be true, but how, precisely, is that principle to complement the theory's claims about moral reasons for action? How is the principle to constitute a meta-ethical or metaphysical truth about morality, one that countenances the appropriately mind-independent status of the rightness or wrongness of particular actions and – crucially – one that helps explain the practicality of putative moral beliefs? If CT3 is to serve *these* purposes, it may be argued, moral cognitivism must, at a minimum, interpret truth in a more-than-minimalist way.[26] Eschewing talk of redundancy, it must take truth to be more than a matter of endorsement, say, or of disquotation. If CT3 is to serve its ostensible purposes, the conception of truth moral cognitivism employs must at least import the notion of distinctive moral features whose presence or absence determines, in substantive fashion, the truth or falsity of putative moral beliefs. Whether it is true that a particular action *is* an act of lying is a substantive matter, it might be said, of whether that action does indeed possess that property. Similarly, the moral cognitivist might

[25] Hume has an easy time scotching proposals to link the evaluability of actions to the truth-evaluability, not of the actions themselves, but of the beliefs, whether moral or nonmoral, that prompt them or that they provoke. Since the problems that beset *these* unprepossessing proposals parallel those we have found in the several variants of CT2, however, we need not rehearse them here.

[26] We shall return to the question how best to construe truth in Chap. 4, Sect. 4.

say, the question whether that action of lying *is* wrong is the substantive question whether it does indeed possess the property of being wrong. Truths about actions, whether they be moral truths or truths of some other sort, are substantive matters of the genuine possession of genuine properties. This is not to deny that what renders a particular act of lying wrong is, say, the effect it has on mutual trust, or on formed expectations, or on the possibility of communication. It is simply to say that this act of lying, an action having the non-moral features mentioned, has the mind-independent feature of being wrong as well.[27] This modestly realist approach to moral truths may be formulated in a principle that, properly interpreted, serves as a metaphysical gloss on CT3:

> CT3.1 An action is right (wrong) if and only if it has the moral feature of being right (wrong).

Together, CT3 (with truth interpreted in a more-than-minimalist way) and CT3.1 complement moral cognitivism. Neither succumbs to Hume's arguments against CT2 and its kin.

Neither singly nor together, however, can CT3 and CT3.1 exhaust the presumptive content of CT1 for, if taken to elucidate the key notion of an action's *conforming* to a moral truth, they have the unwanted implication that an action with moral features cannot fail to do so. An action of promise-keeping (assuming it right) conforms to the moral truth that it is right. But just as clearly an action of breaking a promise (assuming it wrong) conforms to a moral truth, the truth that it is wrong. But the point, surely, is that only one of these actions (by hypothesis, the first) conforms to moral truth: the second action, the breaking of a promise, *fails* to conform. As Hume expresses the moral cognitivist's contention: '[A]ctions... derive their *merit* from a *conformity* to reason, [and] ... their *blame* from a *contrariety* to it' (*T* 458, emphasis added). If the notion of conformity to a moral truth is to complement moral cognitivism, the fact that one's actions conform to a moral truth cannot follow from the fact that they have *some* moral quality or other.

CT3 and CT3.1 capture the requisite measure of moral realism in moral cognitivism of the sort here in question, but they do nothing to explain the notion of conformity the theory needs. Equivalently, they do nothing to sustain moral cognitivist claims to accommodate the practicality of moral beliefs and so to turn Hume's direct argument. A more promising proposal reads CT1 as:

---

[27] Some account must, of course, be offered of the relation between moral and non-moral properties. See the discussion of the first of Hume's three demands in Sect. 4, below.

CT4 An action is right (wrong) if and only if its occurrence (non-occurrence) is required by a moral truth.

Continuing with our previous examples, an act of breaking a promise fails to conform to the moral truth that promise-breaking is wrong, a truth that requires the non-occurrence of promise-breaking. By contrast, an action of promise-keeping conforms to a moral truth: it is an action required by the moral truth that keeping promises is the right thing to do.

Of course, we now need an account of *requiring*. In what sense can a moral truth *require* the occurrence or non-occurrence of an action? Not, surely, in the way in which a report that Smith is lying might be said to require Smith's lying: the sense (a stretched sense, to be sure) in which the report's truth requires that Smith lie. Perhaps commands or prescriptions provide a basis for analogy? A command that Smith lie may be said to require Smith's lying: that is what he must do if the command is to be obeyed. The prescription of a regimen of exercise may be said to require that regimen: only by undertaking that regimen would Smith comply with the prescription. Similarly, moral truths may be said to command and prescribe conduct: the moral truth that lying is wrong prescribes or commands its non-occurrence. Moral truths, let us say, are *prescriptive* ones.[28] A particular action conforms to a moral truth only if that action is what the truth in question commands or prescribes;[29] it fails to conform if its non-occurrence is what the pertinent moral truth prescribes.

How can one wed the prescriptivity of moral truths to their truth-evaluability? How marry a modest moral realism to the requirements on conduct that the cognitivist's moral truths must introduce? How, equivalently, complement moral cognitivism with an account of the practicality of moral beliefs? How turn Hume's direct argument against moral cognitivism, the argument from direction of fit? A seemingly inevitable way in which to *attempt* to do these things is to countenance a peculiarly prescriptive character for the genuine moral features that a modest moral realism requires. One takes prescriptivity to be an intrinsic property of peculiarly moral properties. And one holds that it is in virtue of their

---

[28] The term 'prescriptive' is one associated with R. M. Hare's prescriptivist theory of moral judgement. Use of Hare's helpful term to characterize a possible moral cognitivist theory must not, however, be taken to suggest a blurring of the differences between such a theory and Hare's own non-cognitivist prescriptivism. See R. M. Hare, *The Language of Morals* (Oxford, 1952) and *Freedom and Reason* (Oxford, 1963).

[29] More carefully: only if that action is of a type tokens or instances of which the truth in question commands or prescribes.

prescriptivity that moral properties require agents to act in the ways indicated.[30] Putting the proposal formally, let us introduce, as a metaphysical gloss on CT4:

> CT4.1 An action is right (wrong) if and only if it has the prescriptive moral feature of being right (wrong).

A moral cognitivism that endorses CT4 and CT4.1, allowing their conjunction to constitute the variant of CT1 to which it subscribes, will be prescriptivist about moral truths; it will be prescriptivist in its moral realism as well. It will clearly be a theory immune to the objections Hume levels against CT2 and *its* variants.

It can seem that this prescriptivist form of moral cognitivism is a theory of considerable power. It is a theory that integrates a conception of explicitly moral reasons for action with complementary conceptions both of moral truths and of the relation between moral truth and action that renders an action morally right or morally wrong. It accepts the task of explaining the claimed compatibility of practicality and truth-evaluability for the case of moral beliefs. In seeking explanation it turns to metaphysics, to the metaphysics of what we may call prescriptivist realism. With its introduction of objective prescriptive properties, properties it invokes in explicating the content of explicitly evaluative moral beliefs, it purports to explain just how moral beliefs, though truth-evaluable, can be practical. Explicitly evaluative beliefs are practical precisely because of the peculiarities of their contents. That, the theory continues, is why explicitly evaluative beliefs can have both the mind-to-world and the world-to-mind direction of fit. And that, the theory concludes, is why Hume's *direct* argument for moral conativism fails.

Hume's *indirect* argument is, however, far from finished. As represented thus far, it amounts merely to the sorting out of alternative renderings of the Conformity Thesis—alternative readings of CT1—and the rejection of some of these (CT2 and *its* variants) as false, others (CT3 and CT3.1) as inadequate as they stand. In isolating CT4 and CT4.1 as ways of rendering CT1 we have introduced a prescriptivist form of moral cognitivism that, with *some* show of plausibility, can claim to counter Hume's direct argument for moral conativism. Having articulated this full-dress form of moral cognitivism, however, and having identified what it claims to be competent to do, we must determine what, if anything, it can actually accomplish. Having completed his narrowly focused attack on what he

---

[30] Recall the *non-natural* properties alluded to in Sect. 1, and in n. 4.

takes to be Wollaston's moral cognitivism—having completed, that is to say, his attack on CT2 and the other doctrines he links to Wollaston's work—Hume gives clear expression to the transparently more pertinent task that remains. As a critic of moral cognitivism, a critic here focusing on the Conformity Thesis, he must 'be more particular, and . . . shew, that those eternal immutable fitnesses and unfitnesses of things cannot be defended by sound philosophy' (*T* 463). He invites his reader to 'weigh the following considerations' (ibid.). We must now ask whether the considerations to which he here alludes suffice to show that the moral cognitivist's conception of objective, and particularly of prescriptive, moral properties is indefensible.

4. THE INDIRECT ARGUMENT CONTINUED

It is clear that in raising these considerations Hume has metaphysical matters in mind. The issue, he remarks in a corresponding passage in the second *Enquiry*, is one of 'metaphysics' (*E* 289). The question concerns 'what exists in the nature of things' (*E* 171), what 'exist[s] . . . in nature' (*T* 476), a purported 'natural fitness and unfitness of things' (*T* 465), a purported 'separate being' for moral features of actions, 'that matter of fact, or real existence, which . . . [the moral cognitivist] call[s] *vice*' (*T* 468).

In pursuing these essentially metaphysical questions Hume casts a very wide net. Moreover, he deploys objections that are, many of them, indifferent to many of the differences—in some cases the historically quite important differences—between one version of moral cognitivism and another. He directs his attack against the doctrine of genuine moral features of actions, in particular purportedly prescriptive features of actions, whatever may be said about the structure or standing of the moral truths that claim to capture these features, or about the access agents have to them. Of course he attends to the differences between one kind of cognitivist theory and another, and he recognizes that some of the considerations he raises have limited application. But he makes plain that he takes his target to be—and his central objections to be effective against— *any* variant of moral cognitivism committed to explicitly evaluative content for moral beliefs and to genuine, peculiarly moral, qualities of actions.

Deploying his objections both in the *Treatise* and in the second *Enquiry* Hume makes use of his distinction between necessary and contingent truths. 'Truth is of two kinds', he writes, 'consisting either in the discovery of the proportions of ideas, consider'd as such, or in the conformity of our ideas of objects to their real existence' (*T* 448). In a suitably comprehensive attack on moral realism, then, he must sap the metaphysical foundations both for alleged necessary moral truths and for alleged contingent ones. In the *Treatise*, having rejected the claim that 'vice and virtue consist in relations susceptible of certainty' (*T* 463) he turns to the claim that 'morality ... consists ... in [a] *matter of fact*' (*T* 468). In the second *Enquiry* he reverses the order of treatment, first rejecting 'that matter of fact which we here call *crime*' (*E* 287), then the suggestion of '*moral relations*, discovered by reason' (*E* 288). To be sure, some of the considerations Hume raises pertain only to one of these contrasting claims, not the other. None the less he contends that his main line of objection subverts theories of either kind. Referring to his just-completed argument against the metaphysics of necessary moral truths he writes: 'this reasoning ... if examin'd, will prove with equal certainty, that it [morality] consists not in any *matter of fact*, which can be discover'd by the understanding' (*T* 468). Economical in presentation, he leaves it to the reader to conduct the suggested 'examination' of the alleged metaphysical basis of contingent moral truths.

He endorses a distinction, within the class of necessary truths, between those that are, and those that are not, susceptible of demonstration. The latter 'fall more properly under the province of intuition than demonstration' (*T* 70). He endorses a parallel distinction within the class of contingent truths (*T* 73–4). He pays little attention, however, to the differing forms of moral cognitivism that result from applying this division within the class of purported moral truths. He does note 'a position very industriously propagated by certain philosophers, that morality is susceptible of demonstration', remarking caustically 'that no one has ever been able to advance a single step in those demonstrations' (*T* 463). But he lets the matter drop, fastening instead on what he takes to be the underlying metaphysical assumption common to claims about the necessity of moral truths, the metaphysical claim that 'vice and virtue must consist in some relations' (*T* 463). It is 'this hypothesis' he proceeds to examine. He simply ignores the issue of differing modes of access when he considers the thesis of contingent moral truths.

For reasons deriving from his own way of drawing the distinction between necessary and contingent truths, Hume pays particular attention to realist theories that invoke special moral relations rather than non-relational moral qualities. And some of the considerations he raises are effective, if effective at all, only against relational theories. He does, however, explicitly reject non-relational moral qualities as well as moral relations

(*E* 287–8). And, as we shall see, his central line of argument is indifferent to the particular structures the moral realist advocates.

Hume's indirect argument against moral cognitivism *continues* through three principal stages, corresponding to three demands he makes on moral realism (and so, here, on moral cognitivism).[31]

First, moral realism must provide an articulated, non-obscure account of the special moral features it invokes. Hume insists that the moral realist 'fix those moral qualities', 'point out distinctly the relations, which constitute morality or obligation' (*T* 463), 'shew those relations, upon which such a distinction [namely, that between right and wrong] may be founded' (*T* 466). Persistence here, he suggests, will reveal the moral realist to be committed to 'incomprehensible relations and qualities' of which one can form no 'clear and distinct conception' (*T* 476), to 'an abstruse hypothesis, which can never be made intelligible, nor quadrate to any particular instance or illustration' (*E* 289). If the moral realist *is* thus committed, one has reason to reject his claims.

Second, moral realism must provide a plausible account of cognitive access to its postulated moral qualities and relations, and so of the acquisition of purported moral beliefs. If a sound theory, moral realism must comport with sound theory concerning human cognitive capacities. The moral realist must tell us not only 'wherein they [i.e. the realist's moral features] consist' but also 'after what manner we may judge of them' (*T* 463). The moral cognitivist must both 'point out' the moral quality in question and 'explain the sense or faculty to which it discovers itself' (*E* 287). In the absence of a plausible account of cognitive access, the claim that moral realism complements moral cognitivism is called into question.

Third, the moral realist must explicate the claimed prescriptivity of objective moral qualities and relations. In addition to identifying the postulated moral properties and elucidating the cognitive processes by which they are reached, the realist must provide an account of the bearing those objective properties have on the conduct of moral agents. How could there be such prescriptive properties? How could recognition of their presence lead to action? In Hume's words, the moral realist must 'point out the connexion betwixt the relation and the will' (*T* 465). This third of Hume's three demands is, of course, peculiarly pressing. Failing to meet

---

[31] J. L. Mackie remarks, *Ethics: Inventing Right and Wrong* (Harmondsworth, 1977), 40–1, that if Hume's anti-cognitivist attack is to be successful he must supplement his explicit argument with what Mackie calls 'the argument from queerness'. As will become clear, the present continuation (as we term it) of Hume's indirect argument constitutes that supplement.

it must compromise the moral cognitivist's proposed counter to Hume's otherwise compelling *direct* argument for moral conativism.

Pressing the *first* of his three demands, Hume presents an abstract argument that, when expanded as his objectives require, purports to show that morality cannot be a matter of moral qualities or relations. It cannot be a matter of non-relational moral qualities, for an action, say, has no moral character apart from its relations to the situation in which it occurs. It cannot be a matter of moral relations, for the relations in question—the plausibly relevant relations between an action and its situation—can be instantiated in settings with no moral significance whatever, can be identically instantiated in settings that differ with respect to the possession of moral significance. Candidate relations are to be drawn from Hume's allegedly exhaustive list: 'resemblance, identity, relations of time and place, proportion in quantity or number, degrees in any quality, contrariety and causation' (*T* 69, italics omitted). Relations of any of these seven types can be instantiated in settings with no moral significance: they need only take 'irrational' or 'inanimate' objects as their terms (*T* 464). They can be identically instantiated in relational complexes that differ in terms of the presence or absence of moral significance: two relational complexes—the overtopping and consequent destruction of its parent tree by a sapling, the parricidal killing of a human parent—can be identical in terms of (plausibly relevant) relations despite differing in that the former is not, the latter is, morally significant. The moral character of relational complexes must, then, depend on the character of the terms of the relations in question. '[T]he relations, from which these moral distinctions arise, must lie only betwixt internal actions, and external objects' (*T* 464–5). The 'very essence of morality' cannot, then, 'lie in the relations' (*T* 463–4).[32]

Hume here argues, in effect, against any naturalistic analysis of purported moral relations. It is clear, however, that a moral cognitivist inclined to naturalism, one prepared to share Hume's apparent assumption that moral relations, if there be such, must be identified with natural ones, has room to manoeuvre. Conceding Hume's claim that difference of moral significance depends on the character of the terms of the relations, not just on the relations themselves, such a moral cognitivist could seek an

---

[32] Jenkins comments, *Understanding Hume*, 177: 'We cannot suppose that two situations can be alike in all relevant non-moral respects and that we are free nevertheless to react morally to these two situations in quite different ways…If Hume's argument were valid, moral judgement would be something quite inexplicable and positively *irrational*.' Hume claims, however, not that there are *no* differences but that there are no *relational* differences.

analysis of moral situations that incorporates the characteristics, to which Hume here draws our attention, of the morally significant terms. She could seek relations, more specific than any Hume mentions, that meet Hume's restrictions on the character of the terms, and that are present when and only when situations have moral significance. Making a start in this direction, she could point to Hume's own recognition, elsewhere in the *Treatise*, of a distinction between 'internal' and 'external' relations, the former being 'relations of objects to intelligent and rational beings' (*T* 527).

Each of these naturalistic rejoinders also shares Hume's assumption (*E* 288) that the relevant relations must obtain between the morally significant action and that action's setting, that they are relations internal to the relational complex comprising action and situation. A moral cognitivist committed to naturalism could, however, look to natural relations linking such relational complexes to something else: to the satisfaction of human interests, say, or to the occurrence of affective responses. There are such relational facts, as Hume is well aware. Writing of the relational complex of 'wilful murder' he says that if 'you turn your reflexion into your own breast, and find a sentiment of disapprobation, which arises in you, towards this action' (*T* 468–9) you would discover a 'matter of fact' (*T* 469), a natural relational fact about the action in its situation.

Naturalism has, then, ways around Hume's abstract argument, ways that do not require the introduction of 'incomprehensible relations and qualities' (*T* 476). The trouble with naturalism is not that its moral properties are not comprehensible but that, being natural, they are not prescriptive. They cannot, then, support the practicality of moral beliefs and so cannot counter Hume's direct argument for moral conativism.

Moral cognitivists who reject Hume's assumption that moral relations, if there be such, are to be identified with natural relations of the sort that appear on Hume's list (or on some expanded list) have a different response to make. Admitting that actions have moral features only because of their relations to their settings, they take these relational features as a basis for, rather than as something identical to, their possession of those moral features. The action's being wrong is a consequence of, is *supervenient* upon, its being an act of wilful murder. Its supervenient moral features (whether qualities or relations) are not further natural features of the action: they are non-natural, peculiarly moral, features. Taking this line the moral cognitivist can insist with some plausibility that, whatever the adequacy of Hume's classification of natural relations, his 'enumeration' of relations, more generally of features, is 'not compleat' (*T* 464) for it omits the supervenient non-natural features that explicitly moral beliefs and truths presuppose. Constructing his abstract argument against moral relations, Hume insists the moral realist must identify them with natural ones: 'the whole complicated object, of action and situation, must form certain relations, wherein the essence of vice consists' (*T* 464n.). Our non-naturalist prefers another picture, one that Hume himself articulates but puts aside: 'reason', this moral realist maintains, 'can discover such an action, in such relations, to be virtuous, and such another vicious'(ibid.).[33]

This non-naturalist version of moral realism escapes Hume's abstract argument against moral relations while at the same time introducing a notion, that of supervenience, that it seems *any* satisfactory theory of moral reasons for action, whether conativist or cognitivist, must accommodate. That it evades his abstract argument does not, however, mean that it has met Hume's first demand. Arguably its non-natural properties, precisely because non-natural, remain 'incomprehensible qualities and relations' of which one can form no 'clear and distinct conception' (*T* 476). It seems it must take the supervenience of the moral on the non-moral as a primitive relation incapable of any explication. It is unclear how the theory is to explain the difference in moral significance between sapling and human parricide, or between incest in animals and incest in humans (*T* 466–8). To have recourse to the presence or absence of 'reason sufficient to discover . . . [an action's] turpitude' won't do the trick, for that would simply be 'arguing in a circle' (*T* 467). The theory seems, in short, to have a number of theoretical disadvantages that Hume's first demand is designed to highlight. These disadvantages must be reckoned among the costs of moral cognitivism. It doesn't *follow*, of course, that they are not to be incurred.

The *second* of Hume's three demands—that concerning cognitive access to the moral cognitivist's putative moral features—poses no special problems for naturalistic theories. On the assumption that some sound theory is available for cognitive access to the mathematical, physical, and psychological features of the world, the naturalistically inclined moral cognitivist can simply appropriate the part of that theory that best meets his requirements. Problems of cognitive access are problems for non-

[33] Modern non-naturalists, including Moore and Ross, have made much of supervenience. For some of the difficulties supervenience engenders for moral realism, see Mackie, *Ethics*, 38–42, and especially Simon Blackburn, 'Moral Realism', in John Casey (ed.), *Morality and Moral Reasoning* (London, 1971), 101–24, *Spreading the Word: Groundings in the Philosophy of Language* (Oxford, 1984), and 'Supervenience Revisited', in Geoffrey Sayre-McCord (ed.), *Essays on Moral Realism* (Ithaca, NY, 1988), 59–75.

natural properties. What informative account is to be given of one's acquisition of the concepts in question, or of one's capacity to register peculiar
facts involving the supervenience of non-natural features on unproblematically natural ones? Proposals to model moral cognition on perception,
on introspection, on empirical theory construction, on mathematical reflection, promise nothing of explanatory substance.[34] Nor, more obviously,
does talk of a capacity for moral intuition. Perhaps the moral cognitivist
will claim that only if one postulates intuition of non-natural moral features could one explain, to the limited extent to which one can explain,
the content and incidence of moral judgements. We shall have opportunity
later to explore Hume's response to the implicit challenge.

Neither in the *Treatise* nor the second *Enquiry* does Hume elaborate
on the difficulties the moral cognitivist must encounter when attempting
to meet his second demand. Perhaps he is impatient to get to the purported prescriptivity of the moral realist's special qualities and relations;
and so to the *third* of the three requirements that he sets. There is much
that is misleading in Hume's handling of his argument at this third, and
crucial, stage. He attends as much to peripheral as to central issues. He
raises questions about extending the moral realist's account of the
prescriptivity of special moral properties to the case of 'the Deity himself' (*T* 456) or to that of 'every rational creature' (*T* 465). He alludes to
the phenomenon of weakness of will. But the heart of the matter, the
point on which he must focus, is the role the moral realist assigns to moral
features in the generation of action. And so Hume calls on the moral
realist to 'point out the connexion betwixt the relation and the will' (*T*
465).

According to the prescriptivist moral realism encapsulated in principle
CT4.1, the non-natural moral features of particular actions are objective
properties that themselves have the intrinsic property of prescriptivity.
It is in virtue of their prescriptivity that the moral properties of actions
require agents to act in the ways indicated. The prescriptivity of moral
properties constitutes them properties that prescribe or direct or demand
the doing or the avoidance, as the case may be, of the actions in question.
The prescriptive property constitutive of its wrongness demands that
the killing be avoided; in like manner, the rightness of keeping the promise requires the keeping of one's word. Thus it is that, in registering the

---

[34] To say this is—here emulating Hume—to do little more than register scepticism. A
serious discussion of the issue of epistemic access would need to address the defences of
moral realism collected in Sayre-McCord's *Essays on Moral Realism*. See, too, the discussion
of epistemic access in Harman's *The Nature of Morality*.

presence of such properties, one registers requirements on action. One registers the presence of such properties by forming explicitly evaluative—and correct—moral beliefs. In thus registering what is required one is disposed to act as required.

Putting the doctrine of prescriptive properties so baldly makes plain its obscurity. What sense *is* one to make of properties that are both objective—that is, are part of the fabric of the world in a way at least analogous to that in which the mathematical, or the primary, or even the so-called secondary, qualities of objects are part of the fabric of the world—and intrinsically prescriptive in character? It is one thing to say that the damage a prospective action would cause is an objective property of the action, a property that, for one averse to the damage, requires the action not be done. It seems quite another thing to say, with the prescriptivist moral realist, that the irreducibly prescriptive property of its wrongness requires that the action not be done. When characterized as required by their theoretical role, they seem just the sorts of 'incomprehensible relations and qualities' (*T* 476) whose postulation we have every reason to resist. If 'incomprehensible', however, they cannot help elucidate the practicality of putative moral beliefs—they cannot be enlisted in defence of the possibility of double direction of fit for the case of explicitly evaluative beliefs—and so cannot, in the way envisaged earlier, provide a counter to Hume's direct argument for moral conativism.

It may be objected that the apparent incomprehensibility of prescriptive properties is merely apparent. They appear incomprehensible if one attempts to conceive them in isolation from the other elements in the theory in which they must be embedded. They are comprehensible because of their intelligible location in a full-dress moral cognitivist theory that, taken as a whole, provides a comprehensible account (perhaps, a best explanation) of specifically moral reasons for action. Intrinsically prescriptive objective properties are essential if the full-dress theory is to provide its comprehensible account, but it is other elements in the theory that, by providing a theoretical location for these seemingly incomprehensible prescriptive properties, render them comprehensible. In effect, these properties are to be located by means of relational properties the full-dress theory assigns them in virtue of their intrinsic prescriptivity. Prescriptive properties can affect an agent's conduct only by means of the explicitly evaluative beliefs to which they give rise. The practicality of those explicitly evaluative beliefs serves, then, as an indicator of the prescriptivity of the properties with whose presence those beliefs are concerned. By doing so it renders those properties, and their prescriptivity, intelligible.

On this more holistic approach to prescriptive properties, their comprehensibility is tied to that of the practicality of moral beliefs, and so to the possibility that such beliefs can have a double direction of fit. Given the direction of explanatory dependence, of course, the contention that moral beliefs display both the world-to-mind and the mind-to-world directions of fit can derive no support (of the sort earlier hinted) from an independently intelligible notion of intrinsically prescriptive properties. The explanatory shoe is clearly on the other foot. What, then, are the prospects for an independently intelligible doctrine that explicitly evaluative moral beliefs have both directions of fit?

To have both directions of fit a (single) belief must have both truth-conditions and satisfaction-conditions. Having the mind-to-world direction of fit it has truth-conditions: its task is to fit the world; it succeeds in its task by being true, and its truth-conditions set the conditions on its success. Having the other—the world-to-mind—direction of fit it—the belief—has satisfaction-conditions: the world must fit it; the belief succeeds if it is satisfied and its satisfaction-conditions set the conditions on that success. Now, on the face of it, the suggestion that a belief has satisfaction-conditions makes no sense at all. But let that point go. Let us concentrate on the claim that a (single) belief—an explicitly evaluative belief—can have *both* satisfaction-conditions and truth-conditions.

The conditions on a psychological state's success *correspond* to that state's content. The belief that the coffee is ready is successful—that is, is true—if and only if the coffee is ready. The desire that the coffee be ready is successful—that is, is satisfied—if and only if the coffee is ready. What, then of the *content*, and of the *double* conditions on the success of, an explicitly evaluative belief with—as is claimed—its double direction of fit? Consider the explicitly evaluative belief (as we shall assume it to be) that it would be wrong to tell a lie. The belief is true, presumably, if and only if it would be wrong to tell a lie. It is satisfied, however, if and only if no lies are told.[35] (If it is to do the work the theory assigns it, the belief's truth-conditions and its satisfaction-conditions cannot be the same.) Given the required correspondence between success-conditions (whichever their kind) and content, it follows that the explicitly evaluative belief in question

---

[35] Here we ignore complexities introduced if the putative evaluative beliefs are taken to be prima facie in character.

must, despite appearances, have conjunctive content.[36] It must be a belief both that it would be wrong to tell a lie and that no lies are told. The argument holds, of course, for any putative evaluative belief that can play the major role in a reason for action and that is claimed to have both directions of fit. The absurd consequence is that in holding such an evaluative belief one must, in effect, believe it satisfied. The doctrine of double direction of fit for moral beliefs must, then, be discarded. Without that doctrine, however, standard moral cognitivism succumbs to Hume's direct argument.

This argument against double direction of fit for moral beliefs turns on construing standard moral cognitivism strictly. It turns on taking it to be *beliefs*—albeit explicitly evaluative ones—that possess both the mind-to-world and the world-to-mind direction of fit. Can a version of moral cognitivism be salvaged if that strict constraint is lifted? Moral cognitivism must, to be true to its name, construe ostensible moral beliefs as, indeed, beliefs. In giving up double direction of fit for beliefs it must, then, give up their claimed practicality. Perhaps, however, in the holistic fashion sketched above, it can characterize prescriptive properties as those that prompt explicitly evaluative beliefs that are not themselves practical (for they do not have the world-to-mind direction of fit), but that in turn prompt desires with appropriate descriptive content (and with the world-to-mind direction of fit). The prescriptive property which is the wrongness of a lie, it may be said, prompts the evaluative belief that it would be wrong to tell a lie; that belief in turn prompts the desire that lies not be told. Explicitly evaluative beliefs are truth-evaluable, not practical; the resultant desires are practical, not truth-evaluable; and prescriptive properties are those with the complex relational property just specified.

We have, of course, returned to an inefficaciously complex form of moral cognitivism articulated earlier, a theory with signal disadvantages. It rejects two points that provide common ground for standard moral cognitivism and moral conativism: the claim that a single psychological state will suffice as the major constituent in a moral reason for action; and the recognition that ostensible moral beliefs (whether they be genuine beliefs or not) themselves provide that major constituent. It inherits the problems of standard moral cognitivism with its non-natural properties: the primitiveness of their supervenience on natural ones; the inexplicability of the moral significance of certain natural properties; the puzzles

---

[36] Nothing hinges, here, on possible differences between a conjunctive belief (*A* believes that *p and q*) and a conjunction of beliefs (*A* believes that *p* and *A* believes that *q*).

about epistemic access. It requires, just as moral conativism does, desires with descriptive content. It must postulate a more complex primitive relation than the standard theory, that between prescriptive property, evaluative belief, and descriptive desire. Its claims to explanatory adequacy are, it seems, distinctly uncompelling.

Holding to explicitly evaluative beliefs while rejecting such accompanying desires, moral cognitivism can, of course, eschew the practicality of moral beliefs altogether. To take up this extreme position is, however, to run afoul of Hume's argument, registered earlier, for the practicality of what seem to be explicitly moral beliefs.

Are there other ways in which a moral cognitivist might attempt to blunt the force of Hume's argument from direction of fit? Can some attenuated form of moral cognitivism be constructed that might serve this purpose? What of the thought that the very same non-compound psychological state can be, or be characterized as, both a belief (with evaluative content) and a desire (with descriptive content)? Can the very same non-compound psychological state possess, or be characterized as possessing, both the mind-to-world direction of fit (in virtue of its evaluative content) and the world-to-mind direction of fit (in virtue of its descriptive content)? The thought of a double attribute theory, or of alternative ways of characterizing the very same psychological state, must here be tempting. To be a *cognitivist* rather than a *conativist* theory, however, such an attenuated theory would have, minimally, to view the cognitive, rather than the conative, characteristics of such states as in some way more fundamental or important. To be a *successful* cognitivist theory—one warranting acceptance—it would have to give compelling reason for viewing the cognitive characteristics of these states in this way. And it would have to counter Hume's formidable array of objections to the comprehensibility of the concept of non-natural properties. Whatever be said of the underlying doctrine of alternative characterizations of the very same psychological state, the prospects for an attenuated moral cognitivism resting on that doctrine are, it seems, decidedly dim.[37]

---

[37] We shall consider a similarly attenuated form of moral conativism in Chap. 4, Sect. 4.

4

Moral Sentiments

Hume's direct and indirect arguments constitute a sustained, sophisticated, and—as we have found—compelling attack on standard moral cognitivism and its many variants. *Pari passu*, they constitute a compelling argument on behalf of moral conativism, the doctrine that specifically moral desires, not moral beliefs, play the major role in specifically moral reasons for action. As such, they forward a striking *identity thesis*: what may seem to be *moral beliefs* of a *practical* sort—what Hume himself refers to as action-explanatory 'judgments, by which we distinguish moral good and evil' (*T* 456) or 'opinion[s] of injustice' or 'opinion[s] ... of obligation' (*T* 457)—are in fact *specifically moral desires*.

His direct and indirect arguments cannot, as Hume is well aware, exhaust his case for moral conativism. He must fill out the theory in several ways. He must elucidate its central conception of specifically moral desires and must provide a plausible, wholly naturalistic, account of their formation. With moral conativism as his foundation, he must find ways to incorporate a consonant treatment of those moral 'judgments' and 'opinions' that moral conativism does not itself touch, moral 'judgments' and 'opinions' that, not being practical in the intended sense, are not to be identified with moral desires. He must display moral conativism's ability to accommodate not only those phenomena that resist plausible treatment in cognitivist terms but also those—the apparent intersubjectivity of morality, say, or the seeming truth-evaluability of moral claims—that can make moral cognitivism appear irresistible.

Moral desires (as, for brevity's sake, we may call them) must have propositional content, of course, and must have the world-to-mind direction of fit.[1] They must differ, as other desires do, from affections and

---

[1] Several terminological caveats and clarifications may conveniently be entered here. 'Moral desire' is a term of interpretative art, not Hume's own. 'Moral sentiments', while more nearly a term of Hume's, is here regimented so as to range over both moral desires and what, building on a bit of regimentation from Chap. 2, we shall call 'moral affections'. The inclusive term 'moral sentiments', as used here, is equivalent to the also inclusive 'moral passions'. When the classificatory term 'moral' is used here (as in 'moral sentiment' or 'moral desire' or 'moral affection') it contrasts with 'non-moral' rather than with 'immoral'. As

volitions. But what sets them apart from other desires? What makes them specifically moral ones? Hume's characterization of moral desires is no less sophisticated than is his argument for their acknowledgement. He fastens on features of their content, in particular their *universality*, their *impartiality*, and their several *person-implicating* dimensions. He purports, thereby, to capture the *intersubjectivity* of moral assessment that moral cognitivists rightly emphasize.

If their impartiality helps set moral desires apart, however, it also poses questions about their origin and influence. Humean agents are naturally partial (which is not to say egoistic). How, then, can they come to have impartial concerns? Having such concerns, how can they be governed by them in their actions? In Hume's view the operations of sympathy can extend the range of one's concern for others. Those operations cannot, however, suffice for the explanation of moral desires, with their impartial content, for sympathy, as Hume insists, is naturally partial in its functioning. Mechanisms providing for the *correction of sympathy* must be described; conditions on their functioning must be identified; and the whole psychological or psycho-social tale must be tellable, and plausible, within the constraints of a naturalistic theory. In telling the tale one displays what it is, in Hume's view, that demands the impartiality that marks morality and so adoption of the moral point of view.

An adequate moral conativism must find a way to accommodate, within an expanded theory, those moral 'judgments' or 'opinions' that, not construable as desires, are not practical in the sense of being suited to serve as the major element in a reason for action. Smith's 'judgment' that Jones's conduct is morally execrable, or her 'judgment' that Jones herself is execrable, may prompt Smith's taking of a variety of steps: she may decry Jones in public, take steps to protect the innocent from her influence, avoid her at all costs. But the 'judgments' themselves are patently not desires; and their role in the explanation of Smith's actions is not desire's role. Hume's doctrine of *moral affections*, with its *identification* of ostensible moral beliefs of a *non*-practical sort with specifically moral affections, and with its commitment to the *centrality of moral desire*, constitutes a powerful expansion of his moral conativism. That *expanded moral conativism* locates moral desires and moral affections within a comprehensive configuration isomorphic with the configuration of the passions we explored in Chapter 2, Section 3. An *expanded* moral conativism, it offers an inclusive

---

noted earlier, Hume's 'judgments' and 'opinions' are psychological states, not essentially linguistic occurrences; they are not to be identified with the linguistic occurrences in which such psychological states often find expression.

account of the many kinds of psychological states and occurrences that constitute our moral evaluations.

In his expanded theory Hume identifies what seem to be moral beliefs with passions (sentiments), whether desires (for those suited to play the major role in reasons for action) or affections (for those not so suited). Invoking a conception of calm passions he offers an explanation of the illusion involved when, quite naturally, we take these desires and affections as beliefs, an illusion that finds theoretical articulation in the several forms of moral cognitivism. He says remarkably little about the linguistic expression of moral desires and affections. Perhaps, if pressed, he would postulate illusions embedded in the very language of morals as well. We find it as natural to talk of moral truths as of moral beliefs: one believes that the eradication of poverty is desirable; if one's belief is true it is true that poverty's eradication is desirable. Unless inhibited by philosophical scruples we do not hesitate to append the predicate 'is true' to an explicitly evaluative sentence, or to say 'That's true' or 'That's not true' in response to another's moral contentions about abortion or civil disobedience. The metalinguistic sentence ' "It is desirable that poverty be eradicated" is true' is no more problematic, it seems, than is the sentence ' "Poverty is eradicated" is true'. These and other well-entrenched cognitivist appearances must somehow be reckoned with if Hume's inclusive theory of putative moral beliefs, his expanded moral conativism, is—all said and done—firmly to hold the field. As with ostensible beliefs, so with ostensible truths and predications of 'is true': recourse to talk of illusion must, to Hume, be tempting. Other things being equal, however, an appeal to substantive illusion must here count *against* moral conativism when comparative evaluations of theoretical adequacy are in question. We must, then, look, if only briefly, to other ways—including an attenuated way—in which a moral conativist might attempt to accommodate talk of evaluative truth.

I. MORAL DESIRES

The constructive product of Hume's direct and indirect arguments is the thesis that moral 'judgments' or 'opinions' playing the major role in specifically moral reasons for action are moral desires. Hume *identifies* such practical moral 'judgments'—the 'judgments', say, that promises ought to be kept, or that lying is wrong—with desires of a distinctive, a specifically moral, sort. Such a moral 'judgment'—such a moral desire—has a double responsibility. It both sets moral requirements—marks or makes moral distinctions—and promotes action in accordance with those requirements or distinctions. In Hume's words, it both 'distinguishes moral good and evil' and 'embraces the one and rejects the other' (*E* 294; compare *E* 271, 286). No matter which of these responsibilities is at the focus of his attention, Hume is plain enough on the point of identity. He writes, of the motivational 'sentiments of duty and humanity': 'In these sentiments then, not in the discovery of relations of any kind, do all moral determinations *consist*' (*E* 291, emphasis added).[2] Reflecting on 'moral deliberations' he writes: 'The approbation or blame . . . *is* not a speculative proposition or affirmation, but an active feeling or sentiment' (*E* 290, emphasis added). He commits himself to the identity claim when illustrating, by reference to reasons of justice, a specifically moral reason for action: '*reason* instructs us in the several tendencies of actions, and *humanity*'—as we shall see, 'humanity' is Hume's term in the second *Enquiry* for the primary moral desire—'makes a distinction in favour of those which are useful and beneficial' (*E* 286; compare *E* 172).

Moral desires share the crucial properties of other desires. They are complex psychological states with propositional content that have the world-to-mind, not the mind-to-world, direction of fit. As such, they have no truth-conditions and are not evaluable in terms of truth or falsity. Their content, which must be descriptive, not evaluative, in character, sets their satisfaction-conditions. If their content is descriptive, however, their linguistic expression is explicitly evaluative: desires are expressible in explicitly evaluative sentences that can provide the major premises in arguments supporting actions. Arguably, they are expressible in sentences that are conditional (or prima facie) rather than unconditional (or all out) in character. In virtue of their direction of fit they are practical psychological states, states suited to serve as the major elements in reasons for action, and so can be cited in an action's explanation. With their world-to-mind direction of fit they set (some of) an agent's goals. When functioning as major elements in reasons for action they are suitably linked to causal or constitutive beliefs that, with their own mind-to-world direction of fit, carry information pertinent to the securing of such goals. Both resembling and differing from volitions, they can help explain volitions implicated in the actions that, as major elements in reasons for actions, they help explain. They can compete with or can complement the desires

---

[2] The passage as a whole asserts both of the identity theses we have attributed to Hume: the identity of practical moral beliefs with desires; and the identity of the others with moral affections.

ingredient in other reasons for action. They have a place not only in the basic psychological configuration of desire, belief, and action but also in a more comprehensive configuration that incorporates moral affections, both propositional and person-directed. They prompt propositional moral affections, states of satisfaction or dissatisfaction consequent upon the realization, or the failure of realization, of the satisfaction-conditions specified in their (the moral desires') contents. They are not plausibly to be modelled in the manner of Hume's atomistic official theory, or in that of some modest revision of the official theory. More promisingly, they are to be modelled in terms of a distinctive primitive mode of conception, or in terms of a primitive attitude, that of wanting true, directed towards propositions.

What sets moral desires apart from other desires? When in the thrall of his official theory of the passions Hume thinks of moral sentiments generally, and so of moral desires, in phenomenological terms. He writes of 'that particular feeling or sentiment, on which moral distinctions depend' (T 591), of 'the distinguishing impressions, by which moral good or evil is known' (T 471). 'Nor', he claims, 'is every sentiment of pleasure or pain, which arises from characters and actions, of the *peculiar* kind, which makes us praise or condemn' (T 472). Much more promisingly, he invokes peculiarities of the perspective or point of view adoption of which is implicated in an agent's having these peculiar sentiments. The 'satisfaction or uneasiness' in question is a function of one's adopting '*the general view or survey*' (T 475); it is a 'pleasure or pain' that arises 'whenever we survey the actions and characters of men, without any particular interest in them' (T 617). ''Tis only when a character is considered in general', Hume writes, 'without reference to our particular interest, that it causes such a feeling or sentiment, as denominates it morally good or evil' (T 472). So, too, it is only when the 'interests and pleasures' of individuals are viewed in that same general way that they 'produce that particular feeling or sentiment, on which moral distinctions depend' (T 591). Putting talk of pleasures and pains to the side, we may say that Hume's point is a point about content. For Hume, peculiarities of the moral perspective or point of view reveal themselves, for the case of moral desires, as peculiarities of the content—the non-evaluative content—of those desires. Moral desires are desires that display a certain generality in their content, a certain absence of particular interest.

Let us assume at the start—I shall introduce a host of qualifications later on—that moral desires manifest a concern for the interests of human individuals in so far as those interests are affected by the actions of others. Let us assume, that is to say, that to have a moral desire is to be concerned that such interests be served or at least not subverted. Hume's point about the content of moral desires is that to be distinctively moral such concern must meet very strong conditions of impartiality. The content of one's moral desires must incorporate no essential reference to oneself, or to the peculiarities of one's place or position. It must, in representing the objects of one's concern, employ no devices that characterize individuals in terms of their relations to oneself. In forming moral desires one must, in Hume's words, 'neglect' (*E* 229), 'over-look' (*T* 582), 'forget' (*T* 591) one's own naturally central position in one's representation of other persons, other times and places, other communities and conventions. Adopting the moral point of view, one achieves a perspective informed instead by 'abstract notions' (*T* 585).

There are, of course, a variety of factors – a variety of relations in which a given individual can stand to others – that affect the range and character of that individual's concern (including her instrumental concern) for the others. Ties of blood or friendship (or their absence) have an obvious effect. So, too, does the fact that the other is (or is not) a compatriot, a comrade in arms, a co-operative co-participant in a convention of mutual benefit. Even relations of space and time can play a role: the fact that another person is nearby rather than distant, or that she is a contemporary rather than someone long past, can affect an individual's other-regarding concern, most obviously by determining whether the other is a possible beneficiary of other-regarding action. It is appropriate to describe some of these special relations as *partiality-generating* relations.

Partiality of this sort, however, is perfectly compatible with the impartiality Hume requires in the content of moral desires.

When experience has once given us a competent knowledge of human affairs, and has taught us the proportion they bear to human passion, we perceive, that the generosity of men is very limited, and that it seldom extends beyond their friends and family, or, at most, beyond their native country. Being thus acquainted with the nature of man, we expect not any impossibilities from him. (*T* 602)

In framing our judgements of obligation, then, we accommodate this natural partiality: we acknowledge obligations (say those of friends or parents) that rest on such special relations; we impose no obligations to other-regarding conduct quite beyond what our experience of partiality makes it reasonable for us to expect. Needless to say, we impose no obligations to other-regarding action when, spatial and especially temporal relations being what they are, no action of the agent could affect another's interests. In Hume's view practical moral judgements—which is to say, moral desires—must accommodate partiality-generating special relations of these sorts.

What the impartiality constitutive of moral desire demands is simply that, in so far as one has such a desire, one overlooks *one's own peculiar role* as a term in any such special relation. In so far as one views things from the moral perspective, one overlooks the particularities of one's own ties of blood or friendship, one's own ties to (some) others by way of common membership in a community or common participation in some convention. And one ignores the particularities of one's own spatial and temporal position. One desires that friends perform the offices of friendship for their friends, that parents provide for the welfare of their dependent children, that individuals act in accordance with the conventions to which they are party governing property, or promise-keeping, or sexual conduct. From the impartial vantage-point of morality one desires, in effect, that the friends, the parents, the parties to the conventions act as their essentially partial desires direct.[3] So far as one's moral desires are concerned one's own friends, one's own children, one's own conventions—save in so far as one's own case is a case of one of the kinds in question—have no special place whatever. From the moral point of view 'a person, who liv'd in *Greece* two thousand years ago' is on a par with 'a familiar friend and acquaintance' (*T* 581; compare *E* 273); from the moral point of view, it makes no difference whether individuals are 'persons remote from us' or 'persons near and contiguous' (*T* 603). Adopting the moral point of view we 'consider not whether the persons, affected ... be our acquaintance or strangers, countrymen or foreigners' (*T* 582).

Hume sometimes depicts this intersection of impartiality and special relations in terms, specifically, of the interests of those for whom a partial individual is concerned. It is natural to attend to one's own interests and those of one's friends and relations: one naturally focuses on these and ignores or undervalues the interests of those who fall outside one's 'narrow circle' (*T* 602). Hume frames his account of practical moral judgements, thus of the content of moral desires, so as to reflect this dimension

---

[3] Given Hume's contention that the relevant moral desires are *desire-implicating* desires— a contention discussed in Chap. 5, below—one (morally) desires that the friends, the parents, the parties to the conventions act *from* the appropriate, essentially partial, desires. This contention must be accommodated within a full-dress presentation of a Humean doctrine of the impartiality of moral desire. Such a presentation must accommodate the motivational intersection of partial and impartial desires. It must also reckon with an agent's need to balance competing moral claims, given the facts of his situation.

of human partiality. In doing so, however, he is none the less intent on displaying the fundamental impartiality with respect to interests that the moral point of view introduces. We are 'oblig'd', he writes, 'to forget our own interest in our judgments of this kind' (*T* 602); *so far as* our moral desires are concerned it can make no difference that, or whether, 'our own interest is concern'd, or that of our particular friends' (*T* 583); we 'over-look our own interest in those general judgments' (*T* 582). One's own interests have, of course, a role to play, just as do those of any other; but that those interests are one's own has, from the perspective of moral desire, no role to play at all.

The partiality-generating special relations in which one stands to others are, many of them, subject to change. People come into and go out of one's life. Friends can become enemies and enemies friends. The class of one's compatriots, just as that of the participants of conventions to which one is oneself party, is constantly changing: other members come and go, and one sometimes shifts oneself. Moreover, one's own perspective on things, one's own valuings and predilections, can undergo change, and so bring about changes in one's partiality-generating relations to others. This mutability of human motivational life may well find some reflection in the content of moral desires, but it can do so only subject to the demands of impartiality. Hume requires the content of our moral desires to be impervious to the facts that our 'situation, with regard ... to persons ... is in continual fluctuation' (*T* 581) and that 'the present disposition of our mind' (*T* 582) may well be different, in motivationally significant ways, from what it was and from what it will be. Adopting the moral point of view, one not only ignores the peculiarities of one's own perspective, but also ignores the variability of those peculiarities.

Given their impartiality, moral desires are *intersubjective* in a very strong sense. Abstracting from the peculiarities of one's subjective situation— and making allowances, as above, for the role of special relations—one secures a vantage-point that could be anyone's. One forms desires, shareable by any other, that display concern for the interests of those, whoever they be, who are affected by the actions of others, whoever they be. Despite enormous differences in their own narrow circles of concern different individuals with moral desires have, thus far, the very same—unrestricted— range of concern. The moral point of view is impervious to the fact that 'every particular man has a peculiar position with regard to others' (*T* 581; compare *T* 603, *E* 229). It is a 'common point of view, from which ... [all] might survey their object, and which might cause it to appear the same to all of them' (*T* 591). From that '*steady* and *general* point ...

of view' ($T\,581$–2), we focus on 'the influence of characters and qualities, upon those who have any intercourse with any person' ($T\,582$), on 'those, who have any commerce with the person we consider' ($T\,583$; compare $T\,603$).

Allowing clarity to compensate for the risk of anachronism, we may say that—to a first approximation—the content of moral desire is universally quantified and contains, whether explicitly or surreptitiously, whether by restriction on the ranges of the variables or by specification of the relevant properties and relations, no reference to the individual who has the desire. He and his friends and relations, his communities and conventions, enter in, but only as tokens (or instances) of types (or kinds) of which other individuals, with their friends and relations, their communities and conventions, are equally tokens (or instances). It is because Hume takes moral desires to have such a character that he can describe them as 'impartial' ($T\,583$), as 'disinterested' ($E\,301$) or 'steady' ($T\,582$) or 'stable' ($T\,581$) or 'unalterable' ($T\,603$). It is for the same reason that he can write of forming 'moral determinations or general judgments' ($E\,228$ n.), thinking of such a judgement as a 'sentiment, so universal and comprehensive as to extend to all mankind' ($E\,272$). And it is because of their impartiality and universality that he can characterize the vantage-point such judgements represent as 'common' ($T\,591$).

An obvious qualification, already alluded to, must be made explicit. The requirement that *it* display in *its* content the universality and impartiality we have described seems too stringent a condition on a desire's being a moral desire. Surely a father can make moral judgements about *his* obligations to *his* child and so, on Hume's identity hypothesis, have moral desires concerning *his* contribution to *his* child's well-being. To deal with the difficulty we need only say that a desire is a moral desire provided the desire itself, *or* a desire from which it derives, has the requisite universality and impartiality of content. Does the father's desire derive from a universal and impartial desire concerning parental conduct towards dependent children? If so, the derivative desire is, we may say, itself a moral desire: its introduction of pronominal reference to the desirer himself is the product of his recognizing his own situation to be a token of a type represented in his explicitly universal and impartial desire.[4] If his concern for his child does not derive in this way from an impartial concern, however, his desire for his child's well-being is not, even deriva-

---

[4] Hume's notion of the desire-implicating character of certain moral desires also has a role to play in the development of the present contrast. See n. 3, just above, and the account of desire-implicating desires in Chap. 5.

tively, a moral desire.[5] In such a case his desire does not constitute a moral judgement concerning his obligations to his child.

The relationship between moral and non-moral desires is, for Hume, a complex one. As we shall see in Chapter 5, he even holds that the contents of certain moral desires must themselves make reference to non-moral desires with their own non-moral contents. For present purposes, it is enough to notice that he does insist on a distinction between moral and non-moral desires, and that he does so both for the case of what he terms the artificial, and for that of the so-called natural, virtues. He distinguishes 'sentiments from interest' and 'sentiments from ... morals' (*T* 472) when characterizing the several reasons an individual might have for acting as justice requires. Making the same point he contrasts '[t]he *natural* obligation to justice, *viz.* interest' with 'the *moral* obligation, or the sentiment of right and wrong' (*T* 498). Continuing, he writes that while 'self-interest is the *original motive* to the establishment of justice', a concern for 'public interest is the source of the *moral approbation* which attends that virtue' (*T* 499–500, emphasis replaces Hume's). One may keep one's promises and pay one's debts because it is in one's interest to do so: the non-moral desires from which one acts are partial. Very differently, one may do so because one ought to: one's desires, if that is one's reason, are impartial ones.

At *T* 498 Hume marks the very same division between 'natural obligation' or 'original motive', on the one hand, and 'moral obligation' or 'sentiment of right and wrong', on the other, for the case of what he terms the natural virtues. The virtue of benevolence is a particularly important case in point. The non-moral motive of benevolence is, in Hume's words, 'a desire of the happiness of the person belov'd, and an aversion to his misery' (*T* 367), its partiality being revealed in the mode of its reference to the person loved. This non-moral motive of benevolence must not be confused with the specifically moral motive Hume terms 'humanity'. For Hume, 'humanity'—the principal moral desire—is 'a feeling for the happiness of mankind, and a resentment of their misery' (*E* 286). The comprehensive scope of its concern reveals the presence of the moral point of view. As the principal moral desire *it* is, at bottom, the reason from which one acts whenever one acts from a sense of obligation, whether it be in keeping one's promises or—the point of present interest—in doing what benevolence demands.

In Hume's view, it is clear, non-moral and moral desires can complement

---

[5] This is not, of course, to say that it has no moral value.

one another in the governance of action. Interest and moral sentiment can each contribute to an agent's acting as the rules of justice require: an agent can keep a given promise both because she recognizes that doing so is in her interest (and that of her friends and relations) and because she judges that she is morally obliged to do so. But this is to say that she acts both because she wants to serve her interests (and those of persons near and dear to her) and because she has an impartial desire that individuals keep their promises. In like manner, an agent can act both out of benevolence and out of the thought that she ought so to act. To return to an earlier example, the father's care for his child can (though it need not) manifest both parental love and an impartial concern that parents attend to the needs of their dependent children. Commenting on 'duties, which a man performs as a friend or parent', Hume writes: 'A strong inclination may prompt him to the performance: A sentiment of order and moral obligation joins its force to these natural tyes: And the whole man, if truly virtuous, is drawn to his duty, without any effort or endeavour.'[6]

As remarked above, Hume views 'humanity' as the principal moral desire. Clearly a desire, it 'give[s] a preference to the useful above the pernicious tendencies' of 'qualities and actions', 'makes a distinction in favour of those which are useful and beneficial' (*E* 286). Clearly, too, it is a specifically moral desire. In addition to writing of 'the sentiments of duty and humanity' (*E* 291), Hume calls attention to the universality and impartiality of its content: the 'sentiment of humanity' is 'so universal and comprehensive as to extend to all mankind, and render the actions and conduct, even of persons the most remote, an object of applause or censure, according as they agree or disagree with that rule of right which is established' (*E* 272). It is intersubjective: one moved by 'humanity' is said to 'depart from his private and peculiar situation' and to 'choose a point of view, common to him with others' (*E* 272). While not to be confused with the natural and non-moral motive of benevolence it is a 'benevolent concern for others' (*E* 275). As the principal moral desire it must be distinguished from those 'secondary' or 'subordinate' desires to which, given suitable causal and constitutive beliefs, it gives rise (*T* 394). Given the many different ways in which actions can bear on the interests of

---

[6] David Hume, *The Natural History of Religion*, 89. Following the editions of 1772 and 1777 (as noted by Colver), I here substitute 'moral obligation' for Colver's 'moral beauty'. My attention was drawn to this passage by David Fate Norton, 'Hume, Atheism, and the Autonomy of Morals', in Marcus Hester (ed.), *Hume's Philosophy of Religions* (Winston-Salem, NC, 1986), where the passage is quoted (using 'moral obligation') in n. 41.

others, there is room for a plethora of more specific secondary or subordinate moral desires, such as the desires that parents care for their children, that spouses be faithful to one another, that gratitude be shown to benefactors, that promises be kept, that justice be done. 'Humanity' provides part of the reason for secondary moral desires. As the principal moral desire it stands as the foundation of the motivational structure that is (in part) constitutive of the moral point of view. Whether, given its foundational role in morality, it is itself an *ultimate* desire is, however, a further question, and one that is best deferred until we have discussed convention.[7]

We assumed, when first setting out to characterize Hume's conception of moral desires, that such desires are attentive to human interests. This is faithful to Hume who writes, when representing the moral point of view, of our being 'touch[ed]' by the 'interests' of those for whom we are impartially concerned (*T* 591; compare *E* 218). Equivalently, it seems, we are concerned for 'the good' of those individuals: we are concerned for 'the good of society' (*T* 577); and the psychological mechanism that gives rise to moral desires 'interests us in the good of mankind' (*T* 584). At times Hume writes of our concern, from the vantage-point of morality, for 'the welfare and advantage' (*E* 277) or for the 'pleasure and interest' (*T* 591) of the individuals in question. The proliferation of terms must not be allowed to mask what is central to Hume's conception of moral concern. As he represents the situation, to have moral desires is to be concerned with the satisfaction of the desires of those for whom we are impartially concerned. His conception of a 'man's interest' is tightly tied to that of 'the aversions and desires, which result from it' (*E* 228).

It is tempting to think that, when moved by impartial desire, one wants *impartial* desires, one's own and others', to be satisfied. There is something to this, of course: when adopting the intersubjective moral point of view, one wants those desires satisfied that anyone desiring from that point of view would have. If incoherence is to be avoided, however, the satisfaction of specifically moral desires cannot be the exclusive objective of specifically moral desires. As the earlier discussions of special relations will have suggested, and as the Humean argument concerning moral motivation examined in Chapter 5 will make plain, the satisfaction of *partial* desires, one's own and others', must be the focus of one's *impartial* moral concern. Moved by 'humanity' and by the secondary moral desires one is concerned that individuals' partial concerns for themselves and for their own friends and relations be met.

---

[7] See Chap. 6, Sect. 3.

This being so, one must, in adopting the moral point of view, address the question of the effects, on the content of one's impartial concern, of the recognition that individuals may go astray in their own judgements of partial interest.[8] Hume draws our attention to a variety of ways in which an individual's consulting of his own interests can be unsuccessful. The most obvious ways involve straightforwardly cognitive failing: inadvertence, inattention, ineptness in inference, simple ignorance about the workings of the world, can, singly or together, contribute to an individual's failure to see where his genuine interest lies and so to the formation of unwarranted subordinate desires. The limitations of his imagination can lead an individual to fail to see the value in an unfamiliar course of conduct. Then, too, the force of passion can contribute to specifically cognitive breakdown: as Hume remarks when writing of non-moral motivation in connection with the requirements of justice, 'violent passion hinders men from seeing distinctly the interest they have in an equitable behaviour towards others' (*T* 538). The partiality of one's attention to present or proximate pleasure can stand in the way of one's properly reckoning one's future losses and gains. Hume emphasizes its effects: 'There is no quality in human nature, which causes more fatal errors in our conduct, than that which leads us to prefer whatever is present to the distant and remote, and makes us desire objects more according to their situation than their intrinsic value' (*T* 538).[9] Of course *this* source of misjudgement of one's own interests introduces—though partial interests are alone in question—an interesting failure in impartiality. The realities of one's existence through time and change demand—if one is genuinely concerned about *one's own* partial interests—a certain impartial attention to the claims both of one's present and of one's future selves. It is not clear, it must be said, that Hume takes the point about the partiality of the here and now as far as this. But it is clear that he does think (in a conativist way) in terms of the 'true interests of mankind' (*E* 180) and (in an internalist way) of 'intrinsic value' (*T* 538). This suggests, at least, that impartial moral desires are directed towards the serving of *true*, albeit *partial*, interests. Not having made the suggestion explicitly himself, however, Hume does nothing to address the complex issues that the introduction of true interests raises.

In consulting the true interests of others one must, if impartial, view those interests not from one's own partial evaluative perspective but from that of the others. One must, that is to say, avoid imposing the peculiarities of one's own preferences and predilections, or those of one's own society, when purporting to represent what is in the interest of another individual, an individual from another society. At a sufficiently abstract level, perhaps, one's own partial valuings will match those of the others: each will value displays of concern and friendship, or the well-being of his or her own children, or the fidelity of his or her spouse, or liberty and security. But what counts, concretely, as the offices of friendship, or as a contribution to a child's well-being, or as fidelity, may well differ markedly from one society, and so from one individual, to another. The relative values assigned to competing goods such as liberty and security may also differ. Such differences across individuals and communities are clearly compatible with the absence of the cognitive and other failings implicated in misjudgements of interest. Adopting the moral point of view one is impartially concerned with the true interests of others; that concern requires one to view their interests as they—when not mistaken—do.

Hume does not attend to this dimension of impartiality in the *Treatise* or the second *Enquiry*. In his essay 'A Dialogue' he insists on the diversity of the determinate evaluations that derive, without cognitive or other failing, from an evaluative common ground, but—his eye there on other questions—he draws no conclusions about the content of moral desires.[10] We may take it, however, that his thinking about their content is of a piece with what he says of the impartiality of aesthetic judgement in 'Of the Standard of Taste'. Responding to a culturally foreign work of art the critic must 'preserve his mind free from all *prejudice*, and allow nothing to enter into his consideration, but the very object which is submitted to his examination'.[11] To do that, however, he must view the work from a vantage-point informed by the 'peculiar views and prejudices' of the other culture, 'must place himself in the same situation as the [foreign] audience'.[12] 'A person influenced by prejudice'—that is, by his own culturally bound aesthetic predilections—'complies not with this condition; but obstinately maintains his natural position, without placing himself in that point of view, which the [culturally foreign] performance supposes'.[13] A similar condition must, it seems, be met if one is to adopt the impartial point of view of morality.

[10] David Hume, 'A Dialogue', *Enquiries Concerning Human Understanding and Concerning the Principles of Morals*.
[11] David Hume, 'Of the Standard of Taste', in *Essays Moral, Political, and Literary*, ed. Eugene F. Miller (Indianapolis, Ind., 1985), 239.   [12] Ibid.   [13] Ibid.

One is oneself, of course, an object of one's impartial moral concern: this is a simple consequence of the distinctive content of moral desire. One is, as much as any other, a human individual with partial interests; and it is to the securing of such interests for such individuals that moral desires are directed.

In attempting to explicate Hume's conception of the distinctive content of moral desire we have fastened, as Hume transparently does, on the many dimensions of their impartiality, and on their consequent intersubjectivity. We have also narrowed our attention—conveniently, if perhaps misleadingly—to the effects of human actions on human interests. It is time to take a broader view and so draw attention to a number of other significant dimensions in Hume's all-in account of moral desire's content. It is time to consider the content-specifying ramifications of three distinctively Humean doctrines: his four-part classification of morally relevant features of objects of evaluation; his distinction between natural and artificial virtues; and his representation of the several ways in which, in virtue of their content, moral desires are person-implicating ones.

In the second *Enquiry* Hume writes that an action's or a quality's utility with respect to advancing the interests of others is 'one great source of moral distinctions' (E 218). The other sources he there identifies are 'qualities useful to ourselves' (E 233), 'qualities immediately agreeable to ourselves' (E 250), and 'qualities immediately agreeable to others' (E 260). In the *Treatise*, referring to the 'four different sources' of moral distinctions, he writes: 'we reap a pleasure from the view of a character, which is naturally fitted to be useful to others, or to the person himself, or which is agreeable to others, or to the person himself' (T 591). This four-part classification of moral distinctions reveals two points of importance for the content of moral desires. First, the interests of those for whom we are morally concerned can be affected both immediately and instrumentally by human actions and qualities. They can be affected immediately, as when an individual simply takes pleasure in the wit, the good humour, the *joie de vivre* of a companion. They can be affected instrumentally by another's partial benevolence (if appropriately directed) or by the just actions of persons who are party to conventions to which they are themselves party. Second, their interests can be affected by their own actions and qualities as well as by those of others: his partial benevolence, though directed to the well-being of others, is immediately agreeable to the benevolent person himself; and a person's courage and intelligence can, in obvious ways, be instrumental in the securing of her own interests. (Hume's schema also, of course, provides for the classification of ways in which actions and qualities can be inimical to an individual's interests.)

Actions can be instrumentally related to human interests in two very different ways. For actions of one type, Hume writes, 'the good ... arises from every single act, and is the object of some natural passion' (*T* 579). For actions of the other type it is not the single act 'consider'd in itself' but 'the concurrence of mankind, in a general scheme or system, which is advantageous' (ibid.). We shall explore Hume's crucial contrast of the natural and artificial virtues in the next two chapters. The point to fasten on just here is that moral desire must reckon with the difference between natural and artificial routes to securing the interests of those for whom one is morally concerned.

Moral desires are person-implicating ones in the sense that they concern human interests so far as these can be affected by the actions and qualities of human persons, whether the actions and qualities be those of the person affected or those of some other person.[14] The partial interests to which they are directed are themselves a function of the person-implicating desires of the individuals in question. To be sure, the interests of those for whom one is morally concerned can be damaged without human intervention: by disease, say, or by some other natural disaster. To be sure, from their partial perspectives individuals find the prospect of such damage undesirable. But it is only in so far as partial desires are directed to human actions and qualities that their satisfaction is an object of specifically moral concern.

Person-implicating partial desires can be concerned with any of many desirable and undesirable things: Hume refers inclusively to 'advantages or disadvantages of the *mind, body*, or *fortune*' (*T* 614). They can be concerned with bodily characteristics of persons (health, beauty, soundness or shapeliness of limb), with the possession of 'goods of fortune' (wealth, property, good family), with a host of mental features including conative characteristics (honesty, benevolence), other traits (courage, patience), and intellectual talents or abilities (intelligence, inventiveness, wit). From the vantage-point of moral desire, however, it is only advantageous or disadvantageous *mental* features that enter into consideration. Hume reserves the terms 'virtue' and 'vice' for 'mental qualities': 'whatever mental quality in ourselves or others gives us a satisfaction, by the survey of reflexion, is of course virtuous; as every thing of this nature, that gives uneasiness, is vicious' (*T* 574–5; compare *T* 591, 606, 614). Person-implicating

[14] See the discussion of person-implicating passions, both desires and affections, in Chap. 2, Sect. 3.

moral desires, we may say, focus specifically on the mind-displaying qualities of persons.

As with the case of partial desires, the mind-displaying qualities with which impartial moral desires are concerned include a variety of other-than-conative characteristics of individuals (courage, patience, intelligence, inventiveness, wit, and the like). Of particular theoretical interest, however, is the fact that certain moral desires are focused on conative characteristics—on desires—that persons can possess. We shall explore Hume's difficult doctrine of desire-implicating moral desires in Chapter 5. In Chapter 7, when we consider his conception of moral agents, we shall examine Hume's treatment of the mind-displaying character of intentional actions, and in particular his thesis that actions are intentional only so far as they reveal enduring conative features of the individuals who perform them.

In interim summary of Hume's account of the content of moral desires we may say that such desires manifest an impartial and intersubjective concern for the interests of all human individuals so far as those interests are affected immediately or instrumentally, naturally or artificially, by their own or others' mind-displaying actions or mental qualities.

Despite the fundamental uniqueness of the moral point of view—despite, in Hume's phrase, its being 'the same in all' (*E 275*)—differing individuals in a given community will take themselves to have differing determinate obligations. This is simply to acknowledge that such individuals will recognize themselves to differ from some others in the morally significant characteristics they possess, characteristics whose significance is encapsulated in the content of determinate secondary moral desires. Of course, the members of differing communities will also take themselves to have different determinate obligations. What the members of one group recognize as *their* obligations of justice will be a function of the rules of the conventions to which *they* are party; for others, with differing conventions, the obligations of justice will specify rather different forms of conduct. What counts as parental concern may also differ from one community to another; and what counts as courage. Such variability in the determinate content of secondary moral desires must be admitted even if one ignores the effects of differences in imagination or, more broadly, in cognitive capacity from one individual to the next; and even if one ignores the effects of sheer complexity, or of competition amongst the partial interests of morally significant individuals, or of the diversity of the kinds of secondary moral considerations that must be countenanced, when an individual forms a determinate moral judgement.

As we have represented them, Hume's conditions on specifically moral desires are surprisingly stringent. That being so, is it clear that Hume thinks individuals do, at least some of the time, actually form desires of a specifically moral sort? Does he think that, having formed such desires, agents are ever actually moved by them to action?

Writing of its impartial, specifically moral, form Hume remarks that 'the benevolent concern for others is diffused, in a greater or less degree, over all men' (*E* 275). If the remark has to do with content it introduces the possibility of individuals approximating to one degree or another, in what may tolerantly be called their moral desires, to Hume's demanding standards. Some, perhaps, meet those standards. Others depart from them in one way or another, and to one degree or another: in forming their moral desires (as we tolerantly term them) they fail wholly to eliminate the many kinds of partiality whose absence is the chief mark of specifically moral content. Hume thinks of a minimal approximation when he characterizes the 'rude, untaught savage' as one who 'regulates chiefly his love and hatred by the ideas of private utility and injury, and has but faint conceptions of a general rule or system of behaviour' (*E* 274 n.) (To shift from his primarily partial perspective this individual must, Hume writes, become 'accustomed to society, and to more enlarged reflections', ibid.) He seems to think that in certain circumstances individuals may simply have no need to view their behaviour from the vantage-point of morality, and so, understandably, may fail to do so. Given the constraints of their situation participants in conventions 'on the first formation of society' (*T* 499) would, he maintains, both see reason to act as the rules of justice require and yet fail to see any specifically moral reason to do so. Is a perfect amoralist possible, one whose partiality is such that his desires approximate not at all to the impartiality of moral desire? Hume seems to think an amoralist unlikely (see *E* 272), but perhaps his 'sensible knave' (*E* 282) fits the description.

Moral desires are desires and so, with accompanying beliefs, provide reasons for action and so dispose an agent, thus far, to act as they direct. But they are only some among an agent's many desires and a realistic rendering of their motivational standing must reckon with that fact. Moral desires may well serve as 'settled principle[s] of action', may constitute 'the predominant inclination of the soul' (*T* 419; compare *E* 275). A point that Hume emphasizes, they have the effect of seconding, or even substituting for, the motivation provided, in matters of justice, by an enlightened sense of our own narrow interests (*T* 499–500). Of course, they frequently fail to govern an agent's conduct. That an individual does not, or not consistently, act as his moral judgements require shows, however, neither that the putative moral judgements are not genuine nor that they are not desires; lack of motivational efficacy does not entail their absence. While not pursuing the puzzles this possibility generates, Hume provides a clear representation of the formal features of the situation in a passage cited earlier: 'Let these generous sentiments be supposed ever so weak; let them be insufficient to move even a hand or finger of our body, they must still direct the determinations of our mind, and *where everything else is equal*, produce a cool *preference* for what is useful and serviceable to mankind, above what is pernicious and dangerous' (*E* 271, emphasis added). That she would, everything else equal, act as justice requires entails that she is, thus far, disposed to do so. Does one have moral desires only if they are overriding ones? In Hume's view they may fail to move but be motivational none the less. They display differing degrees of motivational efficacy in different individuals, and in a given individual from one situation to another.

It can seem at times that Hume has doubts about the motivational standing of moral judgements. More accurately, it can perhaps seem that he circumscribes their motivational efficacy in a quite fundamental way, taking them to prompt not the actions they ostensibly demand but only talk that corresponds to them. He certainly strikes a sceptical note (though one should note the 'not always') when he writes, in the *Treatise*, 'the *heart* does not always take part in these general notions [of morality], or regulate its love and hatred by them, yet they are sufficient for discourse, and serve all our purposes in company, in the pulpit, on the theatre, and in the schools' (*T* 603). But he softens the passage significantly when he repeats it in the second *Enquiry*, adding the claim that 'moral differences [have] a considerable influence' to the claim that they are 'sufficient, at least, for discourse' (*E* 229). Presumably he would agree that even extensive hypocrisy is compatible with the reality, and the genuinely practical character, of moral desires. He needn't think that all are hypocrites or that hypocrites are hypocritical all the time. And he would surely say of hypocritical uses of moral language what he says of 'the artifice of politicians', that parasitic uses presuppose in general, if not in the particular case, the reality of the moral sentiments to which they ostensibly give voice (*T* 500, 579).

Of course the principal obstacle to Hume's endorsement of the suggested deflationary doctrine is that it makes nonsense of his theoretically central, and highly elaborated, arguments for moral conativism, arguments that incorporate an explicit claim of the practicality of morals. It makes nonsense, too, of his account of the transition from the narrowly interested to the specifically moral perspective for the case of the conventions of justice.[15]

Given Hume's official theory of the passions, moral desires, just as other desires, have a distinctive phenomenological dimension. They differ from other desires, however, in that they generate little in the way of emotional excitation, little 'disorder in the soul' (*T* 417). Many other desires are typically 'violent' (ibid.); moral desires are typically 'calm' (ibid.), are 'commonly ... soft and gentle' (*T* 470). On occasion, moved by moral desire, we will be much exercised; usually, however, our moral desires play their role without generating much turbulence in our stream of consciousness. Thinking of their typical calmness, Hume classifies moral desires as one of the types of so-called 'calm passions' (*T* 417). Objective concern for one's own interests, despite its partiality, is another of the types (*T* 418).[16]

Should the calmness of a typical moral desire be viewed as a motivational liability? Should we take it that a desire's degree of excitation correlates with its degree of motivational strength? Hume rejects the suggestion. For many individuals, for most individuals on some occasions, a desire's strength does correspond to the degree of its violence. But there are individuals for whom, and situations in which, calm desires, including moral desires, trump violent ones. Thinking of *types* of calm passions—moral desires, objective concern for one's own interests—Hume remarks that 'strength of mind ... implies the prevalence of the calm passions above the violent', even if 'there is no man so constantly possess'd of this virtue, as never on any occasion to yield to the sollicitations of passion and desire' (*T* 418). What, in Hume's view, explains the surprising capacity of calm passions to counter violent ones? He holds that calm desires may be 'corroborated by reflection, and seconded by resolution' (*T* 437). This applies, presumably, to calm desires of whatever (calm) type. In the special case of moral desires, however, he ties motivational efficacy to the pecu-

[15] For this transition see Chap. 6, Sect. 3. It is instructive that Baier, responding to pressures towards a deflationary reading, remarks of *Treatise*, III. i. 1, where Hume's direct argument for moral conativism appears, that Hume must appear 'insincere in his famous claim ... that morality has to be founded on "an active principle"', and that, in seeming to endorse this famous claim, he is not speaking *in propria persona* but is 'appealing to the rationalist moralists' own presuppositions, and trying to reduce their positions *ad absurdum*'. Baier, *A Progress of Sentiments*, 184.

[16] Perhaps it is the calmness of moral desires that Hume has in mind when writing, in the problematic passage just above, that 'the *heart* does not always take part in these general notions [of morality]'. If so, considerations raised in the next paragraph provide further reason to reject a deflationary reading of the passage.

liarities of their content. Though the 'interests and pleasures' of those for whom we are morally concerned 'touch us more faintly than our own, yet *being more constant and universal*, they counter-ballance the latter even in practice' (*T* 591, emphasis added; compare *E* 274). Their intersubjectivity can have a like effect: 'Other passions [than impartial benevolent concern for others], though perhaps originally stronger, yet being selfish and *private*, are often overpowered by its force, and yield the dominion to those social and public principles' (*E* 275–6, emphasis added). Hume attends to the phenomenological features of moral desires but in the last analysis it is their content, not their calmness, that counts.

The very peculiarities of content that provide purported moral desires with their distinctively moral character can seem to call their status as full-fledged desires into question by attenuating—in ways other than those already canvassed—the ties between purported desire and action. Given their universality and impartiality, and so their attention to the interests of individuals 'however remote' (*E* 274), they are unaffected by the fact that the desirer's own actions must, for a vast range of cases, have no conceivable bearing on the promotion of those interests. Given their impartial accommodation of the various partiality-generating relations in which one individual can stand to another, they are impervious to the fact that there are many towards whom the desirer does not stand in those special relations, and so many whose interests could not be affected, in just the ways in question, by any actions of the desirer. Given their inclusion of mental qualities in addition to mind-displaying actions, they incorporate a concern for the effects of features that are at best, and then only minimally, under the desirer's indirect, and limited, control.[17]

Against this line of argument, however, it must be insisted that the desirer *can* affect the interests of those not so remote, *does* stand in special relations to some others, does have *some* measure of indirect control over at least *some* of her mental qualities. It must also be insisted that one needn't stand in a special relation in order for the fact of a special relation to impose requirements on one's own actions by way of one's moral desires: wanting parents to care for their children one can, though childless, take steps to encourage or facilitate parental caring. Despite these obvious considerations, however, misgivings may remain about the full-fledged status of Hume's putative moral desires: his characterization of their content does in fact weaken, in the ways indicated, the links between an individual's moral desires and the range of that agent's possible actions.

[17] For Hume's views on the scope of such control, see my 'Hume's Volitions', 'Locke, Hume and the Nature of Volitions', and (for a briefer account) Chap. 7.

Turning the intended point, Hume can insist that it helpfully highlights the very special status that moral desires have in virtue of the peculiarities of content that define them. They do bear directly on the desirer's own actions when the realities of her situation permit them to do so. But they do so in virtue of features whose proper specification, making no essential reference to herself, can be instantiated in situations in which she is in no interesting sense involved. To restrict the content of moral desires with a view to tightening the connections between an agent's desires and actions within the agent's power would be to eliminate their defining impartiality. It would compromise the identity of practical moral judgement and moral desire that Hume's conativist arguments demand: after all, moral judgements both help constitute an agent's reasons for action and range over situations in which that agent's own actions are nowise in question. It would also reveal a failure to appreciate that being in a state with the world-to-mind direction of fit does not require that one be oneself in a position to secure the realization of its satisfaction-conditions.

His conativist identification of practical moral judgements with full-fledged, if impartial, desires is the key element in an inclusive theory that provides economical explication of several phenomena that, when examining Hume's indirect argument for moral conativism, we found troublesome for the moral cognitivist.

Hume rejects the moral cognitivist's doctrine that the moral character of a particular action is a function of its conforming or failing to conform to a moral truth. There is point, however, to the claim that an action's moral character is a function of its conforming or failing to conform to a moral desire. Its conforming or failing to conform is, of course, its fitting or failing to fit. It is right if it is a token of a type of action that, having adopted the intersubjective and impartial moral point of view, one desires to occur; it is wrong if its occurrence is something to which, from the moral point of view, one is averse. The relevant concept of conformity requires no prescriptive moral truths, no putatively prescriptive non-natural properties. It provides an economical foundation for talk of an action's being 'conformable to our abstract rule' (*E* 274).

We have seen reason to reject the standard moral cognitivist's rendering of the supervenience of moral features on non-moral ones: it postulates theoretically unprepossessing non-natural properties and a primitive relation of supervenience between them and natural ones. Within a Humean framework supervenience is a perfectly intelligible product of the fact that practical moral judgements are conative states with descriptive

content. Why does one think of the wrongness of an action as supervenient on its being the breaking of a promise, say, or a failure to pay
one's debts? Because its being such an action is just what prompts one to
want—impartially—it not to occur. An economical doctrine, moral
conativism secures supervenience with no departure from an attractive
naturalism.

We can be mistaken about our moral desires. We can be mistaken in
believing that, in acting or assessing as we do on an occasion, we are
viewing things from the moral point of view. 'Our predominant motive
or intention', Hume writes, 'is frequently concealed from ourselves when
it is mingled and confounded with other motives which the mind, from
vanity or self-conceit, is desirous of supposing more prevalent' (*E* 299).
We have reason not to recognize that it is the voice of partiality, not that
of impartial concern, that speaks. Thinking in terms of his official theory
of the passions, Hume would find remedy for such illusions, so far as it is
available, in the exercise of heightened care in the making of introspective judgements. More helpfully, he recommends attempting to view our
actions as others view them (*E* 276).

We can also be subject to the illusion of thinking that moral desires
are explicitly evaluative beliefs. This is the illusion that fuels the moral
cognitivist's theoretical constructions. Hume traces it back to the calmness of typical moral desires: because they are 'calm, and cause no disorder in the soul, they are very readily taken for the determinations of
reason, and are suppos'd to proceed from the same faculty, with that,
which judges of truth and falshood' (*T* 417). He might better trace it to the
peculiar properties of moral desires that he links to their typical calmness,
to the universality, impartiality, and intersubjectivity of their content.
Given such content it is not surprising, perhaps, that moral judgements
would seem to be reason's products. One can dispel *this* illusion by reflecting on the need to accommodate the practicality of morality and on the
possibility that desires have impartial descriptive content. In stressing the
impartiality and intersubjectivity of moral desire one offers, of course, a
moral conativist explanation of features of moral judgements that the
moral cognitivist claims to be alone able to capture.

2. SYMPATHY AND ITS CORRECTION

Hume does not just provide a characterization of moral desires in terms
of their content; he also offers a psychological account—a psychological

theory—of the formation of such desires. Despite the peculiarities of their content moral desires are perfectly intelligible natural phenomena, and his theory of their formation is designed to show them to be such. *Sympathy* and its *correction* are the two chief components in Hume's explanatory account. Sympathy serves to expand the range of our concern to individuals outside the narrow circle of our friends and relations: in Hume's words it 'takes us . . . out of ourselves' (*T* 579). Sympathy's correction introduces the universality and impartiality, and thus the intersubjectivity, of moral desires. Attention to the two elements in Hume's explanatory account—attention both to sympathy and to its correction—will help confirm that the analysis we have offered of moral desires is Hume's. It will throw additional light on his views about their content. It will also reveal what he takes to be their quite distinctive functional location in the psychological economies of human agents.

Sympathy is not itself a desire: it must not be identified with pity, say, or with compassion or benevolence. None the less, one can sympathize with the desires of others, just as one can sympathize with their affections or with their beliefs. That Hume assigns a broad scope to sympathy is clear: he writes of sympathizing with another's 'sentiments, and way of thinking' (*T* 592), with his 'passions, sentiments and opinions' (*T* 365). That he includes desires within its scope is clear from his account of its role in the generation of pity (*T* 385) and from his talk of sympathy with the 'interests' (*T* 364, 369, 384, 388, 499–500, 580) and the 'concerns' (*T* 386, 389) of others. Given the complex interrelations that hold amongst desires, affections, and beliefs there is, it must be said, an element of abstraction in focusing narrowly on sympathy with another's desires. Given the centrality of moral desires in Hume's moral psychology, however, there is much to be gained by doing so.

The product of sympathizing with another's desire is, we may say, a *sympathetic desire*. Ignoring needed qualifications, a sympathetic desire is a desire with two crucial relational properties. First, it is type-identical with—is of the same type or kind as—a desire (let us call this the *original desire*) that the other person has. Second, it stands in a special causal relation to that original desire. (Sympathetic beliefs and affections stand in similarly special causal relations to original beliefs and affections with which they are, in ways that need to be spelled out, type-identical.) Let us start with the special causal relations.

The most important point is a negative one. Sympathetic desires have psychological causes, in particular (as Hume has it) beliefs about the desires of those with whom one sympathizes. But in sympathy the psychological causes operate neither by prompting love for, and so benevolence directed towards, the individual with whose desires one sympathizes, nor by providing one with reasons for having the sympathetic desires one has. It is not that something about the other individual prompts one to love her and so to be concerned about her well-being. And it is not that an antecedent desire that the other's desires be satisfied gives rise, given beliefs about her determinate desires, to a desire that they be satisfied. In sympathy—more accurately, in sympathy when operating at a foundational level—the desires one forms *initiate* one's concern for the other individual. So it is that sympathy 'takes us . . . out of ourselves' in a radical way: it can bring within the range of our concern individuals whom we do not love and in whose interests we take, antecedently, no interest at all.[18] That a friend is in danger of drowning provides one a perfectly intelligible reason for wanting him to be rescued: as Hume has it, one loves him and feels a consequent desire of benevolence ('a desire of the happiness of the person belov'd, and an aversion to his misery'). On the assumption that specifically moral desires are playing no role, however, the fact that a perfect stranger is in such a danger can provide one with no motivational reason for wanting him to be rescued, but it *can* prompt a sympathetic desire that he be rescued. Coming to have that sympathetic desire would constitute the beginning of one's concern for that stranger. By giving rise to sympathetic desires sympathy does not necessarily turn strangers into friends, but it does turn them into objects of similarly benevolent concern.

Distinguishing between the phenomenon of sympathetic desire and the explanation of that phenomenon (T 317, 319), Hume takes the occurrence of sympathetic desires to be unquestionable but their explication to be a matter of difficult theory. He offers what we may think of as a *thin theory* of sympathetic desires: one individual, A, comes to believe that another, B, has a desire of a certain type D; given suitable similarities between A and B, A comes to have a desire of type D. (Alternative thin theories postulate A's imagining herself in B's shoes, or imagining herself to be B, or imitating B's behaviour, as a crucial condition on the formation of A's sympathetic desire of type D.) He elaborates this thin theory—we may think of the elaboration as his *thick theory* of sympathetic desires—along three lines. First, he renders the beliefs and desires in question (A's and B's type-identical desires, A's beliefs about B's desires) in terms of his

---

[18] The point, it must be emphasized, pertains only to sympathy's operations at a foundational level. For Hume, sympathy has, of course, a significant role to play in the full development of our benevolence towards those we love.

narrow official doctrines of impressions and ideas: desires as simple impressions, beliefs as lively ideas. Second, he assigns to A's purported impression of herself the causal role of enlivening the already lively idea that constitutes A's belief that B has a desire of type D. Third, he claims that the effect of this further enlivening is to convert A's belief (her lively idea of B's desire) into a desire (construed as a simple impression) type-identical to—qualitatively, but not numerically, identical to—B's desire.

The claimed conversion of A's belief about B's desire into a desire type-identical with B's (the whole business implicating Humean ideas and impressions, strictly construed) is prominent when Hume writes:

When any affection is infus'd by sympathy, it is at first known only by its effects, and by those external signs in the countenance and conversation, which convey an idea of it. This idea is presently converted into an impression, and acquires such a degree of force and vivacity, as to become the very passion itself, and produce an equal emotion, as any original affection. (T 317)

It is equally prominent when he writes:

When I see the *effects* of passion in the voice and gesture of any person, my mind immediately passes from these effects to their causes, and forms such a lively idea of the passion, as is presently converted into the passion itself. In like manner, when I perceive the *causes* of any emotion, my mind is convey'd to the effects, and is actuated with a like emotion. (T 576; compare T 595)

He invokes the enlivening role of the impression or conception of one's self when remarking that '[t]he stronger the relation is betwixt ourselves and any object, the more easily does the imagination make the transition, and convey to the related idea [A's idea of B's desire, say] the vivacity of conception, with which we always form the idea of our own person' (T 318). In staccato summary of the thick theory he writes: 'In sympathy there is an evident conversion of an idea into an impression. This conversion arises from the relation of objects to ourself. Ourself is always intimately present to us' (T 320).

Having glanced at Hume's thick theory of sympathetic desires, let us now ignore it.[19] An implausible contribution to mental chemistry, its interest for us lies in its confirming that the thin theory sketched above is Hume's and that that thin theory incorporates his crucial negative claim about the generation of sympathetic desires.

Whatever the significant stages in their generation, sympathetic desires

[19] For a helpful account of Hume's thick theory of sympathy, one that compares Hume's theory with Adam Smith's, see Árdal, *Passion and Value in Hume's Treatise*, 41–61.

are type-identical with the causally relevant original ones: A's sympathetic desires are type-identical to B's original desires. Hume has A 'feel the passion [B's passion] itself' (T 371), but he must have types, not tokens, in mind. More carefully, he writes of 'an emotion similar to the original one' (T 369), of being 'actuated with a like emotion' (T 576). Expanding on the similarity in question he refers to 'a secondary sensation correspondent to the primary', to a 'conformity in the tendency and direction of ... [the] desires' (T 385): their 'motion' is 'conformable' (T 386), their 'impulses or directions are correspondent' (T 381; compare T 576, T 605, E 223), they have a 'parallel direction' (T 384). Acquiring sympathetic desires that thus correspond to B's, A 'enters into' B's sentiments and 'embrace[s] them' (T 318), 'enter[s] into his [B's] interest[s]' (T 364; compare T 588–9), 'share[s] them [B's interests], in some measure' with B (T 364), makes B's desires his 'own concern' (T 386). Sympathy 'interests us in the fortunes of others, good or bad' (T 385); but '[t]he sentiments of others can never affect us, but by becoming, in some measure, our own' (T 593).

Interpreting Hume, we may take it that sympathetic desires are, with a qualification to be noted, identical in content to the original desires to which they correspond. By way of A's beliefs, B's desire that he (B) be rescued from the sinking sailboat prompts A's desire that B be rescued from the sinking sailboat: the desires are parallel in that each is directed towards B's being rescued. It is not that A desires that *he* (that is, A) be rescued: we may assume that he is standing safely on shore and is free from delusion. To be sure, there is *a* crucial difference in the contents of A's and B's desires: B thinks of *himself* being rescued, A of *that other person* being rescued. Their desires differ, we may say, *indexically*. The difference is of a kind with that which Hume invokes when characterizing one's sympathizing with the self-estimations, and the estimations of others (including one's self), that others make. It is not, Hume writes, 'in any way material upon what subject he and I employ our thoughts': 'Whether we judge of an indifferent person, or of my own character, my sympathy gives equal force to his decision: And even his sentiments of his own merit make me consider him in the same light, in which he regards himself' (T 592). On the strong assumption that the difference in indexicals does not affect content, we may say that A's and B's desires are type-identical. Alternatively, we may say they are type-identical so far as differences in indexicals are discounted. After all, the very same state of the world— B's being rescued from the sinking sailboat—would satisfy both A's sympathetic and B's original desire.

There is, incidentally, no requirement that A's desires be second-order desires with respect to B's. A desires that B be rescued, not that B's desire that he (that is, B) be rescued be satisfied. Second-order desires would introduce a needless, and a textually unmotivated, complication into Hume's account of sympathetic concern for the interests of others. To accommodate generality, Hume need only countenance dispositions to sympathize with the several determinate desires of the other individual(s).[20]

It follows from our characterization of sympathetic desires that they are not egoistic in content. Hume makes the anti-egoistic point explicitly: 'in sympathy our own person is not the object of any passion nor is there any thing, that fixes our attention on ourselves' (T 340). The other's sentiments must, to repeat, 'become, in some measure, our own'; despite this our sympathetic desires constitute a concern for the other's, not our own, interests.[21]

Hume's doctrine of sympathetic desires is compatible with a recognition that desires are non-atomistically linked to other desires, to passions other than desires, and to the ramifying elements in complex networks of beliefs. It is compatible, as well, with the diachronically complex character of the individuals with whom one sympathizes. Despite his own officially atomistic leanings, Hume displays some sense of the need to extend his doctrine of sympathetic desires along such lines. In 'extensive ... sympathy' (T 387) or 'compleat sympathy' (T 388) one sympathizes with a wide range, diachronic as well as synchronic, of the other person's cognitive, conative, and affective states: one's sympathetic response is 'not confin'd merely to the immediate object, but diffuses its influence over all the related ideas, and gives ... [one] a lively notion of all the circumstances of that person, whether past, present, or future; possible, probable or certain' (T 386). Continuing in this vein, Hume points out that 'the future prospect ... is necessary to interest ... [one] perfectly in the fortune of another' (ibid.). Needless to say, Hume has no need to deny that, when sympathizing with some desire of another, one can come by standard means to form desires derivative from that desire. One can come, that is to say, to have desires for which one has a reason and which are, perhaps, type-identical to derivative desires that the other person has as well. As envisaged, this process begins with sympathetic desire. Granting the

---

[20] This suggestion is pursued below.

[21] The *original* desires with which one sympathizes are, of course, covered by Hume's arguments against psychological egoism and psychological hedonism examined in Chap. 2, Sect. 1.

possibility of overdetermination, the derivative desire could be a sympathetic desire as well.

For the most part, sympathetic desires correspond to actual desires, past or present, of the other person. '[T]o sympathize', Hume writes, is 'to receive by communication' (*T* 316); sympathy is 'the communication of sentiments from one thinking being to another' (*T* 363); desires of the appropriate type 'are first present in the mind of one person, and afterwards appear in the mind of another' (*T* 369). Hume's conception of sympathetic desires can, however, accommodate cases in which no *actual* desire (past or present) serves as original. One can sympathize with desires one believes the other person will, or will perhaps, have: 'in considering the future possible or probable conditions of any person, we may enter into it with so vivid a conception as to make it our own concern' (*T* 386). It is attention to such cases that prompts the modest measure of holism contained in Hume's remarks about 'extensive' or 'compleat' sympathy. One can also sympathize with desires one believes the other person neither has nor will have, but which one believes he would have were certain conditions (including certain psychological conditions) not present. His 'greatness of mind' may prevent a man's being moved as others are by some misfortune. None the less, in a display of sympathy 'of a partial kind' (*T* 371)—which is to say sympathy that is not 'compleat' in the sense intended—one may have sympathetic desires type-identical to desires the other would have were he not as he in fact is. In either case[22] 'the communicated passion of sympathy ... arises from affections, which have no existence' (*T* 370).[23]

His introduction of the notion of 'extensive' sympathy would facilitate Hume's making a distinction, one he wants to make, between sympathy with desires tied to the true interests of another and those not thus tied. It also has some tendency to suggest that it is other psychologically complex individuals, and not just individual psychological states, with whom, properly speaking, one sympathizes. When 'extensive' sympathy is in question, one sympathizes with the interests of individuals with integrated cognitive, conative, and affective lives—and so with the integrated elements in those lives—rather than with the atomistically rendered desires of some individual who is, thus far, of no further concern.

---

[22] One can also, of course, have sympathetic desires that rest upon false beliefs.

[23] This passage is unhappy in two respects. In seeming to treat sympathy as itself a passion it runs counter to Hume's thesis that sympathy is a psychological mechanism, not a passion. (Clarity would be better served were Hume to write not of 'the communicated passion of sympathy' but of 'the passion communicated by sympathy'.) In seeming to countenance the communication of non-existent passions it runs the risk of incoherence.

There is, perhaps, a pronominal hint of this when Hume uses the phrase 'my sympathy with *him*' (*T* 592, emphasis added). (Hume's emphasis, when developing his thick theory of sympathy, on the role of one's sense of oneself, encourages the same focus on psychologically complex individuals rather than on their individual desires.)

The character of his thin theory in turn encourages emphasis on the desires that the *other person* has, or had, or will have; or that the *other person* would have in the counterfactual situations envisaged. Sympathetic desires are taken to be type-identical with *the other's* desires, not those the sympathizer would have were she in the other person's shoes—or were she, with her own general goals and projects, that other person. This said, limits must be admitted. Sympathy is easier the more like the other person the sympathizer is. And, at least if certain remarks about literature apply here, sympathy with sentiments is easier the closer the original sentiments are to those one experiences *in propria persona*. 'We enter', Hume writes, 'more readily into sentiments, which resemble those we feel every day' (*E* 222). If more difficult, however, sympathy with unfamiliar sentiments is not impossible, for there is no sentiment 'of which every man has not, within him, at least the seeds and first principles' (ibid.).

Sympathy—the formation of sympathetic desires, affections, and beliefs—is implicated in a diverse array of psychological phenomena. Hume invokes sympathy in his explanations of: our affection for relations and acquaintances despite their failure to display any markedly valuable or admirable qualities (*T* 353f.); our 'esteem for power and riches' and 'contempt for meanness and poverty' (*T* 362); a concern for one's reputation (*T* 316 f.); pity (*T* 362) and malice (*T* 369); many characteristic cases of 'pride, ambition, avarice, curiosity, revenge or lust' (*T* 363). He takes it to play a role in '[p]opular seditions, party zeal, a devoted obedience to factious leaders' (*E* 224; compare *E* 275). He emphasizes the part it plays in the formation of aesthetic responses (*T* 363, 576 f.), in particular one's responses to stage tragedies (*T* 369). And—our present concern—he assigns it a critical causal role in the formation of moral responses, including in particular moral desires.

The diversity of sympathy's explanatory contributions has, for Hume, a methodological significance. That the same mechanism *can* be invoked in the explanation of each of the types of phenomena mentioned suggests that it *should* be invoked for each of them. That sympathy can be invoked to explain so much of our emotional, aesthetic, and moral life encourages the thought that one is right to appeal to it in explaining each of these otherwise diverse psychological phenomena (compare *T* 577–8, 618).

Equally explicable through sympathy, these diverse phenomena are, of course, equally natural phenomena, and equally unmysterious. So far as explicable by sympathy, moral desires, despite the peculiarities of their impartial content, are no more mysterious than feelings of pity or malice, no less a part of the natural order of things than a love of fame or a sense of beauty. In this sense moral desires are 'necessary and infallible consequences of the general principles of human nature, as discovered in common life and practice' (*E* 230).

As should be plain, however, sympathy's role in generating sympathetic desires is, if necessary, not sufficient for the generation of specifically moral ones. Presumably, given the person-implicating content of moral desires, it is sympathy with a restricted range of desires, with specifically person-implicating ones, that contributes to their formation. More pressingly, it is plain that one naturally sympathizes more readily and more deeply with some than with others. (With some, for quite banal reasons, one naturally sympathizes not at all.) But moral desires are marked by the universality and impartiality of their content. Blurring the boundaries between moral desires and moral affections, Hume underscores the limitations to what sympathy can explain:

But as this sympathy is very variable, it may be thought, that our sentiments of morals must admit of all the same variations. We sympathize more with persons contiguous with us, than with persons remote from us: With our acquaintance, than with strangers: With our countrymen, than with foreigners. But notwithstanding the variation of our sympathy, we give the same approbation to the same moral qualities in *China* as in *England*. They appear equally virtuous, and recommend themselves equally to the esteem of a judicious spectator. The sympathy varies without a variation in our esteem. Our esteem, therefore, proceeds not from sympathy. (*T* 580–1)

Hume does not, of course, subscribe to the ostensible conclusion expressed by the last sentence in this passage: as we have seen, he holds the workings of sympathy to be essential if we are to have any concern at all for those outside the narrow circle of our friends and relations. Sympathy, he says, 'produces our sentiment of morals in all the artificial virtues ... [and] also gives rise to many of the other virtues' (*T* 577–8).[24] His point, in the long passage cited, is rather that something additional must be introduced if the variability natural to sympathy is not to prevent the projected formation, by means of the operations of sympathy, of specifically

[24] Presumably he means not that sympathy 'gives rise to' the natural virtues but rather that it helps generate the 'sentiment of morals' we have with respect to those virtues. The reason for the hesitation intimated by 'many' is difficult to fathom.

moral desires. Our moral desires proceed not from sympathy alone but from *corrected sympathy*. Hume views the correcting of sympathy as a natural response to an intolerable situation in which individuals would otherwise find themselves. Seeing corrected sympathy as a remedy for this intolerable situation is essential if one is to appreciate Hume's functionalist conception of an individual's adoption of the moral point of view.

Regimenting somewhat, we may say that Hume characterizes two predicaments in which, in the absence of corrected sympathy, individuals would find themselves, one of them *intrasubjective*, the other *intersubjective*. He appears to distinguish two aspects of the intersubjective predicament, a *conative* aspect and a specifically *linguistic* one. He argues explicitly for a *modest* thesis about the connection between the intersubjective predicament, including the linguistic aspect of that predicament, and that predicament's remedy. He also hints, however, at a *bold* thesis about that connection. Hume's modest thesis appears too weak to secure his explanatory objectives, his bold thesis too strong. In drawing attention to the specifically linguistic dimension of the intersubjective predicament, however, he has posed an exceptionally difficult question whose pursuit might well shed much light on the character and place of moral desire.

Suppose that one's concern for others, at a given time, were wholly a function of the determinate relations in which one then stood to those individuals. Suppose, for example, that one's benevolence, ill-will, or indifference towards others, at a given time, depended wholly on their impact, at that time, on one's own interests, at that time; or that whether, or the force with which, one felt sympathetic desires correspondent to the desires of a given individual, at a given time, depended wholly on the relations of similarity, proximity, and the like, in which one stood to that individual at that time. One's conative life, so far as it concerns others, would be in constant flux: since the desire-affecting relations in which one would stand to others would themselves be in constant flux one's desires would follow suit. One would—or so Hume claims—find the conative turmoil intolerable. Given the character of one's predicament, remedy would require introduction of a measure of conative constancy, some element of *intrasubjective stability* in one's desires, some range, that is, of desires unaffected by the constant changes in one's relations to others. Hume draws attention to the changeability of our relations to, and so of our conative attitudes towards, others: 'Our situation, with regard both to persons and to things, is in continual fluctuation; and a man, that lies at a distance from us, may, in a little time, become a familiar acquaintance' (*T* 581; compare *T* 603). He alludes to the unsatisfactoriness of the uncorrected situation, and to what its correction requires, by citing our need to 'arrive at a more *stable* judgment of things' (T 581), our desire to avoid the 'uncertainty [arising] from the incessant changes of our situation' (T 583).

Suppose—ignoring intrasubjective variability—that one's conative attitudes towards others were wholly a function of the relations in which one stood, oneself, to those individuals. Suppose, that is to say, that the character and range of one's concerns were wholly determined by how things appeared from one's own 'peculiar point of view' (T 581). Suppose, too, that others, with *their* conative attitudes towards others, were likewise governed by the appearances from *their* 'peculiar points of view'. There would, it is clear, be no conative common ground one would share securely with those others. Save accidentally, there would be no sharing of concerns: no sharing of objects—or of degrees—of benevolence or ill-will; no sharing of sympathetic desires. Given the practicality of conative thinking each would be disposed to differ markedly in behaviour from every other. Each—or so Hume holds—would find the situation intolerable. Given the character of the predicament, a solution would demand the generation of *intersubjectively shareable* desires, some range of desires not affected by the peculiarities of each person's position relative to that of each of the others. It would require each to form sympathetic desires in ways insulated from the effects of those peculiarities.[25]

The intersubjective predicament would have, as Hume represents it, a linguistic dimension as well. Assuming the individuals to give voice to their essentially unshareable desires, there would be no agreement in what each would *say* of the needs of others, or in what each would *say* of another in response to the bearing of that other's conduct or qualities on those needs. Each would *speak*, evaluatively, from his own 'peculiar point of view'. Addressing the linguistic aspect of the intersubjective predicament, Hume writes: 'every particular man has a peculiar position with regard to others; and 'tis impossible we cou'd ever converse together on any reasonable terms, were each of us to consider characters and persons, only as they appear from his peculiar point of view' (T 581); 'we every day meet with persons, who are in a different situation from ourselves, and who cou'd never converse with us on any reasonable terms, were we to remain constantly in that situation and point of view, which is

---

[25] Individuals would, of course, have similar desires even without the correction of sympathy: each would desire food and warmth; each would desire the well-being of his or her friends and relations. The point is that they would none the less differ radically with respect both to the individuals for whom they were concerned and to the degrees of concern directed to a given object of joint concern.

peculiar to us' (*T* 603). We would, he takes it, find such linguistic discord most unsatisfactory: we would desire 'to prevent those continual *contra-dictions*' (*T* 581), would seek to prevent the 'many contradictions to our sentiments in society and conversation' (*T* 583).[26] Seeking a solution to the linguistic side of our predicament we would look for 'some other standard of merit and demerit, which may not admit of so great variation' (ibid.), some standard that would lead to agreement in what we say.

The intersubjective predicament, both conative and specifically linguistic, is not, in Hume's view, a parochial predicament, one in which only those who are near neighbours, say, or fellow countrymen, might find themselves. Hume's individuals would likewise find it distressing to share no conative common ground, no voiceable evaluations, with individuals quite distant from themselves in time, place or culture. They would be similarly dissatisfied were there no agreement in sentiment, and so no agreement in what is said when voice is given to sentiment, between themselves (assuming them to be contemporary Europeans) and someone in China, say, or someone (Brutus, for example) who lived in ancient Rome. Hume's envisaged individuals seek some range of desires and evaluative ways of speaking shareable, despite enormous differences amongst the peculiar points of view in question, with those long dead or far distant—and even with those yet to come.

Solution to the intersubjective predicament—the solution we devise by adopting the moral point of view—lies fundamentally in the formation of specifically moral desires, desires intersubjectively shareable in virtue of the universality and impartiality of their content. It is their content that insulates such desires from the peculiarities of point of view that generate the intersubjective predicament. Representing the common vantage-point that specifically moral desires make possible, Hume writes:

'Tis therefore from the influence of characters and qualities, upon those who have an intercourse with any person, that we blame or praise him. We consider not whether the persons, affected by the qualities, be our acquaintance or strangers, countrymen or foreigners. Nay, we over-look our own interest in those general judgments. (*T* 582)

The predicament's solution is, equivalently, a matter of the correction of sympathy. Were individuals to form their sympathetic desires from a standpoint that systematically discounts the peculiarities introduced by each one's particular point of view, their sympathetic desires would not

---

[26] Obviously, admission of such 'contradictions' does nothing to undercut Hume's anti-cognitivism.

display the intersubjective variability that, when exclusive, generates the intersubjective predicament. Perhaps Hume's thought is that, when corrected, sympathy is governed by a recognition that '[a]ll human creatures are related to us by resemblance' (*T* 369). Concretely, he suggests that, in corrected sympathy, each sympathizes similarly with the desires of each of those, whoever they be, who are affected by the actions or characteristics of others, whoever they in turn may be. In a context of corrected sympathy, it makes no difference whether the individual with whom one sympathizes is friend or foe, fellow countryman or foreigner, a contemporary or of some other time. Hume adumbrates such a perspective for sympathy when he writes: 'Being thus loosen'd from our first [i.e. our particular] station, we cannot afterwards fix ourselves so commodiously by any means as by a sympathy with those, who have any commerce with the person we consider' (*T* 583).

Hume apparently thinks that the suggested solution to the intersubjective predicament brings a solution for the intrasubjective predicament in its train: one would secure some measure of intrasubjective stability by adopting the moral point of view, a point of view from which one would attend no more to the temporally bound, than to the other, peculiarities of one's position. He clearly holds that, were the moral point of view adopted, individuals would be able to converse in reasonable ways with one another about the objects of their conative attitudes. Given intersubjectively shareable, because impartial, desires individuals would have available a novel (segment of a) language, 'another language' to complement 'the language of self-love'. Hume writes:

When a man denominates another his *enemy*, his *rival*, his *antagonist*, his *adversary*, he is understood to speak the language of self-love, and to express sentiments peculiar to himself, and arising from his peculiar circumstances and situation. But when he bestows on any man the epithets *vicious* or *odious* or *depraved*, he then speaks another language, and expresses sentiments, in which he expects all his audience are to concur with him. (*E* 272)

Hume's examples have to do with the evaluation of persons, but the point pertains to the language of moral desires as well. Shifting from one language to the other the speaker shifts from 'his private and peculiar situation' to 'a point of view, common to him with others' (ibid.). Speaking this latter language, individuals can agree in what they say of the needs of others despite deep differences founded in the particularities of their individual positions.

Hume thinks of desire's double predicament, and its solution, as having a parallel in the case of perceptual experience. He compares the two cases in the second *Enquiry*:

> The judgment here [in the case of moral sentiments] corrects the inequalities of our internal emotions and perceptions; in like manner, as it preserves us from error, in the several variations of images, presented to our external senses. The same object, at a double distance, really throws on the eye a picture of but half the bulk; yet we imagine that it appears of the same size in both situations ... [W]ithout such a correction of appearances, both in internal and external sentiment, men could never think or talk steadily on any subject; while their fluctuating situations produce a continual variation on objects, and throw them into such different and contrary lights and positions. (*E* 227–8; compare *T* 602–3)

As with desire, so with perception: both intrasubjective and intersubjective difficulties are envisaged; and the intersubjective difficulties have both linguistic and non-linguistic dimensions.

With allowances for the differences—differences central to Hume's moral psychology—between desire and perception, the solution for the latter case resembles that for the former: each of many perceivers shifts to a shareable perceptual vantage-point; each becomes capable of speaking the language of objective perceptual reality, not just that of appearances. Taking the point of Hume's analogy between perceptual representations and moral desires, we may say that the latter, by virtue of the universality and impartiality of their content, and so their intersubjectivity, are *objective* desires, not merely subjective ones. And the language expressive of such objective desires is a language of objective, not merely subjective, evaluation.

As set out thus far, Hume's claims about the role of intersubjectively shareable desires, and about the origin and function of the objective language of moral evaluation, constitute, whatever their merits, a *modest* thesis. So, too, do his parallel claims concerning language and perceptual experience. Obviously—and fortunately—neither rules out a subjective dimension to language, a language of perceptual appearances, say, or 'the language of self-love'. On the face of it, however, each countenances language when intersubjectivity—whether of sense or sentiment—is absent. The modest thesis is simply that conative and perceptual objectivity, and the consequent availability of objective languages of desire and perception, provide remedy for conative and perceptual situations that individuals would have reason to reject. They do so by enabling individuals to 'think or talk steadily'—both evaluatively and perceptually—'on any subject' (*E* 228).

Hume hints, at least, at a much *bolder* thesis about objectivity and language: that a condition on having a language is the presence of shared perceptual perspectives; and further, that having a language requires shared desires and so shared adoption of the moral point of view. He writes of the conditions on our being able to 'talk steadily on any subject' (*E* 228), or on our being able to 'converse together on any reasonable terms' (*T* 581). Sketching his modest thesis we have read 'steadily' and 'on reasonable terms' in a minimal way, as suggesting modes of linguistic expression whose employment reduces the discord-generating effects of our widely differing individual perspectives, both perceptual and conative. That individuals be able to talk 'steadily' or 'reasonably'—whether on perceptual or evaluative matters—could, however, be taken as a condition on their having *any* linguistic capacity at all. *Perhaps* Hume is tempted by that line of thought. In any event, he does explicitly strike a decidedly bolder note when he writes, discussing impartial sentiments, that "twere impossible we cou'd ever make use of language, or communicate our sentiments to one another, did we not correct the momentary appearances of things, and overlook our present situation' (*T* 582). He strikes the same bolder note in the second *Enquiry*, when commenting on 'general preferences and distinctions, without which our conversation and discourse could scarcely be rendered intelligible to each other' (*E* 228). 'General language', he there writes, 'being formed for general use, must be moulded on some more general views, and must affix the epithets of praise and blame, in conformity to sentiments, which arise from the general interests of the community' (ibid.). Shared desires—and a shareable perceptual perspective—are, that is to say, a condition on *any* communicative use of language. Given his account of the conditions on the requisite shareability of desires, it follows that mutual adoption of the impartial vantage-point of morality—as also of a common perceptual perspective—is a condition on the having of a public language.[27]

Hume elaborates neither his modest nor his bold thesis about the link between objectivity, whether conative or perceptual, and language. Providing no more than sketches, however, he cannot convince. Whatever be said on the perceptual side, it is not obvious that his modest thesis is strong enough to serve his explanatory purposes for the case of morality. It postulates a common need for a measure of conative and linguistic compatibility as the spur to formation of an impartial conative concern for individuals outside the 'narrow circle' of one's friends and relations

---

[27] Presumably, neither his bold nor his modest thesis would prompt Hume to deny the possibility of parasitic or hypocritical uses of the objective language of moral evaluation.

and so the devising of a language of shareable evaluation. The thesis being so economically stated, however, it is not obvious that the formation of moral desires, with their substantive demands on one's conduct, has been convincingly explained. On the face of it, some deeper source for impartial desire must be sought. The weak thesis's claim about the standing of the objective language of moral evaluation (as also that of perceptual judgement) is also suspect, for it countenances a language of perceptual appearances, and of partial evaluations, prior to the objective languages that the thesis purports to explain.

Were adoption of the moral vantage-point—or, more inclusively, joint adoption of objective perceptual and conative frameworks—essential to the very use of language a deeper source of impartial desire would, it seems, have been identified. Given the mutual dependency, at least in humans, of thought and language,[28] and the mutual dependency of cognitive and conative thinking, objective thinking and objective language, both evaluative and perceptual, would be a condition on the possibility of doing any thinking or talking at all. Objective thinking, both conative and perceptual, would be a condition on partial desire and subjective perception. An objective language of impartial evaluation and objective perceptual description would be a condition on the language of perceptual appearances and of partial desires. In the absence of objectivity, whether conative or perceptual, one could neither think nor speak.

Hume does no more than hint at this bolder line on objectivity and evaluative language. He can, then, have done nothing to subvert suspicion that the bold thesis is, on the presently central point, too strong. Suppose it be granted that the capacity to use language, and so the capacity to think, requires human individuals to agree, in quite fundamental and extensive ways, in their valuations and in what they say, evaluatively, in giving voice to their evaluations. Suppose it be granted, that is to say, that having those capacities they must share a good deal of conative common ground, must share the same basic values. Does it follow that they must share the peculiar desires that, with their impartiality of content, constitute adoption of the moral point of view? Does impartiality follow from shareability? Having only hinted in the bold doctrine's direction, Hume has done nothing to show that it does. Failing that, he has failed—at least

---

[28] Whatever Hume's own views about the suggested dependency for the human case, he allows thinking for the case of (presumably) non-linguistic animals. See the *Treatise* sections 'Of the reason of animals', 'Of the pride and humility of animals', and 'Of the love and hatred of animals'. Contrast Davidson's unqualified claim of mutual dependency in two essays, 'Thought and Talk', in *Inquiries into Truth and Interpretation*, 155–70, and 'Rational Animals', *Dialectica*, 36 (1982), 317–27.

in bold fashion—to explain the origin of corrected sympathy and so of the moral point of view.[29]

Hume has elaborated neither his modest nor his bold thesis about impartiality of desire and the language of evaluation. In setting out his arguments so sketchily (for the modest thesis) or not at all (for the bold thesis) he has shown neither that the modest thesis is strong enough, nor that the bold is not too strong, to serve his elucidatory purposes. In posing the question of morality's origins as he has, however, and particularly in fastening on the role of shareable desires (and perceptions) in the use of communicative language, he has at least opened a line of investigation that promises, if pursued, to produce genuine, and genuinely naturalistic, illumination of the nature both of mind and of morality.

Whatever the explanatory merits of his modest and bold theses about impartiality of desire and the language of evaluation, how precisely does Hume envisage the transition from the predicament he has characterized to its solution? What—so far, at any rate, as his weak thesis is concerned—are the steps that take individuals from the intolerable turmoil of intra-subjective instability and intersubjective conflict of language and sentiment to joint adoption of the moral point of view? What, that is to say, are the mechanisms by which the correction of sympathy comes about?

Hume says little, but on one point, at least, he is reasonably clear: reflection, knowledge, and experience have a role to play. How do we arrive at objective aesthetic responses? '[W]e know what effect it [a beautiful countenance] will have in such a position, and by that reflexion we correct its momentary appearance' (*T* 582). How arrive at objective perceptual judgements? '[C]orrecting the appearance by reflexion, [we] arrive at a more constant and establish'd judgment concerning them' (*T* 603). How, in particular, do we correct for 'the several variations of images, presented to our external senses' (*E* 227)? 'The same object, at a double

[29] The bolder thesis is proto-Davidsonian in making substantive agreement in evaluation a condition on having an interpretable language. It is much stronger than Davidson's own thesis, however, in that it makes the condition not (just) a large measure of agreement in attitude but, more specifically, joint adoption of the impartial conative vantage-point of morality. For Davidson's defence of his thesis, see *Expressing Evaluations*, as well as 'Judging Interpersonal Interests', in Jon Elster and Aanund Hylland (eds.), *Foundations of Social Choice Theory* (Cambridge, 1986), 195–211, and 'The Structure and Content of Truth'. Of course, given Davidson's views about the mutual dependency of thought and language, a large measure of agreement in valuation is a condition not only on language but also on thought. Hume, it should be noted, writes not only of talking steadily but also of thinking steadily.

Had Hume developed the present line of thought he would surely have represented matters in a developmental, rather than in a conceptual, way, but—just as in the case of his analysis of convention—that might well be viewed as an excisable feature of the account.

distance', Hume writes, 'really throws on the eye a picture of but half the bulk; yet we imagine that it appears of the same size in both situations; because we know that on our approach to it, its image would expand on the eye, and that the difference consists not in the object itself, but in our position with regard to it' (*E* 227–8). Something similar occurs in the formation of objective affections directed towards persons. Despite the particularities of our position we judge Brutus 'as represented in history' to be 'more laudable' than our own faithful servant. What explains our reaching this objective vantage-point? 'Experience', Hume writes, 'teaches us this method of correcting our sentiments' (*T* 582): '[w]e know, that were we to approach equally near to that renown'd patriot, he wou'd command a much higher degree of affection and admiration' (ibid.).[30]

Reflection, knowledge, and experience enter into the formation of impartial desires and corrected sympathy as well. They do so by providing knowledge of the causal and constitutive conditions on a solution to the predicament. Hume assumes individuals capable of learning that adoption of what comes to be called the moral point of view would provide a solution, as would, equivalently, the joint formation of specifically moral desires or a joint capacity for the impartial formation of sympathetic desires. He assumes individuals capable of realizing, upon reflection, the predicament's source in the countless sources of subjectivity, including the subjectivity of uncorrected sympathy. He assumes them capable of realizing that the product of (uncorrected) sympathy is 'much fainter than our concern for ourselves, and a sympathy with persons remote from us much fainter than that with persons near and contiguous' (*T* 603; compare *E* 229), that this is a source of the predicament, and that the solution lies in learning to 'neglect all these differences' (*E* 229). He offers no recipe for learning to neglect these differences, unless it be the recommendation that we 'fix on some *steady* and *general* points of view; and always, in our thoughts, place ourselves in them, whatever be our present situation' (*T* 581–2).

Does Hume take the formation of specifically moral desires, or the operations of a corrected sympathy, to be things subject to *reason explanations*? Is adoption of the moral point of view something that, in Hume's view, individuals do for the reasons indicated? The question raises intractable

---

[30] Here one must not confound one's corrected *sentiment* with one's *belief* about the character of the sentiments one would have were one to make the imagined approach. Within the framework of Hume's expanded moral conativism, the belief *helps explain* the occurrence of the corrected—and so the impartial—sentiment that *constitutes* one's moral judgement.

issues in interpretation, and in methodology, but this much, at least, can be said with confidence. Hume does envisage individuals finding a certain situation intolerable, recognizing the sources of their difficulties and so what is needed for their remedy, acquiring information about possible steps to be taken, and so on. There is ample room here for Hume to think of reasons for *desire*. There is rather less room, however, for reasons for *action*. Given his restrictive views on what one is free to do,[31] Hume's individuals can have no very direct route to impartial desires and corrected sympathy. At a minimum, they must be heavily dependent on the use of various indirect strategies that provide no guarantee that they will come to have the impartial desires they want to have, will come to sympathize in the impartial way in which they want to sympathize. Granted what they want and know, Hume's individuals have reason to adopt the moral point of view. As Hume would surely insist, however, their doing so is not wholly in their own hands.

Does Hume take adoption of the moral point of view to involve *conventions* amongst individuals resolved to remedy their predicament? The question is best deferred until we have considered, in Chapter 6, Hume's explicit analysis of convention. It will be obvious, however, that an individual has the reason Hume cites for adopting the moral point of view only if others adopt it as well: did others not do so there would be no shared impartial desires and so no solution to the intersubjective predicament. Of course, Hume would take the devising of an objective language of evaluation to require convention (see *T* 490). As it happens, however, when analysing convention he offers no special account of specifically linguistic ones.

On the reading here developed, the intersubjective predicament's solution is equivalently (1) a matter of the joint formation of specifically moral desires, person-implicating desires intersubjectively shareable in virtue of the universality and impartiality of their content, or (2) a matter of corrected sympathy's generation of sympathetic (person-implicating) desires. It can seem, however, that there is something suspect in the suggested equivalence. Moral desires are impartial, but sympathetic desires are, save accidentally, partial ones: in sympathizing with another, one comes to have desires type-identical with his partial desires. Moral desires are universal in their content: they constitute a concern for the interests of each individual in so far as those interests are affected by the mind-displaying actions or qualities of human agents. Given the role of belief

---

[31] See n. 17, above.

in Hume's thin theory of sympathy, however, one's sympathetic desires must originate with one's beliefs about the particular desires of particular individuals. What, then, of desires of which one is simply unaware, or the many individuals of whom one has no knowledge at all? How, given the thin theory, could one be said to sympathize with them?

Hume does not address these questions explicitly, but the outlines of Humean answers are readily supplied. Suspicions on the point of partiality rest on confusion: as we saw earlier, Humean moral desires constitute an impartial concern for the admittedly partial concerns of others (or of the desirer herself). Suspicions on the point of universality can be countered by recalling that the sympathy in question is corrected sympathy, and by thinking of corrected sympathy in terms of a disposition to sympathize similarly with each individual of whom one becomes apprised and with any person-implicating desire that comes to one's attention.[32] One cannot sympathize with desires of which, or with persons of whom, one knows nothing at all. One can none the less be prepared to sympathize with such desires and persons were one's cognitive situation to provide the occasion. *Perhaps* Hume is thinking in dispositional terms when he writes, discussing the links between sympathy and adoption of the moral point of view: 'The *general rule* reaches beyond those instances, from which it arose' (*T* 499). His sense that those adopting the moral point of view are disposed to think in certain ways of individuals of whom they have not thought before, provided they are prompted to think of them at all, is apparent when he writes: 'if you represent a tyrannical, insolent or barbarous behaviour, in any country or in any age of the world, I soon carry my eye to the pernicious tendency of such a conduct, and feel the sentiment of repugnance and displeasure towards it' (*E* 273). Hume's weak thesis granted, such dispositions would be sufficient for the predicament's solution.

A thoroughly naturalistic theory, Hume's theory of corrected sympathy—provided it is prised free of the exaggerations of the thick theory of sympathy—has much to recommend it. It renders the universality and impartiality of moral desires in relatively non-mysterious, plausibly concrete,

---

[32] Is the suggestion that one sympathizes with *any* person-implicating desire? There is an important issue here, but not one to which Hume pays more than glancing attention. At *T* 389 he offers an account of why, for a range of cases, we sympathize with the person suffering misfortunes, not with the author of those misfortunes. Perhaps, for the general case of corrected sympathy, he would take holistic considerations, as well as an emphasis on person-implicating desires, to introduce the restraints that he seems to need? Or the fact, stressed at *T* 354 and 604, that one sympathizes most readily, and extensively, with someone whose sentiments are akin to one's own?

terms. It avoids each of two equally unattractive (and equally un-Humean) assumptions: that of a wide-ranging and primitive altruism in human motivation; and that of continuing and exclusive concern for one's own interests (or for those plus the interests of one's friends and relations). If not in a wholly convincing fashion, it represents the altruism peculiar to morality as a development, along intelligible lines and for intelligible reasons, from a point that does not presuppose its presence. Its mechanism of correction, if needed for the understanding of perceptual experience and aesthetic response as much as for morality, cannot be dismissed as an *ad hoc* source of the distinctiveness of morality. That mechanism permits a sense of the objectivity of moral desires—and so practical moral judgements—that is not tied to their being evaluable as true or false: objectivity is not, as for the moral cognitivist, a matter of standards utterly independent of the proclivities and preferences of those who adopt the moral point of view; it is, very differently, a product of the non-partiality of the standpoint from which each person sympathizes similarly with the person-implicating desires of each of the others. It is, then, 'founded entirely on the particular fabric and constitution of the human species' (*E* 170), is something 'arising from the internal frame and constitution of [human] animals' (*E* 294). The objectivity that originates in corrected sympathy comports effortlessly with the conative character of practical moral judgements. It does so while accommodating, as it must, the fact that agents often fail to act in the ways that, as they recognize, morality requires.

3. MORAL AFFECTIONS

Hume's arguments for moral conativism concern *practical* moral 'judgments' or 'opinions', those that can play the major role in reasons for action and so can be cited in explanation of what an agent does. Assuming the arguments sound, *such* moral judgements or opinions are in fact moral desires, desires that (as we have just seen) have a distinctive impartial and person-implicating content. As we have represented them, however, Hume's arguments for moral conativism say nothing directly about moral judgements or opinions that are not practical in the intended sense. They simply ignore the many types of moral judgements that can neither play the major role in a reason for action nor be cited, in straightforward fashion, as part of an action's explanation. In effect, they ignore those moral judgements—judgements about the actual mind-displaying actions and

qualities of individuals, judgements about the individuals themselves—
that cannot plausibly be identified with desires, even desires with a distinctive impartial and person-implicating content. To sustain a thoroughgoing non-cognitivism with respect to moral judgements, then, Hume
must find a way to accommodate *non-practical* moral judgements within
an essentially conativist theoretical framework. He must, that is to say,
devise an *expanded* moral conativism that accommodates both approval or
disapproval of a person's mind-displaying actions or qualities and approval
or disapproval of the persons who perform those actions or possess those
qualities.

He does so by identifying non-practical moral judgements with person-
implicating *moral affections*, whether propositional or person-directed, that
presuppose moral desires.[33] *Some* such judgements are person-implicating
propositional affections that are consequent upon the realization of, or
upon the non-realization of, the satisfaction-conditions on specifically
moral desires. These judgements, themselves instances of satisfaction or
dissatisfaction, are specifically moral isomorphs of the affections Hume
calls 'joy' and 'grief'.[34] They are person-implicating both because they
are consequent upon beliefs about the realization (or the non-realization)
of person-implicating moral desires and because they in turn give rise, as we
shall see, to person-directed affections. More narrowly, they are satisfactions or dissatisfactions prompted by the presence or absence of mind-
displaying human actions or qualities. They are specifically moral affections
because they are consequent upon desires with the universality and impartiality of content that marks the moral. They are, we may say, instances of
impartial satisfaction or dissatisfaction that arise in light of one's beliefs
with respect to some or other human individual's meeting, or failing to
meet, one's moral desires. In thinking Jones's conduct morally execrable
one has or experiences such an impartial moral affection: viewing things
from the moral vantage-point, one is dissatisfied that he has behaved as he
has. In thinking that one's own conduct has been morally objectionable
one is dissatisfied with one's own doings in that they have failed to accord
with what, morally speaking, one impartially wants. Thinking that one's
own, or another's, mind-displaying actions or qualities have met morality's
requirements one is pleased: finding one's own, or the other's, mind-displaying actions or qualities to accord with what, impartially, one desires
one has, in consequence, a sense of (propositional) satisfaction. In cases of

---

[33] In characterizing this identity thesis—as also the allied thesis of the centrality of
moral desire—I revert to the regimented account of the affections in Chap. 2, Sect. 3.

[34] Here, for simplicity's sake, I overlook the more complicated cases of hope and fear.

the kinds canvassed, one morally approves or disapproves of one's own, or of another's, mind-displaying conduct or qualities.

Other non-practical moral judgements are non-propositional, person-directed affections that take persons as their objects. Non-propositional instances of satisfaction or dissatisfaction, they are specifically moral isomorphs of the affections Hume terms 'pride', 'humility', 'love', and 'hatred'. They presuppose, and correspond to, instances of the specifically moral, person-implicating, propositional affections just described. Though non-propositional, they are specifically moral: they are impartial responses to human individuals – either self-directed or other-directed affective responses – that, depending on beliefs about that individual's meeting or failing to meet the requirements that moral desires set out, are based upon the propositional affections those beliefs prompt. Dissatisfied with one's own (or with Jones's) conduct one is, in consequence, dissatisfied with oneself (or with Jones): one experiences an impartial form of humility or shame directed towards oneself (or of hatred directed towards Jones). Satisfied with one's own actions or qualities (or Smith's actions or qualities)—they match one's impartial moral desires—one is (thus far) satisfied with oneself (or with Smith): one experiences a specifically moral form of pride (or of love). In having such affective responses, one morally approves or disapproves of oneself or of some other person.

Moral affections of these two types, along with the moral desires on which they directly or indirectly depend, have their place within a comprehensive configuration of moral sentiments that parallels the one we explored in Chapter 2, Section 3. For moral desires and affections, just as for non-moral ones, Hume traces a causal route from person-implicating desire, through person-implicating affection of joy or grief, to person-directed affection of pride or humility, love or hatred. In tracing the route he displays moral desire's *centrality* with respect to moral approval, whether of actions and qualities or of persons. In doing so he develops the *expanded moral conativism* that his thoroughgoing non-cognitivism with respect to moral judgements requires.

In a passage cited earlier from *Treatise*, III. iii. 1 ('Of the origin of the natural virtues and vices'), Hume traces much of this route for non-moral cases:

The most immediate effects of pleasure and pain are the propense and averse motions of the mind; which are diversified into volition, into desire and aversion, grief and joy, hope and fear ... But when along with this, the objects, that cause pleasure or pain, acquire a relation to ourselves or others: they still continue to excite desire and aversion, grief and joy: But cause, at the same time, the indirect passions of pride or humility, love or hatred, which in this case have a double relation of impressions and ideas to the pain or pleasure. (*T* 574; compare *T* 438–9)

As its location in the *Treatise* makes plain, this passage is intended to set the stage for his subsequent discussion of the formation of specifically moral sentiments, both desires and affections, in the case of the so-called natural virtues. Both in that subsequent discussion and elsewhere he explicitly locates moral desires and the two kinds of moral affections at their appropriate functional positions in the intimated comprehensive configuration of specifically moral sentiments.

He represents the link between moral desires and propositional moral affections when he distinguishes 'the benevolent concern for others' (where it is impartial benevolence that is meant) from 'the blame and approbation, consequent on it' (*E* 275), a person's 'humanity' (his impartial concern for others) from his 'consequent censure or approbation' (*E* 230). Assuming the presence of specifically moral desires, he writes that 'reflecting on the tendency of characters and mental qualities, is sufficient to give us the sentiments of approbation and blame' (*T* 577). The approbation or blame here invoked are of the propositional, not the person-directed, sort. Hume is thinking of one's affective responses to a person's mind-displaying qualities: he writes of 'qualities [that] acquire our approbation, because of their tendency to the good of mankind' (*T* 578), of 'that esteem, which attends such of the natural virtues, as have a tendency to the public good' (*T* 580), of '[t]he approbation of moral qualities' (*T* 581), of 'approbation or blame, satisfaction or displeasure towards characters and actions' (*E* 218). He proposes to investigate 'the principles, which make us feel a satisfaction or uneasiness from the survey of any character' and that thus explain our judgements that 'the character is laudable or blameable' (*T* 471). He writes, in the same vein, that 'virtue is distinguished by the pleasure, and vice by the pain, that any action, sentiment or character gives us by the mere view and contemplation' (*T* 475).[35]

Given propositional approbation or blame—given affective responses of satisfaction or dissatisfaction consequent upon the belief that a person's actions or qualities meet or fail to meet the requirements moral desire sets—person-directed approbation or blame follow. Perhaps Hume represents

---

[35] Here it is assumed that the approbation or blame is prompted by the belief that some or other individual actually performs or possesses some desirable or undesirable mind-displaying action or quality. Without that assumption, approbation or disapprobation of mind-displaying actions or qualities of some sort or other would simply be a matter of relatively determinate moral desire.

this link in the comprehensive configuration when he writes, of an individual whose qualities he has described, that 'we approve of his character, and love his person' (*T* 602). He appears to do so when writing, of a person who is 'possess'd of a character, that in its natural tendency is beneficial to society', that 'we esteem him virtuous, and are delighted with the view of his character' (*T* 584). He is explicit about this link, and also alludes to that between moral desire and propositional moral affection, when he writes: 'The *pain or pleasure*, which *arises from* the general survey or view of any action or quality of the mind, constitutes its vice or virtue, and *gives rise to* our *approbation or blame*, which is nothing but a fainter and more imperceptible love or hatred' (*T* 614, emphasis added). He is plain on the point at *Treatise*, ii. i. 7 ('Of vice and virtue'), when offering his associationist explanation of pride and humility when they result from recognition of the virtues or vices of the person in question:

To *approve of a character* is to feel an original delight upon its appearance. To *disapprove* is to be sensible of an uneasiness. The pain and pleasure, therefore, being the primary causes of vice and virtue, must also be the *causes* of all their effects, and consequently of *pride and humility*, which are the unavoidable attendants of that distinction. (*T* 296, emphasis added)

He makes what can seem a puzzling claim that 'these two particulars are to be consider'd as equivalent, with regard to mental qualities, *virtue* and the power of producing love or pride, *vice* and the power of producing humility or hatred' (*T* 575). They are equivalent precisely because a mental quality of the kind envisaged 'gives us a satisfaction, by the survey or reflexion' (*T* 574–5) or 'gives uneasiness' (*T* 575) and that satisfaction or uneasiness both prompts and is presupposed by the person-directed sentiments of pride and love, or humility and hatred, as appropriate. Satisfaction or uneasiness of the former sort both prompts and is presupposed by appropriate 'judgments of persons' (*T* 583).[36]

---

[36] In *Passion and Value in Hume's Treatise*, Árdal has convincingly argued for the importance, in Hume's theory of moral sentiments, of objective variants of pride and humility, love and hatred. Given the reading forwarded in the present chapter, however, such person-directed moral affections can only be understood within a framework that displays their dependencies on moral desires, and on person-implicating propositional moral affections. Árdal poses the question: 'Is there any justification for thinking that Hume considers reference to the indirect passions absolutely necessary in accounting for morality?', 112–13. In answer, he cites Hume's claim: 'The pain or pleasure which arises from the general survey or view of any action or quality of the *mind*, constitutes its vice or virtue, and gives rise to our approbation or blame, *which is nothing but a fainter and more imperceptible love or hatred*' (*T* 614, Árdal's emphasis). He neglects to emphasize those other moral sentiments that, as the passage makes plain, *give rise to* the person-directed moral sentiments to which he rightly draws our attention.

In the case of non-moral sentiments one must distinguish yet another position in Hume's comprehensive configuration for desires and affections, a position for desires that are consequent upon person-directed affections. The non-moral affections of love and hatred, as we have seen, in their turn give rise to the desires of benevolence and anger, respectively. Hume locates the very same position in the configuration for moral sentiments as well. Assuming an underlying impartial concern for the interests of anyone concerned, he locates the position of *consequent* moral desires when setting out almost the whole of the configuration:

As to the good or ill desert of virtue or vice, 'tis an evident consequence of the *sentiments of pleasure or uneasiness*. These sentiments *produce love or hatred*; and love or hatred, by the original constitution of human passion, is *attended with benevolence or anger*; that is, with a desire of making happy the person we love, and miserable the person we hate. (*T* 591, emphasis added)

Moral desires prompt propositional moral affections; these in turn prompt person-directed moral affections; some of these, in their turn, prompt further moral desires. Thinking it morally desirable to help the homeless, one approves of Sally's efforts to help, thus thinks highly of Sally, and so is led to want to praise or in some other way please her. Judging it wrong to ignore the needs of others, one disapproves of Sam's having done so, thus disapproves of Sam, thus is prompted to want to censure or in some other way discomfort him.

Once their several links, both direct and indirect, to the moral desires they presuppose or prompt are set out in terms of the comprehensive configuration, it is clear both (1) that moral affections, whether propositional or person-directed, cannot play a quite straightforward role in action explanations, and (2) that they none the less play a perfectly intelligible oblique role in such explanations. They cannot play a quite straightforward role for they are not suited to serve as the major elements in reasons for actions. Being cognizant of the comprehensive configuration, however, one can understand an agent's action when told that she acted as she did because she disapproved of his being so narrow-minded and grasping—or because she disapproved of him—even though such explanations cite moral affections rather than moral desires. Disapproving of *his* being so narrow and grasping she tried not to be so herself. Disapproving of his being so narrow and grasping, thus disapproving of him, she rallied the others to reprove him.

Within Hume's naturalistic framework, corrected sympathy must play a role in the generation of specifically moral affections, whether propositional or person-directed. It plays an indirect role in so far as it is implicated in the formation of the specifically moral desires that hold the central position in the conative and affective structure that we have just examined. Corrected sympathy is requisite for specifically moral desires, but, given such desires, one has specifically moral affections, both propositional and person-directed, when those desires are met or go unmet.

Given the measure of holism that Hume introduces into his account of sympathy's operations, however, there is both room for, and a requirement of, corrected sympathy not only with another's partial desires but also with that person's partial affections, both propositional and person-directed. One can sympathize with, and so have corrected sympathy with, the person-implicating satisfactions or dissatisfactions another has when her person-implicating partial desires are satisfied or go unsatisfied. Similarly, one can have corrected sympathy with another's (partial) pride or humility, love or hatred. Hume invokes such direct dependence of moral affections on corrected sympathy with the partial affections of others when he explains our moral response to acts of injustice: 'We partake of their uneasiness [the uneasiness of those injured by the unjust actions in question] by *sympathy*; and as every thing, which gives uneasiness in human actions, upon the general survey, is call'd Vice, and whatever produces satisfaction, in the same manner, is denominated Virtue; this is the reason why the sense of moral good and evil follows upon justice and injustice' (*T* 499). The 'uneasiness' with which we sympathize in the cases imagined is the partial, person-implicating, propositional dissatisfaction of the person injured by the unjust action. That the sympathy in question is corrected sympathy is indicated by Hume's reference to 'the general survey'. He invokes corrected sympathy with the partial person-directed affections of others when remarking on the especially important case, for the formation of specifically moral judgements, of sympathy with another's responses to oneself: 'we naturally', Hume writes, '*sympathize* with others in the sentiments they entertain of us' (ibid.).

There are difficulties, to which Hume does not attend, in the specification of the content of the sympathetic affections the theory introduces, difficulties stemming in particular from indexical elements in the content of person-directed affections: sympathy with another's hatred for oneself introduces such difficulties; so does sympathy with another's self-directed humility or shame. As with the case of sympathetic desires, Hume must set conditions on type-identity for affections that do not require identity of pronominal ingredients in their contents.

Hume's official theory of moral sentiments, whether desires or affections, displays the psychological atomism to which we have objected when discussing their non-moral counterparts: he writes that 'the distinguishing impressions, by which moral good or evil is known, are nothing but *particular* pains or pleasures' (*T* 471), that 'moral distinctions depend entirely on certain peculiar sentiments of pain and pleasure' (*T* 574). If he is to provide an expanded conativist theory that will prove adequate to its explanatory tasks he must eschew atomism in favour of a theory, not only of moral desires, but also of moral affections, that addresses, in ways considered earlier, the issues of content, truth-evaluability, and direction of fit. He must acknowledge the propositional content of certain moral affections, and the absence of direction of fit for all. He must recognize the content-mediated dependence of moral affections, whether propositional or person-directed, on prior beliefs and specifically moral desires. He must offer an adequate metaphysical model—perhaps one invoking modes of conception, perhaps one introducing primitive attitudes towards the truth of propositions, or towards persons—of moral sentiments. He must provide a corresponding account both of the role of moral sentiments in reasoning and of the features of the sentences in which such sentiments find verbal expression. A non-atomistic Humean theory of the objective, specifically moral, variants of joy, grief, pride, humility, love, and hatred will be isomorphic, we may take it, with the non-atomistic theory of these partial affections that we considered in Chapter 2, Section 3.

When examining Hume's indirect argument for moral conativism we encountered his claim that moral cognitivism provides no plausible account of the difference in moral significance between the destruction of its parent tree by a sapling and the parricidal killing of a human parent. From the vantage-point of Hume's own expanded conativist theory the difference in moral significance is perfectly intelligible. It is a function of the fact that moral sentiments, just as the partial sentiments of which they are the impartial variants, are person-implicating.[37] Our conative and affective responses to trees differ from those we have towards persons, ourselves and others. Those differences are no more puzzling when the sentiments are specifically moral than when they are the partial sentiments with which moral sentiments are isomorphic. The differences in moral significance are an intelligible product of deep and intelligible features of the life of human emotion. What prompts moral sentiments, just as what prompts their partial counterparts, 'must necessarily be plac'd either in ourselves or others, and excite either pleasure or uneasiness;

[37] This is, of course, not to say that all sentiments are person-implicating.

and therefore must give rise to one of these four passions [pride, humility, love, hatred]; which clearly distinguishes them from the pleasure and pain arising from inanimate objects, that often bear no relation to us' (*T* 473).

Hume's direct and indirect arguments secure *moral conativism*, a theory specifically about moral reasons for action, *not* the *expanded moral conativism*—the comprehensive theory of moral desires and affections—to which he is committed and which we have now elaborated. Directed against moral cognitivism construed narrowly as a theory about moral reasons for action, they do not as such rule out essentially cognitivist accounts of other-than-practical moral judgements.[38] Given the case for moral conativism, however—a case that includes Hume's constructive characterization of specifically moral desires—the requirements of simplicity and comprehensiveness of theory, and the requirement of a theory that fits moral thinking to a background theory of human cognitive, conative, and affective capacity, conspire to make a nearly compelling case for Hume's expanded theory, for his complex and inclusive theory of moral judgements as moral sentiments. What misgivings remain require Hume's attention to the facts that we do commonsensically think and talk in terms of moral beliefs and moral truths. To be quite compelling, Hume's expanded moral conativism must be seen successfully to subvert—or somehow to accommodate—*these* seemingly cognitivist appearances.

4. MORAL BELIEFS AND MORAL LANGUAGE

We have achieved a hard-edged representation of the character and scope of Hume's direct and indirect arguments for moral conativism. We have, at least in outline, a clear picture of the ways in which his expanded moral conativism mirrors his doctrine of non-moral desires and affections. We have a detailed rendering both of his account of the distinctiveness of moral sentiments and of his views about their origin in the correction of sympathy. Thus equipped, we can remain unmoved by hints of a residual moral cognitivism that some readers find in the text of the *Treatise* or the second *Enquiry*.

[38] Variants on that part of Hume's *indirect* argument which is concerned with the characterization of peculiarly moral properties can, it seems, be readily devised for these other-than-practical moral judgements. Presumably some of the same (more general) evaluative predicates are employable in the expression both of practical and of other-than-practical moral judgements.

Could Hume be an *ideal observer* theorist? If the thought is that he identifies moral judgements or opinions with beliefs about the responses of an impartial or otherwise ideal observer, it is clear that it cannot capture Hume's thinking. Such beliefs—just as any others—must be amongst the targets of his direct and indirect arguments concerning moral reasons for action. With their focus on observers, they also fail to capture Hume's own sustained attention to the valuations that agents make, as distinct from observers. Hume has, of course, the conception of an impartial desirer, as also the complementary conception of an individual whose consequent affective responses are impartial: these conceptions are essential constituents of his expanded conativist theory. He can have no objection to introducing requirements of cognitive success into the characterization of such an individual's moral desires and affections. After all, as desires and affections they implicate beliefs in a variety of ways. Nor can he object to the suggestion that, in adopting the vantage-point of conative and affective impartiality, an individual may, or may typically, have an accompanying belief that others who share that vantage-point— and who have similar cognitive success—will thus far want, and be satisfied by, what she herself wants and finds satisfying.[39] He can surely countenance the suggestion that, in having that accompanying belief, the individual will think of herself and such others symmetrically, as each approximating to an ideal, and ideally reflective and informed, impartiality in desire and affection. He must insist, however, that such accompanying beliefs not be confounded with the impartial desires and affections they accompany and presuppose.[40]

Does Hume at times intimate a doctrine of *moral perception*?[41] The putative products of moral perception would, presumably, be moral beliefs with evaluative content, and would, as beliefs, have the mind-to-world direction of fit and be evaluable in terms of truth and falsity. As our representation of Hume's direct and indirect arguments for moral conativism shows, however, he could not take *practical* moral judgements to be construable on such a perceptual model. As the considerations he presents in elaboration of his expanded moral conativism make plain, a perceptual

[39] Room must, of course, be left for variations of the sort examined earlier in the more determinate moral sentiments of persons from differing periods and cultures.

[40] He must similarly insist that more narrowly subjective beliefs about one's own conative and affective responses not be confounded with any moral desires and affections they accompany and presuppose—or that they may cause. Compare n. 30, above.

[41] Compare David Fate Norton, *David Hume: Common-Sense Moralist, Sceptical Metaphysician* (Princeton, NJ, 1982).

model is no better placed for illuminating moral judgements of a *non-practical* sort.

To be sure, Hume writes of 'the moral sense' (*T* 588), compares sympathy to sense perception on the point of correction, and introduces an analogy between moral judgements or opinions and the perception of so-called secondary qualities as traditionally understood. 'Vice and virtue', he writes, 'may be compar'd to sounds, colours, heat and cold, which, according to modern philosophy, are not qualities in objects, but perceptions in the mind' (*T* 469).

In his usage, however, the products of moral sense are 'moral sentiments', 'sentiment[s] of approbation or blame' (*E* 102), 'sentiments of duty and humanity' (*E* 291), 'sentiment[s] of ... vice and virtue' (*E* 294), 'sentiment[s] of right and wrong' (*T* 498). These are one and all 'emotions' (*E* 102), and it is by generating such emotions that the moral sense gives 'the sense of moral good and evil' (*T* 499). Hume is explicit on the point: '*To approve* of a character *is to feel* an original delight upon its appearance. To disapprove of it is to be sensible of an uneasiness' (*T* 296, emphasis added). 'In these sentiments', he writes, 'do all moral determinations consist' (*E* 291); '[t]o have the sense of virtue, is nothing but to *feel* a satisfaction of a particular kind from the contemplation of a character' (*T* 471); 'our approbation or blame ... is nothing but a fainter and more imperceptible love or hatred' (*T* 614). Hume's terminology is closer to Jane Austen's than to J. L. Austin's: he associates moral sense with moral sensibility, not with moral sensibilia.

That both perception and sympathy's operations are subject to correction does nothing to reduce the fundamental differences between objective sensory perception and the moral sentiments that are corrected sympathy's products. That there are analogies between perceptual experience that implicates secondary qualities, and moral sentiments that 'gild ... or stain ... all natural objects with the colours, borrowed from internal sentiment' (*E* 294), likewise does nothing to diminish the gap that separates them. Such perceptions and such sentiments are alike, perhaps, in deriving from peculiarities of our 'frame and constitution' (ibid.). They are none the less most unlike in that the former are cognitive states, the latter conative or affective ones.

Is Hume perhaps committed to saying that moral sentiments are like experiences of secondary qualities in that each at least seems to present a perceiver with the presence of objective, or mind-independent, qualities? Has he, perhaps, the view that one's moral sentiments prompt the projection of seemingly objective features, thus the formation of (illusory) beliefs in the presence of such features, thus the (illusory) belief, of one's moral sentiments, that they are moral beliefs?[42] This seems not in fact to be *Hume's* explication of the illusory belief that moral judgements are moral beliefs: he fastens on the calmness of moral judgements, not on projection, when offering the needed explanation.[43] As is obvious, however, even adoption of the suggested diagnosis would leave Hume's identification of moral judgements with moral sentiments quite firmly in place. As seems equally obvious, the ways in which one's desires and affections do in fact colour one's perceptions of objects are quite different from the ways in which one's perceptions of secondary qualities are sometimes thought to do.[44]

Hume's theory—an expanded conativist theory of moral judgements—is an identity theory, one identifying what *seem* to be moral beliefs with specifically moral desires and affections. The very statement of his identity thesis, however, reveals Hume's recognition of cognitivist intuitions embedded in our common-sense thinking about moral matters, intuitions to which he himself gives expression when writing of 'the distinguishing impressions, by which moral good or evil is *known*' (*T* 471, emphasis added), of 'the *opinion* of injustice, and ... that of obligation' (*T* 457, emphasis added), of 'those *judgments*, by which we distinguish moral good and evil' (*T* 456, emphasis added). As we have seen, Hume proposes to deal with *such* cognitivist intuitions by declaring them illusory and by invoking the calmness of moral sentiments to help explain the illusion. (As noted earlier, he might more compellingly have called upon their impartiality in this connection.) For Hume, it is understandable that we think, at times, in terms of moral beliefs, but those thoughts must not, when doing theory, be taken at face value. When doing theory one discovers that these putative beliefs are, one and all, desires and affections. To this his critics may well, of

---

[42] Compare Mackie's discussion of objectification and the varieties of sentimentalism in *Hume's Moral Theory*, 64–75. Colin McGinn considers Hume's suggestion of an analogy between moral judgements and the perception of secondary qualities in *The Subjective View: Secondary Qualities and Indexical Thoughts* (Oxford, 1983), 145–55. For broader discussions of the suggested analogy, see John McDowell's essays: 'Non-Cognitivism and Rule-Following', in Steven H. Holtzman and Christopher M. Leich (eds.), *Wittgenstein: To Follow a Rule* (London, 1981), 141–62; 'Values and Secondary Qualities', in Ted Honderich (ed.), *Morality and Objectivity* (London, 1985), 110–29; and *Projection and Truth in Ethics*, The Lindley Lecture (Lawrence, Kan., 1988), 1–14. See, too, Simon Blackburn's *Spreading the Word*, and 'Reply: Rule-Following and Moral Realism', in Holtzman and Leich (eds.), *Wittgenstein: To Follow a Rule*, 163–87.

[43] If projection were the source of the illusion it seems illusion should be generated for sentiments generally, not just for specifically moral ones.

[44] It must be emphasized that Hume himself *rejects* the contrast between primary and secondary qualities that lies in the background here. See *Treatise*, I. iv. 4 ('Of the modern philosophy'). See, too, the discussion in my *Hume's Philosophy of Mind*, Chap. I.

course, retort that having recourse to talk of illusions reveals an unhappy failure to see moral beliefs for what they are in themselves. Hume would, one assumes, simply hold the line. His expanded moral conativism would, however, be somewhat better positioned had he some way to meet his imagined critics half way.

Hume says very little directly—and not much more by implication—about *evaluative language*. He has a conception of explicitly evaluative terms: 'every tongue', he says, 'possesses one set of words which are taken in a good sense, and another in the opposite' (*E* 174). He also has a conception of expressing moral evaluations: 'when [a man] ... bestows on any man the epithets of *vicious* or *odious* or *depraved*, he speaks another language [than the language of self-love], and expresses sentiments, in which he expects all his audience are to concur with him' (*E* 272). These linked conceptions inform his comments—whatever the contribution these much-discussed comments make to his arguments for moral conativism[45]—on the 'new relation or affirmation' involved when one employs 'propositions ... connected with an *ought*, or an *ought not*', and on the possibility of 'this new relation ... [being] a deduction from others, which are entirely different from it' (*T* 469). He does nothing, however, to illuminate the relation he has in mind between moral sentiment and its linguistic expression. '[W]hen any action, or quality of the mind, pleases us *after a certain manner*', he writes, 'we say it is virtuous; and when the neglect, or non-performance of it, displeases us *after a like manner*, we say that we lie under an obligation to perform it' (*T* 517). Again: 'when we receive those feelings [of pleasure or pain] from the general consideration of any quality or character, we denominate it vicious or virtuous' (*T* 608–9). But how are we to understand the *saying* or *denominating* to which Hume here alludes?

Perhaps Hume would, if pressed for an explanation, call upon a doctrine of performative utterances?[46] He has a concept of performatives available from his theorizing about promising: 'there is', he maintains, 'a *certain form of words* ... by which we bind ourselves to the performance of any action', a 'form of words [that] constitutes what we call a promise' (*T* 522). It is far from clear, however, how the concept of a performative utterance can help illuminate the use of explicitly evaluative sentences.

[45] For a sample of views about the contribution these remarks make to Hume's argument for moral conativism, see: Harrison, *Hume's Moral Epistemology*, 69–82; A. C. MacIntyre, 'Hume on "Is" and "Ought"', in V. C. Chappell (ed.), *Hume: A Collection of Critical Essays* (Garden City, NY, 1966), 240–64; Mackie, *Hume's Moral Theory*, 61–3; Snare, *Morals, Motivation, and Convention*, 38–40; and Stroud, *Hume*, 186–8.

[46] For the concept of a performative utterance, see J. L. Austin, *How to Do Things with Words*, ed. J.O. Urmson (Oxford, 1962).

Perhaps, if pressed, he would invoke a doctrine of illocutionary force?[47] When discussing volitions he displays some sense of the peculiarities of imperatives. Perhaps, then, he would find thoughts of the imperatival or prescriptive force of evaluative sentences appealing?[48] Whatever its interpretative merits, the root philosophical difficulty in this proposal lies in its neglect of the central role of semantics, its neglect of the autonomy of meaning.[49] Perhaps, anticipating modern emotivist theories, Hume would insist on construing the evaluative expression of moral sentiment as nothing more than the venting of feeling?[50] The defects of this crude doctrine of linguistic expression are, however, such that, were his moral conativism ineluctably wedded to emotivism, the credibility of that central doctrine in his moral psychology must, despite his constructive arguments on its behalf, be called into question.

Whatever its independent philosophical significance, Hume's undeveloped contention that the use of language is a product of convention (*T* 490) throws no light on the peculiarities of specifically evaluative language.[51] His bold thesis that the possibility of a communicable language demands the availability of a language of objective evaluation,[52] while effecting (were it correct) a remarkable tie between moral sentiment and talk of anything under the sun, says nothing, as such, about the tie between moral sentiment and evaluative sentence.

Hume writes: 'when you pronounce any action or character to be vicious, you *mean* nothing, but that from the constitution of your nature you have a feeling or sentiment of blame from the contemplation of it' (*T* 469, emphasis added). He also writes: 'We blame equally a bad action, which we read of in history, with one perform'd in our neighbourhood t'other day: The *meaning* of which is, that we know from reflexion, that the former action wou'd excite as strong sentiments of disapprobation as the latter, were it plac'd in the same position' (*T* 584, emphasis added). Does he perhaps take evaluative expressions of moral sentiments to be equivalent to autobiographical reports of their actual or projected pres-

---

[47] For discussions of illocutionary force, see, in addition to Austin's *How to Do Things with Words*, John Searle's *Speech Acts: An Essay in the Philosophy of Language* (Cambridge, 1969) and *Expression and Meaning* (Cambridge, 1979).

[48] The *loci classici* for this line of thought are R. M. Hare's *The Language of Morals* and *Freedom and Reason*.

[49] Compare Davidson, *Expressing Evaluations*.

[50] See A. J. Ayer, *Language, Truth, and Logic* (London, 1946), and C. L. Stevenson, *Ethics and Language* (New Haven, Conn., 1944) and *Facts and Values: Studies in Ethical Analysis* (New Haven, Conn., 1963). On the prospects for an emotivist reading of Hume, see Harrison, *Hume's Moral Epistemology*, 117–20.

[51] See Chap. 6, Sect. 1, for his analysis of convention.   [52] See Sect. 2, above.

ence? They would then, of course, be evaluable as true or false, but this would come at no direct cost to his moral conativism. They could not, however, serve as major premises in the practical arguments that provide an agent's justification of his actions. The autobiographical rendering of evaluative sentences being so utterly implausible, it is fortunate that there is no reason whatever to think that Hume here means by 'meaning' what, when concerned with language, we now mean.

Neglecting the task of providing a conativist characterization of evaluative language, Hume does nothing to accommodate cognitivist intuitions embedded in our handling of that language. He comments not at all on syntactical similarities between evaluative and other predicates, on the fact that 'x is true' is as naturally predicable of evaluative as of many other sentences, on the syntactic soundness of sentences in which 'It is true that' prefaces an embedded evaluative sentence, on the fact that one can express one's agreement or disagreement with another's moral claims by saying, simply, 'That's true' or 'That's false'. He fails to remark the remarkable fact that the very sentences—the evaluative sentences—one employs to give canonical expression to moral desires and affections are both syntactically subject to truth and suited to provide the content-clauses in sentences designed, to all appearances, for the attribution of explicitly evaluative beliefs. 'One ought not lie', one says, expressing—assuming Hume right—a moral desire. But that very sentence can appear in 'It is true that one ought not lie', and in 'He believes that one ought not lie'. To all linguistic appearances, it can be used to give voice to an explicitly evaluative belief.

Just to insist, as Hume presumably would, that such uses of 'true'—such seeming transactions with truth—are out-and-out illusory is heroic, perhaps, but unhappily unhelpful. As in the connected case of seeming moral beliefs, so here: some convincing tale must be told – Hume tells none – of the illusion's origins. As for putative moral beliefs, so, again, here: his case for moral conativism would be strengthened had Hume some way to accommodate rather than dismiss common-sense talk of evaluative truth.

What of the suggestion that seeming transactions with evaluative truth are illusory, but only in so far as they are taken to involve a *substantive* notion of truth? Perhaps—truth not being a substantive notion—*no* transactions with truth involve a substantive notion of truth? Perhaps, much more cautiously, the substantive notion of truth employable in other contexts is unavailable for that of moral evaluation? Perhaps there is *more* to mathematical or empirical truth, say, than there is to the truth of evaluative sentences?

Countenancing other-than-substantive truth—the same for both evaluative and descriptive sentences—must at least appear to compromise Hume's case for moral conativism. Were he to be tempted by either of the ways just suggested for accommodating ostensible transactions with evaluative truth, he would face the challenge of showing just how the tempting proposal comports both with his interdict against double direction of fit and with the crucial contrast between desire and belief.[53] It seems, however, that he would in fact reject the first of the alternatives mentioned, and that he has independent reason to reject the second.

Hume would reject the suggestion that *no* sentences are evaluable using a substantive notion of truth. At least he would do so if what he says of the truth of psychological states mirrors what he would say when the subject is sentences. 'Truth', he writes, 'is of two kinds, consisting either in the discovery of the proportions of ideas, consider'd as such, or in the conformity of our ideas of objects to their real existence' (*T* 448). In so writing he represents truth as a substantive matter of a relational property—in the empirical case, at least, as a conformity—linking a truth-bearer (by present hypothesis, a sentence) and what renders that truth-bearer (that sentence) true.

According to the more cautious alternative, (1) some other-than-substantive element is common to truth in evaluative and in other (mathematical, empirical) contexts, and (2) in some contexts (mathematical, empirical), but not in others (evaluative), there is a substantive element as well. What would count as other-than-substantive common elements? Whether for evaluative or (as we shall say for short) descriptive sentences, truth is disquotational: ' "*p*" is true if and only if *p*.' Whether for evaluative or descriptive sentences, prefacing such sentences with 'It is true that' adds nothing to what the sentences, unadorned, convey. For sentences of either kind, use of 'That's true' signals endorsement of, or serves to express agreement with, what has been said. On the present proposal some such other-than-substantive elements exhaust what is involved in truth

---

[53] For some of the difficulties in this area, see: Crispin Wright, *Truth and Objectivity* (Cambridge, Mass., 1992) and 'Truth in Ethics', *Ratio* (New Series), 8 (1995), 209–26; Michael Smith, 'Why Expressivists about Value should Love Minimalism about Truth', *Analysis*, 54 (1994), 1–11; John Divers and Alexander Miller, 'Why Expressivists about Value should Not Love Minimalism about Truth', *Analysis*, 54 (1994), 12–19; Paul Horwich, 'The Essence of Expressivism', *Analysis*, 54 (1994), 19–20; Michael Smith, 'Minimalism, Truth-Aptitude and Belief', *Analysis*, 54 (1994), 21–6; and Frank Jackson, Graham Oppy, and Michael Smith, 'Minimalism and Truth-Aptness', *Mind*, 103 (1994), 287–302.

for evaluative sentences. Talk of the truth of descriptive sentences, however, introduces something more, the concept of conformity, or some other similarly substantive element. Should Hume seek, in *some* such way, to countenance the truth-evaluability of evaluative sentences while not compromising his expanded moral conativism?[54]

Let us assume the proposal introduces no equivocation on '*x* is true' and its kin. Its asymmetrical treatment of truth for descriptive and evaluative sentences appears, however, to be multiply *ad hoc*. The *common* presence of other-than-substantive elements in otherwise very different cases goes, on the face of it, wholly unexplained. Something—conformity or something such—appears to *constitute* truth for descriptive sentences; but nothing appears to do so for evaluative ones. *That* the other-than-substantive elements have a role to play seems explicable for the descriptive case; no such explanation, it seems, is in the offing for the other-than-substantive truth-evaluability of evaluative sentences. Perhaps its *ad hoc* appearance is merely that. If tempted by such an asymmetrical treatment of truth, however, Hume must either lessen or live with that appearance.

Hume would surely have no inclination towards replacing this asymmetrical treatment of truth with one that (1) acknowledges substantive truth on *both* sides of the descriptive/evaluative divide, while (2) insisting that substantive truth for evaluative sentences *differs* from substantive truth for descriptive ones. It is nevertheless instructive to inquire into the prospects for combining moral conativism—in a form not Hume's—with some such treatment of truth.

A version of moral conativism can be envisaged that appears compatible with—indeed, required by—a well-conceived approach to semantic theory that is unflinchingly committed both to (1) the specification of truth-conditions for, and so the truth-evaluability of, all explicitly evaluative sentences, and to (2) a substantive conception of truth for sentences on either side of the descriptive/evaluative divide. On the approach to semantics in question one provides a theory of (literal) meaning for a language if one provides, on an empirical basis, an axiomatic truth theory,

---

[54] Three terminological remarks are in order. Talk of the truth of *sentences* is, here, convenient shorthand for talk of the truth of utterances of sentences, or that of the statements made by the use of sentences (or whatever more careful theory may require as truth-bearers). We are here concerned with the truth of evaluative *sentences*, not that of the *judgements* (in the terminology used thus far) such sentences are used to express. I use the contrasting terms 'substantive' and (especially) 'other-than-substantive' to mark the contrast with which we are presently concerned precisely because, being relatively *non*-specific, they leave room for any of several more determinate contrasts to be found in the contemporary literature on this topic.

more or less in Tarski's fashion, for that language. The axiomatic theory will contain, as theorems, statements of the truth-conditions for every sentence—and so for every evaluative sentence—of that language. It will be an empirical theory on condition that it is achievable, in principle, from the perspective of a radical interpreter intent on devising a unified theory of meaning and action.[55] This approach to an empirical semantics eschews correspondence (as also coherence) conceptions of truth, but maintains that both the structure and the content—and so, as we may say, both other-than-substantive and substantive dimensions—of truth must find a place within the interpreter's explanatory theory.

How does this approach to semantics bear on—how does it require— moral conativism? From the vantage-point of the radical interpreter, it might be said, one must make a hard-and-fast distinction between inter-dependent, but mutually non-reducible, beliefs and desires, each with descriptive content, and one must assign to desires the major role in reasons for action. One must also recognize that states characterizable as desires with descriptive content are alternatively characterizable as beliefs with explicitly evaluative content, and that, in whichever way characterized, such states are expressible by the use of explicitly evaluative—and truth-evaluable—sentences. If characterizable in alternative ways, however, it is when characterized as desires with descriptive content that such states are characterized in the palmary—the explanatorily fundamental—way. For it is only on condition that they are thus characterized that unified theories of meaning and action can be secured.[56] Practical evaluative be-liefs are, then, at bottom, or basically, desires with descriptive content, albeit desires expressible using explicitly evaluative (and truth-evaluable) sentences.

[55] As commonly understood, the task of a radical interpreter is to solve for two unknowns—belief and meaning—on the basis of unquestionably empirical evidence. The task of a (more) radical interpreter intent on construction of a unified theory of meaning and action is to solve for three: (degree of) belief, (relative strength of) desire, and meaning. For discussion of the character, and of the philosophical point of discussing, radical interpretation, see Davidson's 'Radical Interpretation' and 'Belief and the Basis of Meaning', both in *Inquiries into Truth and Interpretation*, and David Lewis, 'Radical Interpretation', *Synthese*, 27 (1974), 331–44. Davidson explores the conditions on a unified theory of meaning and action in *Expressing Evaluations* and 'The Structure and Content of Truth', and in 'Towards a Unified Theory of Meaning and Action', *Grazer Philosophische Studien*, 11 (1980), 1–12, and 'A New Basis for Decision Theory', *Theory and Decision*, 18 (1985), 87–98. For his defence of a truth-theoretical approach to semantics, see 'Truth and Meaning', in *Inquiries into Truth and Interpretation*, 17–36.

[56] The thought is that for a unified theory to be constructible one must begin with preferences with respect to the truth of descriptive sentences; and one must think of the explanatory primitives, in the first instance, in terms of differing attitudes (wants true, holds true) towards the very same (descriptive) sentences.

From the perspective of the radical interpreter, it is wholly *un*surprising that the very evaluative sentences that serve to express desires provide the content-clauses for sentences used to attribute explicitly evaluative beliefs, and serve to express those beliefs. There is no illusion in the thought of moral beliefs, but only in the thought that such beliefs are, at bottom, like descriptive ones.

On this approach to empirical semantics, understanding the primitive evaluative predicates in such sentences requires both a grasp of their syntactic similarities to other predicates and attention to their role in expressing psychological states that are at bottom, or basically, desires. In securing that understanding, one incorporates, in a non-metaphorical but systematic way, considerations that have fueled so-called projectivist readings of Hume.[57] And—here acknowledging the differences in substantive truth in the two cases—one must take into account differences in the procedures for ascertaining truth and falsity for descriptive sentences expressive of (descriptive) beliefs, on the one hand, and for evaluative sentences expressive of desires, on the other. One must not confound what constitutes truth in the case of *desire-expressing* truths with what constitutes the truth of (descriptive) belief-expressing ones.

Such an *attenuated* moral conativism—*assuming* it capable of deploying in cogent fashion its contrast of the differing conditions constitutive of truth—appears to accommodate, in convincing fashion, the cognitivist intuitions embedded in talk of evaluative belief and truth that Hume has, for the most part, simply ignored.[58] Of course, it is a form of moral conativism quite different from Hume's own. If resting, just as Hume's moral conativism does, on an inquiry into the explanation of action, it incorporates as part of that inquiry a study of language. With its introduction of alternative characterizations, it displays none of Hume's own atomist and introspectionist inhibitions in its theorizing about psycho-

---

[57] See the references to Blackburn and Mackie in n. 42, above.

[58] This attenuated conativist theory is Davidsonian in inspiration but not obviously—certainly not explicitly—Davidson's own. If suggested by his work on the unified theory of meaning and action, it goes past anything Davidson explicitly says both in its argument for taking characterizations as desires (rather than as explicitly evaluative beliefs) as explanatorily fundamental, and in its treatment of the differently substantive character of truth for descriptive and for evaluative sentences. In setting out this attenuated theory, I have been inattentive to the affections, and to the boundary between moral and other desires. In articulating the tasks that, in the present context, the attenuated theory is designed to perform, I have been influenced by Wright's *Truth and Objectivity* and 'Truth in Ethics'. For an attempt to employ a truth-theoretical approach to semantics to forward moral cognitivism, rather than moral conativism, see Platts, *Ways of Meaning*, especially 243–63, and 'Moral Reality and the End of Desire'.

logical states. Its legitimization, within an essentially conativist frame-work, of talk of explicitly evaluative beliefs, and of their truth, sets it quite apart from Hume's theory. So does its rejection of an assumption Hume shares with his traditional (and his modern) cognitivist opponent, the assumption that moral cognitivism follows from either of two equivalent claims: that moral judgements are legitimately characterizable as moral beliefs; and that they are expressible in evaluative sentences that can be true or false. From the perspective of this attenuated, but none the less genuine, moral conativism moral judgements are properly characterizable as moral beliefs, to be sure, but they are at bottom—and so, at least for certain purposes, can better be characterized as—moral desires. And the truths expressed when using explicitly evaluative sentences are, at bottom, desire-expressing ones.

To adopt such an attenuated theory is to compromise the interdict against double direction of fit that, on Hume's behalf, we have deployed in setting out his argument for moral conativism: it is to allow a single non-compound psychological state to have both truth-conditions—when it is characterized as an evaluative belief—and satisfaction-conditions—when it is characterized as a desire.[59] This is, however, consistent with endorsement of a *revised* interdict that, while not Humean, appears to capture much, at least, of the intuitive force of Hume's own doctrine. In revised form, the interdict rules out a single non-compound psychological state's being related to truth in *both* of the substantive ways that we have distinguished. It bars a non-compound psychological state's being related to truth both in the way that a state also characterizable as a desire is, and in the way a (descriptive) belief is. In this way it registers a recognition that for evaluative beliefs the concept of fitting the world can get no serious grip.

To substitute this revised interdict against double direction of fit for Hume's unrevised interdict is, if surprisingly, not wholly to subvert the latter's contribution to Hume's all-in argument for his expanded moral conativism. Understood not as firmly entrenched assumption but as a re-buttable presumption, his unrevised interdict would still enable Hume to display the explanatory inadequacies of standard, and of standardly vari-ant, forms of moral cognitivism. It would enable him to advance the dis-cussion of moral cognitivism to the point at which an attenuated form of that theory—a form of moral cognitivism that itself employs a doctrine

---

[59] It does not, of course, allow a single *belief*—or a single *desire*—to have both truth-conditions and satisfaction-conditions.

of alternative descriptions of a single non-compound psychological state—
can be seen, on independent grounds, to be insupportable.[60] Even if viewed
only as a rebuttable presumption, Hume's unrevised interdict would have
a substantive part to play in what we have seen to be a many-stranded
argument designed to display moral conativism's ability to best its
cognitivist competitors in the explanation of the phenomena. Taken in
this way, it is only when one attempts to go past the point at which Hume
himself—neglecting language—stopped, that one perhaps finds compelling reason to revise it.[61]

---

[60] See Chap. 3, Sect. 4, the very end.

[61] For an effort to *sustain* the unrevised interdict against double direction of fit, see
Smith, 'The Humean Theory of Motivation', 55–8.

5

From Moral Desire to Convention

Specifically moral desires, just as the partial desires of which they are impartial variants, are *person-implicating*: their contents make essential reference to the actions and qualities of human persons. More narrowly, they are *mind-implicating*: their contents make essential reference to the mind-displaying actions and qualities—the conative characteristics, the traits, the intellectual talents and abilities—of such individuals. Among the mind-displaying features with which moral desires are concerned are, then, the desires that prompt human actions. From the moral point of view, there are certain desires that one wants individuals to have, certain desires that one would have govern their actions; for example, the desire Hume terms benevolence. Some moral desires, that is to say, are *desire-implicating* desires.

Within the framework of Hume's expanded moral conativism, it follows that some propositional moral affections are likewise desire-implicating ones. Within that framework, of course, *all* propositional moral affections presuppose moral desires. Additionally, however, *some* propositional moral affections—those consequent upon the satisfaction or non-satisfaction of desire-implicating moral desires—are themselves desire-implicating. Having the impartial moral desire that individuals have and act from benevolence one is (impartially) pleased that a given individual has that desire and acts accordingly.

Given Hume's thin theory of corrected sympathy, and its contribution to his theory of impartial moral desires, some of the *partial* desires with which one sympathizes must also be desire-implicating desires, must have contents that make essential reference to the desires of human persons. Some partial desires, as we have remarked, are person-implicating, but not all are. Some of these partial person-implicating desires are desire-implicating. Similar things must be said of partial propositional affections.

Desire-implicating moral desires make reference, in their contents, to the *non-moral* desires of the individuals with whom they are concerned: they are, after all, directed to the partial desires of those individuals. These non-moral desires are of two kinds, *natural* desires and *artificial* desires.

Artificial desires require the presence of conventions; natural desires do not. Desire-implicating moral desires concerned with natural desires play the central structural role in Hume's theory of the so-called natural virtues (including, for example, the virtue of benevolence). Those concerned with artificial desires play that structural role in his theory of what he terms the artificial virtues (including, to take the chief example, the virtue of justice).

Attention to this complex taxonomy, and in particular to the theoretically central conception of desire-implicating moral desires, assists in the understanding of a dense and difficult argument Hume deploys at *Treatise*, III. ii. 1 ('Justice, whether a natural or artificial virtue'). That argument (hereafter, 'the Artificiality Argument') proceeds from consideration of the desire-implicating character of (some) moral desires, through defence of the claim that the implicated desires must (with a qualification to be registered later) be non-moral ones, to the thesis that justice is an artificial virtue. It moves from an examination of the conditions on desire-implicating moral desires to the thesis that moral desires concerned with matters of justice presuppose the existence of complex human conventions. Reflection on the content of (some) moral desires, when joined to reflection on the non-moral desires that do, or can, prompt action in accordance with rules governing property, say, or sexual conduct, leads to the conclusion that moral obligations concerning justice (and sexual conduct) rest on human conventions that in turn rest on the non-moral desires of the participants. In this way the Artificiality Argument sets the stage for Hume's elaborate naturalistic explication, at *Treatise*, III. ii. 2–6, of the non-moral and moral claims that the rules of justice make on human conduct. 'I . . . shall endeavour', he writes, 'to defend . . . [the] opinion [that justice is an artificial, not a natural, virtue] by a short, and, I hope, convincing argument, before I examine the nature of the artifice, from which the sense of that virtue is derived' (*T* 477).

Daunted, perhaps, by the difficulties that stand in the way of interpreting and assessing the Artificiality Argument, most commentators have neglected it.[1] To do that, however, is to neglect Hume's elaboration of

---

[1] The results achieved by those commentators who *have* attended closely to *Treatise*, III. ii. 1, have not been encouraging. Mackie examines Hume's argument for the artificiality of justice in *Hume's Moral Theory*, 76–82; Harrison does the same in *Hume's Theory of Justice* (Oxford, 1981), 1–23. Mackie, having described Hume's argument as 'complicated and difficult' (77), fails to produce an interpretation that both provides Hume with a coherent view and employs only principles that Hume accepts. In his more miscellaneous examination of Hume's argument, Harrison gives no very explicit account of its structure; and the theses of importance that he does attribute to Hume do not, it seems, promise much in the way of a

some of the most central claims in his moral psychology, including his emphasis on the centrality, and the action-explanatory role, of moral desires and his specifications of the person-implicating character of moral sentiments. It is also to be poorly placed to appreciate his subtle constructive treatment of the connections between convention and adoption of the moral point of view.

A terminological point will assist our examination of the Artificiality Argument. When characterizing desires, Hume uses the term 'natural' in two very different senses. In the first, a natural desire is any *non-moral* one (*T* 475 n., 498). In the second, a natural desire is one that does not rest on convention, and so is *not*, in Hume's usage, *artificial*. In the Artificiality Argument's first part, Hume contends that desire-implicating moral desires implicate natural—that is to say, non-moral—desires. In the course of its second part he distinguishes two types of desire-implicating moral desires. Moral desires of one of these types implicate *natural* non-moral desires, desires that do not require conventions. Moral desires of the other of these types implicate *artificial* non-moral desires, desires that require the presence of conventions.

1. MORAL DESIRES AS DESIRE-IMPLICATING

Hume presents the Artificiality Argument in full at *Treatise*, III. ii. 1, and offers a compressed, more specialized, version at *Treatise*, III. ii. 5 ('Of the obligation of promises').[2] He states, as its conclusion: 'justice is an artificial, and not a natural virtue' (*T* 526). He employs, in its first part, the frequently emphasized 'principle' that 'all virtuous actions derive their merit only from virtuous motives, and are consider'd merely as signs of those motives' (*T* 478). (In the words of the first *Enquiry*: 'actions are objects of our moral sentiment, so far only as they are indications of the internal character, passions, and affections', *E* 99.) He employs, that is to say, the principle that certain moral sentiments are desire-implicating in the sense we have introduced: they make essential reference, in their contents, to the desires of the agents, actual or prospective, whose actions

path to Hume's ostensible conclusion. (David Gauthier's helpful 'Artificial Virtues and the Sensible Knave', *Hume Studies*, 18 (1992), 401–27, focuses on issues pertinent only to the second part of the Artificiality Argument, issues discussed in Sect. 2, below.)

[2] Hume supplements the Artificiality Argument with a series of 'new arguments' (*T* 526) at *Treatise*, III. ii. 6 ('Some farther reflexions concerning justice and injustice').

they concern.[3] And he argues, in this first part of the Artificiality Argument, that the implicated desires must be non-moral ones.

As stated, Hume's principle ranges over both moral desires and propositional moral affections. Not surprisingly, then, he writes inclusively of one's regarding an action as '*virtuous, or morally good*', of having 'regard' to 'the virtue of the action', or to its 'merit', or to its 'moral obligation'. And he takes the moral sentiments in question to include ones in which one has '*the sense of* . . . [an action's] *morality*', a 'sense of duty', a 'sense of morality or duty', a 'sense of duty and obligation' (*T* 478–9). If inclusive with respect both to moral desires and propositional moral affections, however, it is restrictive with respect to the content of these moral sentiments. Ignoring intellectual talents and abilities, as well as such traits as courage or patience, it fastens on the conative characteristics—that is to say, on the desires—that in fact prompt, or that might prompt, an agent's actions. If limited to the case of favourable moral sentiments, Hume's principle may be stated as follows:

P1 Moral sentiments directed towards actions are directed towards those actions as prompted by virtuous desires.

P1 incorporates, it will be clear, a narrower principle that focuses specifically on moral desires:

P2 Moral desires directed towards actions are directed towards those actions as prompted by virtuous desires.

For a given individual, of course, P2 pertains not only to her impartial moral desires concerning the actions of others but also to her impartial moral desires concerning her own actions. P2 has implications, that is to say, for the central case of moral agency, the case where moral desirer and moral agent are the same.[4]

P1 and P2 are straightforward consequences of the expanded moral

---

[3] Later in the *Treatise* he takes as 'self-evident' (and as of 'the utmost importance') the perhaps broader principle: 'If any *action* be either virtuous or vicious, 'tis only as a sign of some quality or character' (*T* 575). If this 'self-evident' principle *is* broader, it is simply the claim that moral sentiments from a certain range are *mind*-implicating: they make reference to some or other mental quality, perhaps conative, perhaps intellectual. Perhaps, however, it is simply a less perspicuous rendering of the claim that moral sentiments from a certain range are, specifically, *desire*-implicating.

[4] As stated P1 and P2 can seem to allow explicitly evaluative content to moral sentiments, including moral desires. References to virtuous desires must, however, be read as references to desires that are valued when one adopts the moral point of view, and so are desires that one impartially desires people to have, desires that one approves of their having.

conativism that we attributed to Hume in Chapter 4.[5] They also capture, Hume claims, commitments revealed in the illustrative cases he considers as the Artificiality Argument opens.

The first case concerns 'praise and approbation' (*T* 477). ''Tis evident', Hume writes, 'that when we praise any actions, we regard only the motives that produced them, and consider the actions as signs or indications of certain principles in the mind and temper' (ibid.). Being pleased by the consequences of an agent's action need require, of course, no reference to his intentions in acting, and so no reference to the desires that prompted that action: he may well, quite unintentionally, have forwarded one's own interests. But propositional affections of a specifically moral sort must— being mind-implicating sentiments—attend to those desires.

'After the same manner', Hume writes, 'when we ... blame a person for not performing [some morally obligatory action] ... we always suppose, that one in that situation shou'd be influenced by the proper motive of that action, and we esteem it vicious in him to be regardless of it' (*T* 477). The negative moral affection (the state of esteeming the agent's mind-displaying omission vicious) makes essential reference to the agent's motives or desires. The presupposed moral desire (the state represented as the supposition that agents ought to be motivated by the 'proper motive' in question) does so as well. Consider the 'proper motive' of parental benevolence. One thinks that parents ought to have, and be moved to action by, that motive or desire. One has, that is to say, an impartial moral desire that parents have that motive and act accordingly. The consequent moral affections one feels must in turn correspond, in their content, to that of the moral desire they presuppose. To acknowledge that a father's action has in fact benefited his child is not necessarily, then, to acknowledge that he has done what he ought to do. The beneficent effect may well have been just the opposite of what he intended. Though intentionally beneficent, he may have acted as he did only to avoid the attention of the courts. Such situations, though involving beneficent action on the part of a parent, do not suffice to prompt those favourable moral affections that are keyed to parental benevolence. Emphasizing the critical role of motivation, Hume insists that a father may well have done what, morally, one wants of him even though he has failed to act in a way that in fact benefited his child. Perhaps, moved by a concern for his child's well-being, he took steps that—nature being grudging—proved ineffective. Perhaps he was simply unable to act. As Hume remarks: 'If we find, upon

---

[5] We shall consider further aspects of the person-implicating character of moral desires and affections in Chap. 7.

enquiry, that the virtuous motive was still powerful over his breast, 'tho check'd in its operation by some circumstances unknown to us, we retract our blame, and have the same esteem for him, as if he had actually perform'd the action, which we require of him' (*T* 477–8; compare *T* 584).[6]

Moral desires are impartial. Assuming their conditions met, one's moral desires impose obligations on oneself just as on any other. If they are desire-implicating they are so with respect to one's own case as much as to the case of some other agent. They are desire-implicating even when, as moral agent, one views one's own prospective actions through the lens of one's moral desires. Hume acknowledges this implication of P2 when, adapting the Artificiality Argument for use in the special case of obligations to keep one's promises, he attends to our thinking of an action as 'requir'd of us as our duty' (*T* 518). To think of an action in this way is to think of ourselves as required to have, and to act from, a given (virtuous) motive or desire. It is to have an impartial moral desire to have, and to act from, the virtuous desire in question. A person who thinks parents ought to act towards their children from the motive of parental benevolence, and who recognizes that she is herself a parent, is committed to thinking that she herself ought to act towards her children from that motive. Impartially desiring any parent to act from such a desire she is committed to desiring that she herself act from that desire. When acting specifically out of a sense of the obligatoriness of parental benevolence, that is the impartial desire-implicating desire from which she acts. P2 applies even when moral desirer and moral agent are identical.

It must be noted—parenthetically—that his notion of duties to act from virtuous motives can be squared with Hume's views about the scope of one's freedom to act. Hume does think that one's motives or desires are not directly within one's control: ''tis certain', he writes, 'we can naturally no more change our own sentiments, than the motions of the heavens' (*T* 517). And he seems committed to *some* version of the claim that 'ought' implies 'can'. At least he explains the fact that, in determining obligations, we defer to the norms revealed by common human conduct by saying: 'Being . . . acquainted with the nature of man, we expect not any impossibilities from him' (*T* 602).[7] It is clear, however, that P2 can coun-

---

[6] To be sure, the matter is a good deal more complicated than Hume's brief remarks concerning his second case suggest. A more carefully crafted characterization would need to consider the bearing of competition amongst moral considerations, and of the presence of culpable ignorance or ineptness, among other things. Introducing these considerations would not, however, affect Hume's central contention.

[7] See the discussion of Hume's 'undoubted maxim' UM, just below.

tenance judgements of obligation geared to desires the moral desirer does not himself possess: the implicated desires need only be those humans generally possess.[8] And Hume's doctrine of freedom does leave room for indirect strategies designed for the acquisition of desires or motives. Indeed, he thinks a recognition of one's duties provides one with reason for acquiring, and so perhaps prompts steps towards one's acquiring, motives one thinks one ought to have (*T* 479). In the cases envisaged an agent *can* perform the 'external' (*T* 477) action (he *can* act in such a way as to benefit his children); what he cannot (yet) do is act from the motive of parental benevolence, and so he cannot (yet) do his duty. Of course, a benevolent parent *can* do what duty requires; his sense of duty provides additional motive for doing what he is naturally motivated to do.[9]

Given P2, desire-implicating moral desires are second-order desires: they are desires that agents have, and so act from, certain (virtuous) desires. What renders the implicated desires *virtuous* ones? This is not the place to set out Hume's full answer to this question. We have seen something of what he says in answer in Chapter 4, Section 1; we shall see more in Chapter 6. Here it must suffice to notice a condition on the virtuousness of the implicated desires that Hume makes much of in the course of the Artificiality Argument, and that must be carefully distinguished from P1 and P2.

Early in the Artificiality Argument Hume introduces an 'undoubted maxim': '*no action can be virtuous, or morally good, unless there be in human nature some motive to produce it*' (*T* 479). Arguing for the artificiality of the obligation to keep promises he says much the same again: 'No action can be requir'd of us as our duty, unless there be implanted in human nature some actuating passion or motive, capable of producing the action' (*T* 518). The maxim lays down a necessary condition on the *virtuousness* of the desires to which moral sentiments must, in accordance with P1 and P2, make reference. In Hume's view, moral assessment, not being concerned with impossible standards (*T* 602), looks to what may reasonably be expected, in the way of useful or agreeable motivation, of human agents. Determinations of what may reasonably be expected in turn rest (at least in large part) on facts about the desires human agents tend to have, and about the relative strengths those desires tend to possess. Stating what he terms a 'corollary' of the central thesis for which he argues in the Artificiality Argument's first part, Hume says:

[8] See below for Hume's discussion of two cases of this kind.
[9] We return to many of the issues raised in this paragraph when we consider Hume's views about moral agents in Chap. 7.

we always consider the *natural* and *usual* force of the passions, when we determine concerning vice and virtue; and if the passions depart very much from the
common measures on either side, they are always disapprov'd as vicious. A man
naturally loves his children better than his nephews, his nephews better than his
cousins, his cousins better than strangers, where every thing else is equal. Hence
arise our common measures of duty, in preferring the one to the other. Our sense
of duty always follows the common and natural course of our passions. (*T* 483–4;
compare *T* 488–9, 518–19)

A given agent may, as we shall see, fail to possess a desire that is in this
sense 'implanted in human nature'.

A number of questions can be raised about Hume's attempt to tailor
the virtuousness of desires to empirically determined human proclivities. Does it rule out thoughts of moral ideals, or of supererogation? Are
only common motives, at common levels, to be construed as virtuous? It
seems that Hume could, if needed, accommodate the recognition of ideals,
and of desirable actions beyond the call of duty, by restricting his maxim's
scope to judgements of obligation. Does his maxim comport with recognition of the differing roles that the several virtues play in different—and
differently desirable—constellations of virtues? There is no reason to think
it does not. Does its gearing of obligation to inclination make a sense of
obligation otiose? No, as our discussion of convention and moral motivation in Chapter 6 will make plain.[10]

Hume's 'undoubted maxim' is not to be confused with his 'principle'
P1 (or with the narrower P2): it concerns the character of the implicated
desires to which P1 and P2 refer. It plays, as we shall see, an important
role in the second part of the Artificiality Argument. With misgivings
about its scope already registered, this 'undoubted maxim' may be stated
in summary fashion as follows:

UM A desire is a virtuous desire only if it is a desire that human
agents commonly have (and only if it is had in its usual strength).

A desire is virtuous, we may say, only if it is a *normal* desire (and only if at
normal strength). When combined with P1 (and, of course, P2) UM gives
the result that favourable moral sentiments directed towards actions make
essential reference to normal human desires or motives.

This normality condition is a necessary, not a sufficient, one: even if

---

[10] For some discussion of such questions concerning Hume's 'maxim', see Harrison,
Hume's Theory of Justice, 2–5, 14–15, 18, 22.

common the motives of envy, small-mindedness, and malice would be virtuous only if, when considered from the impartial standpoint of morality, they were useful or agreeable to the person who has them, or to others.[11]

Hume claims to 'conclude' from P1 (and so from P2) that 'the first virtuous motive, which bestows a merit on any action, can never be a regard to the virtue of that action, but must be some other natural motive or principle' (*T* 478). 'A virtuous motive', he writes, 'must precede the regard to the virtue; and 'tis impossible, that the virtuous motive and the regard to the virtue can be the same' (*T* 480). The point concerns not just a 'regard to virtue' but also a 'sense of duty' (*T* 518), a 'regard to ... moral obligation' (*T* 479), a 'regard to ... honesty' (*T* 480), a 'sense of ... morality' (*T* 479).

The 'virtuous motives' or 'first virtuous motives' to which Hume here refers are the implicated desires to which the moral sentiments that fall within the scope of P1 and P2 make essential reference. Hume's 'conclusion' is that these implicated desires cannot themselves be specifically moral desires but must be 'natural'—which is to say, *non-moral*—desires. Equivalently, they must be partial, not impartial, desires. They must, of course, be *virtuous* non-moral or partial desires, but that is just to say that they must, when judged from the vantage-point of morality, be viewed as desirable desires. And that in turn is just to say that they are desires that, when adopting the impartial point of view of morality, one desires agents to have. Such virtuous natural or non-moral desires as benevolence, pity, or parental affection can serve as the requisite implicated desires. The specifically moral desires that constitute judgements of moral obligation, or of moral desirability, cannot. With P1 as premise Hume's 'conclusion' is, to a first approximation:

C1 Moral sentiments directed towards actions are directed towards those actions as prompted by (virtuous) non-moral desires.

With a view to the narrower principle P2 his 'conclusion' is, again to a first approximation:

C2 Moral desires directed towards actions are directed towards those actions as prompted by (virtuous) non-moral desires.

---

[11] Harrison, *Hume's Theory of Justice*, 2, 18, 22, apparently interprets Hume to intend the normality condition as a *sufficient* condition for a virtuous motive. He writes of 'Hume's view that a motive is virtuous *if* it is one that is usual for human beings to have' (2, emphasis added).

Given UM, of course, the virtuous non-moral desires in question must be normal ones.[12]

Is it Hume's view that specifically moral desires can *never* be the implicated desires that, given P1 and P2, moral sentiments demand? Does he perhaps think that specifically moral desires cannot fit the bill because they cannot themselves be *virtuous* desires? Bracketing the first question for the moment, let us consider the second. There is, it seems, no compelling reason to think that Hume denies the virtuousness of specifically moral desires. On the face of it, he holds that specifically moral desires meet the normality condition UM imposes on virtuous desires: 'the sentiments of morality', he writes, 'are so rooted in our constitution and temper, that without entirely confounding the human mind by disease or madness, 'tis impossible to extirpate and destroy them' (*T* 474). Presumably he also holds that specifically moral desires meet the disjunctive condition of being useful or agreeable to the desiring agent or to others. That being so, it is at least open to Hume to view moral desires as themselves virtuous. He must, it seems, have some other reason for denying that specifically moral desires can be the implicated desires P1 and P2 demand.

'To suppose', Hume writes, 'that the mere regard to the virtue of the action, may be the first motive, which produc'd the action, and render'd it virtuous, is to reason in a circle' (*T* 478). To suppose, that is to say, that a specifically moral desire may be the implicated desire that P1 and P2 demand, and that renders the agent's action morally desirable, is to 'reason in a circle'. Hume thinks the circularity will be clear to one reflecting on cases involving justice: ''tis a plain fallacy to say, that a virtuous motive is requisite to render an action honest, and at the same time that a regard to the honesty is the motive of the action' (*T* 480). It is plainly fallacious, that is to say, to allow a specifically moral desire with respect to the performance of just actions to be the implicated desire that P1 and P2 demand in such cases, the implicated desire that—when viewing matters of justice from the moral point of view—one must desire agents to have and to act from. Presumably, the same fallacy occurs if one allows a specifically moral desire to play the role of implicated desire when the moral issue is a matter not of justice but of benevolence. Given P1 (and P2), to

---

[12] That the desires in question are *virtuous* is, of course, perfectly compatible with their being *non-moral*. Virtuous desires contrast with non-virtuous, perhaps with vicious, ones. Moral desires—desires with the generality and impartiality integral to the moral point of view—contrast with non-moral desires, whether virtuous or vicious, whose content is partial.

deny C1 (or C2) is, in Hume's view, to 'reason in a circle' and to commit a 'plain fallacy'.

What, precisely, is the fallacy? Where, precisely, is the alleged circularity in allowing specifically moral, rather than non-moral, desires to provide the implicated desires P1 and P2 require? Hume writes: 'Before we can have such a regard [i.e. a regard to the virtue of the action], the action must be really virtuous; and this virtue must be deriv'd from some virtuous motive: And consequently the virtuous motive must be different from the regard to the virtue of the action' (*T* 478).[13] Granted, the moral sentiment Hume calls 'regard to the virtue of the action' must make reference to the virtuous desire that prompts the action. This, plainly, is what P1 requires. But if (as suggested above) a specifically moral desire can itself be a virtuous desire, P1's requirements would seem to be met if one has a specifically moral sentiment directed towards some action an agent performs, that action having been performed from a specifically moral desire to act in the way in question. Where, once again, is the fallacy or circularity, the avoidance of which requires commitment to C1 and C2?

Perhaps Hume's point is this. Given P2, the *implicated* specifically moral desire just countenanced must in its turn make reference, via its content, to a virtuous desire. Suppose *that* virtuous desire were itself a moral desire. Given P2 *that* moral desire must make reference, via its content, to a virtuous desire. *That* virtuous desire, in its turn, must, if it is a specifically moral desire, implicate yet *another* virtuous desire. Provided specifically moral desires are allowed, quite generally, to serve as the implicated desires P2 demands for any specifically moral desire, one can generate an indefinitely extended series of embedded references to specifically moral desires. While adhering to P2, one can interrupt the generation of such a series of references to specifically moral desires only by requiring *some* implicated desires to be non-moral ones. Since non-moral desires are not themselves subject to P2, they do not, it will be clear, automatically generate reference to still other desire-implicating desires.

Without C2, that is to say, one could, following the requirements of P2, have a moral desire that children be cared for by their parents out of a specifically moral desire that children be cared for by their parents out of a specifically moral desire that children be cared for by their parents, and so on. For the case where initial moral desirer and agent are identical

[13] This bit of the Artificiality Argument is sufficiently important to be repeated at *T* 478, and again at *T* 480 and *T* 518.

one could have an agent who desires that he attend to the needs of his children out of an impartial desire that he attend to his children's needs out of an impartial desire that is in turn an impartial desire that he attend to their needs, etc., etc. He thinks he ought to act from the thought that he ought to act from the thought that he ought to act, and so on and on. With the introduction of C_2, however, the series can come to a (very early) halt. One has a moral desire that children be cared for by their parents, that care being motivated by the parents' parental benevolence. For the case where one is both moral desirer and prospective agent, one impartially desires that one care for one's own children from the promptings of parental benevolence.

It is *not* clear that the line of argument just sketched does in fact constitute Hume's own reason for endorsing C_1 and C_2. It provides at best *an* intelligible rendering of what he might have had in mind when writing of fallacy and circularity if C_1 and C_2 be denied. Reading Hume's argument in this way does, however, have a number of signal advantages. It does not require him to hold that specifically moral desires are not themselves morally desirable. It assigns a perfectly clear role to the principles, P_1 and P_2, from which Hume claims to 'conclude' to C_1 and C_2. It serves, incidentally, to highlight the roles that P_2 and C_2—the 'principle' and the 'conclusion' concerned specifically with moral desires, rather than with moral sentiments generally—are given to play. These are surely virtues in an area where convincing interpretation has proved uncommonly difficult to come by.

Allowance for the virtuousness of specifically moral desires calls for a modest modification of C_1 and C_2. Each of these conclusions requires, we might better say, that the relevant moral sentiments be directed towards actions *either* as prompted by (virtuous) non-moral desires *or* as prompted by (virtuous) moral desires that themselves make reference to (virtuous) non-moral desires. Perhaps Hume's talk of the '*first* virtuous motive' (*T* 478, emphasis added) marks his recognition of the need for the suggested modification. Having noted that need, however, we may continue—in this, sticking closely to Hume's text—to render his conclusions from P_1 and P_2 as C_1 and C_2.

Perhaps uneasy about the intricacy of the argument on which it rests, Hume remarks that C_1 is not 'merely a metaphysical subtilty' for it 'enters into all our reasonings in common life' (*T* 478). Further reflection on sentiments of approbation, blame, and duty (the three sentiments Hume considers when defending P_1 and P_2), and of the reasons offered in their support, reveals, he claims, our commitment to C_1, 'tho' perhaps we may not be able to place it in such distinct philosophical terms' (ibid.). If these reflections add nothing essential to Hume's case for C1, they at least help confirm its status as his conclusion. 'We blame a father for neglecting his child', he writes, 'because it shews a want of natural affection, which is the duty of every parent' (ibid.). He then continues: 'Were not natural affection a duty, the care of children cou'd not be a duty; and 'twere impossible we cou'd have the duty in our eye in the attention we give to our offspring.' In such cases, he says, we 'suppose a motive to the action distinct from a sense of duty'. Consider the non-moral desire of humanity or benevolence. We take that desire to 'bestow ... a merit on' a man's actions; and '[a] regard to this merit is ... a secondary consideration, and deriv'd from the antecedent principle of humanity, which is meritorious and laudable' (ibid.).[14]

C2 requires an agent's specifically moral desires to make reference to (virtuous) natural or non-moral desires; it does not, however, in general require an agent with specifically moral desires to have (and so be capable of actions caused by) the virtuous non-moral or natural desire that some specifically moral desire 'supposes' (T 518). Thus Hume can say: 'But may not the sense of morality or duty produce an action, without any other motive? I answer, It may: But this is no objection to the present doctrine' (T 479). A man can both recognize an obligation to be motivated by (and so act from) parental benevolence, and be moved by that sense of obligation to act in ways beneficial to his child, and yet not be moved by parental benevolence: such an agent acts 'merely out of regard to its [i.e. the action's] moral obligation' (ibid.).

Hume describes two such cases. In the first, the agent hopes that, by emulating an affectionate parent so far as 'external performance' (T 477) goes, he will come to have the desire of parental benevolence and so be and do (thus far) what he judges he is morally obliged to be and do. He hopes, that is to say, that he will thereby come to be and do what he impartially desires that he be and do. The agent, 'feel[ing] his heart devoid of that principle [i.e. in our illustration, parental benevolence], may hate himself upon that account, and may perform the action [i.e. the external performance] without the motive [i.e. parental benevolence], from a certain sense of duty, in order to acquire by practice, that virtuous principle [i.e. parental benevolence]' (T 479).

The second case is similar to the first, save that the agent, moved by his recognition of a moral obligation, is concerned not to change, but to de-

[14] Humanity, as introduced here, must not be identified with the fundamental moral desire that Hume calls 'humanity' in the second *Enquiry*.

ceive himself about, his conative character. He hopes to 'disguise to him-self, as much as possible, his want of it [i.e. parental benevolence]' (ibid.). An essential ingredient in this self-deception, in Hume's handling of it, is that, if successful, it weakens the agent's purchase on the truths enunci-ated as P1 and P2. 'Actions are at first only consider'd as signs of motives' (ibid.): the agent subscribes to P1 and P2. 'But 'tis usual, in this case, as in all others, to fix our attention on the signs, and neglect, in some measure, the thing signify'd' (ibid.): the agent's hold on P1 and P2 weakens, as it must if he is to delude himself into thinking he has done his duty.

C1 and C2 apply not only to moral sentiments concerned with the so-called natural virtues but also to those concerned with the virtues Hume terms 'artificial'. Hume is explicit about their application to cases of ar-tificial virtue (as he says, to 'the present case', T 479) when he remarks on one's duty to repay loans. What '*reason or motive*', he asks, has one to make repayment (ibid.)? One may have a specifically moral reason for doing so: 'my regard to justice, and abhorrence of villainy and knavery, are suffi-cient reasons for me, if I have the least grain of honesty, or sense of duty and obligation' (ibid.). Given C2, however, this specifically moral desire implicates a non-moral (but virtuous) one, a desire other than 'regard to the honesty of the action' (T 480). The need to specify this non-moral desire is the point of Hume's emphasized question: '*Wherein consists this honesty and justice, which you find in restoring a loan, and abstaining from the property of others?*' (ibid.).

Their very generality can seem to undercut any contribution C1 and C2 might be thought to make to an argument that some, but not all, of the virtues are artificial. Their intended contribution is, however, obvi-ous. As we shall see, Hume argues that moral sentiments pertaining to obligations of honesty, promise-keeping, and the like (pertaining, that is to say, to the so-called artificial virtues) can meet the conditions C1 and C2 impose *only* given the presence of 'an artifice or contrivance, which arises from the circumstances and necessities of mankind' (T 477). The virtues in question are artificial, he maintains, precisely because of the artificiality, or the convention-presupposing character, of the non-moral desires to which the moral desires in question make essential reference. ''Tis requisite', he writes, 'to find some motive to acts of justice and hon-esty, distinct from our regard to the honesty; and in this lies the great difficulty' (T 480). The requirement, of course, is the one C1 and C2 lay down. The difficulty—this is Hume's point—would prove to be an im-possibility were we not able to tie the implicated non-moral desires to human conventions. To talk of this difficulty is, however, to anticipate the second part of the Artificiality Argument.

2. MORAL DESIRE AND CONVENTION

The theoretical task that C_1 and C_2 set is that of identifying the non-moral desires that the chief kinds of moral sentiments—and so the chief kinds of moral desires—make essential reference to in their contents. Hume takes it that the task poses no special difficulties when the moral sentiments in question pertain to benevolence, say, or to gratitude, or to other of what he calls the natural virtues. In their case, the implicated desires are readily recognizable, are normal (and thus accord with his 'undoubted maxim' UM), are unproblematically characterizable in terms of their agreeableness or utility, either for the individual in question or for others.

The problematic cases are those of moral sentiments that pertain to matters of justice, and to certain other similarly complex constraints on human conduct. Agents have specifically moral desires concerning the avoidance of theft, or the repayment of loans, or the keeping of promises—to cite the examples Hume uses—and they are, at times, moved to act accordingly. What, in the case of *such* moral desires, are the implicated non-moral desires that C_1 and C_2 require? Three candidates suggest themselves: 'self-love' or 'a concern for our private interest' (T 480);[15] 'public benevolence' (T 482) or 'the *regard to publick interest*' (T 480); and '*private benevolence*, or a *regard to the interests of the party concern'd*' (T 482). Taking each candidate in turn, Hume pursues a series of interrelated questions. Is the candidate non-moral desire a desire human agents actually have? Is it a normal desire in the sense specified in his 'undoubted maxim' UM? Do its claims on conduct correspond to those that acknowledged moral sentiments impose? (Failing any of these conditions it could not, of course, provide the virtuous non-moral desire C_1 and C_2 require.) Is it one that might move an agent to actions of the kind in question even in the absence of a supporting structure of social practices or conventional regularities in behaviour? (If it would not it could not be a natural—in the sense, now, of a non-artificial—desire.)

Hume argues that none of the three candidates is a desire that would

---

[15] Opening the discussion Hume writes not just of 'private interest' but of 'concern for our private interest or reputation'. He proceeds, however, to ignore the question of reputation, and we shall here follow him in this.

move an agent to the requisite actions (avoiding theft, repaying loans, keeping promises) in the absence of conventions. On the assumption that the list of candidates is exhaustive, it follows that any non-moral desires implicated (as C1 and C2 require) by the moral sentiments in question must rest on artifice or convention, and so cannot be natural—cannot be non-artificial—ones. That being so, the moral sentiments in question are themselves *artificial sentiments*, which is to say, they are convention-presupposing ones. And so justice, as Hume typically puts the Artificiality Argument's conclusion, is an artificial virtue. (It is, of course, a genuine virtue none the less: Hume's argument for the artificiality of the moral sentiments in question has no tendency whatever to show them up as ersatz.)

Which of the three candidates is, assuming the presence of appropriate conventions, the non-moral desire that artificial moral sentiments make essential reference to in their contents? Hume argues that neither 'the regard to publick interest' ('public benevolence') nor 'regard to the interests of the party concern'd' ('private benevolence') is fitted for the job. Neither of these is a virtuous desire for neither meets the normality condition that UM imposes. Neither prompts action in ways that correspond to the requirements that artificial moral sentiments set. If the first of these candidates, 'regard to publick interest', is construed as 'love of mankind' it is not even a non-moral desire that humans actually have. If construed more narrowly as 'love for the members of the individual's own community' it is not a non-instrumental non-moral desire that normal desirers have. The second candidate is, even more obviously, not a normal non-instrumental desire. The other candidates having been rejected, it follows that 'a concern for our private interest' ('self-love') is the non-moral desire that, as C1 and C2 require, artificial moral sentiments, whether affections or desires, implicate.[16]

With this map of a very dense part of Hume's text to guide us, let us turn to his examination of each of the candidate non-moral desires he considers.

Can *self-love* be the requisite non-moral desire? If it is, then a normal agent must, quite generally, have a self-interested reason to act as justice requires. (As Hume writes: 'it wou'd follow [on the proposal in question], that wherever that concern ceases, honesty can no longer have place', *T*

---

[16] As we shall see below, what Hume initially characterizes as 'a concern for our private interest' gives way, as the discussion of justice advances, to a combination of private interest and partial benevolence (where the admitted non-moral desire named 'partial benevolence' is not to be confused with the rejected non-moral desire termed 'private benevolence').

480.) In Hume's view, however, self-interest, *if unrestrained*, does not correlate in the needed way with acknowledged claims of justice. "[T]is certain', he writes, 'that self-love, *when it acts at its liberty*, instead of engaging us to honest actions, is the source of all injustice and violence' (ibid., emphasis added). If self-interest is to provide the implicated non-moral desire for moral sentiments concerned with justice, then, some device for 'correcting and restraining the *natural* movements of that appetite' must be introduced (ibid.). To introduce the restraining effects of competing other-regarding desires would, of course, be simply to subvert the projected tie between justice and self-interest. If the projected tie is to be sustained, then, some other source of restraint must be found. Having made this point, Hume quickly turns to an examination of his other candidates.

Can *public benevolence* be the non-moral desire that sentiments of justice presuppose? If *unrestrained*, public benevolence is no better suited to the task than unrestrained self-interest is. More precisely, if a putative public benevolence (a putative non-instrumental concern for the interests of the members of an individual's own society) were not constrained by a framework of appropriate conventions, the actions it would prompt would not correspond to the acknowledged requirements of justice. If considered apart from a setting of social practices, actions such as repaying loans or keeping promises would not correlate, as required, with the public interest. Given suitable conventions, however, such actions would, or so Hume suggests, serve the public interest. He endorses both the negative and the positive claim when writing that 'public interest is not naturally attach'd to the observation of the rules of justice; but is only connected with it, after an artificial convention for the establishment of these rules' (*T* 480). He emphasizes his negative claim when he writes:

A *single act of justice* is frequently contrary to *public interest* ... When a man of merit, of a beneficent disposition, restores a great fortune to a miser, or a seditious bigot, he has acted justly and laudably, but the public is a real sufferer. (*T* 497, initial emphasis added)

Again emphasizing the negative he claims that '*considering each case apart*, it wou'd as often be an instance of humanity to decide contrary to the laws of justice as conformable to them' (*T* 579, emphasis added). *Unrestrained* public benevolence, that is to say, cannot provide the sought-for non-moral desire.[17]

---

[17] Hume adds that in the case of *secret* loans (those both made in secret and to be repaid in secret) justice requires repayment but 'the public is no longer interested in the actions of

Neither, however, can *restrained* public benevolence for that is not, or so Hume claims, a *normal* non-moral motive that correlates, in the way required, with moral sentiments pertaining to justice. Suppose the putative public benevolence to be an individual's non-instrumental concern for the interests of the several members of his own society (a concern for the interests of those individuals towards whom he does or could have the specific obligations that justice imposes). Even given a functioning society, that is not a non-instrumental desire that most members of the society would have and that would prompt them to act as that society's rules of justice require. So, at least, Hume appears to claim when he writes:

experience sufficiently proves, that men, in the ordinary conduct of life, look not so far as the public interest, when they pay their creditors, perform their promises, and abstain from theft, and robbery, and injustice of every kind. That is a motive too remote and too sublime to affect the generality of mankind, and operate with any force in actions so contrary to private interest as are frequently those of justice and common honesty. (*T* 481)

It follows, for Hume, that public benevolence (even when restrained) cannot meet C1's requirements for it is not, in the requisite sense, a *normal* desire and so not one that meets the requirements on *virtuous* non-moral desire.[18] (This is not, of course, to deny that actions of the kinds in question are in fact, within the framework of convention, in the public interest.)

If non-instrumental public benevolence were assumed to be a concern not just for the members of an individual's own society but, far more broadly, for all human beings (Hume writes of 'love of mankind', *T* 481, and of 'regard to the interests of mankind', *T* 482), this line of objection would apply with even greater force. For if Hume is right, there is simply no such non-moral desire. '[T]here is no such passion in human minds', he writes, 'as the love of mankind, merely as such, independent of personal qualities, of services, or of relation to ourself' (*T* 481). To appreciate Hume's point one must advert to his associationist theory of the links

---

the borrower' (*T* 481). The point of the example is obscure. Perhaps, however, this is supposed to be an especially clear example of the gap between obligatory action and public interest *if* the role of convention is ignored.

[18] In remarking on the inefficacy of public benevolence with respect to actions 'so contrary to private interest as are frequently those of justice and common honesty' (*T* 481), Hume is not denying that just actions are in the agent's interest. Here, as elsewhere in the course of the Artificiality Argument, he confusingly fails to make plain that the point concerns actions that are viewed from the vantage-point of *unrestrained* self-interest or of self-interest in isolation from convention.

between love and benevolence. He alludes to that theory when writing 'that man in general, or human nature, is nothing but the object both of love and hatred, and requires some other cause, which by a double relation of impressions and ideas, may excite these passions' (*T* 481–2). Only humans, he holds, are objects of human love and benevolence, but they are objects of these affections only in virtue of some other qualities they possess, qualities that set them apart from (some) others. There is genuine non-instrumental (and non-moral) concern for others, that is to say, but it is an essentially partial benevolence that is normally quite limited in its scope. ''Tis true', Hume writes, 'there is no human ... creature, whose happiness or misery does not, in some measure, affect us, when brought near to us, and represented in lively colours' (*T* 481). But this phenomenon, a product of the workings of sympathy, confirms the point: it is only those thus brought 'near' to us who are objects of non-moral concern. '[P]erhaps a man wou'd be belov'd as such, were we to meet him in the moon' (*T* 482)? But this would not display even a love of *that* man 'merely as such, independent of personal qualities, of services, or of relation to ourself' for in the case imagined the love 'proceeds only from the relation to ourselves' (ibid.). *A fortiori*, the imagined case provides no support for the comprehensive non-moral benevolence (a 'universal affection to mankind', *T* 481) here in question.

It might be suggested that these reflections about love and benevolence undercut Hume's dismissal of non-instrumental public benevolence directed towards the members of an individual's own society. Surely the members of her own society are sufficiently closely 'related' to the agent? Surely the members of her society are the source of 'services' to the agent? After all, it may be said, *their* according with her society's conventions are a condition on the agent's reaping the advantages to be had from living in that society. And so, it may be suggested, the members of her society must be—given Hume's own account of love and benevolence—objects of the agent's non-instrumental concern. Hume himself gives an example, elsewhere in the *Treatise*, that suggests this very possibility:

Suppose ... that two merchants, tho' living in different parts of the world, shou'd enter into co-partnership together, the advantage or loss of one becomes immediately the advantage or loss of his partner, and the same fortune necessarily attends both. Now 'tis evident, that ... love arises from ... [the] union [of their interests]. (*T* 383)

Hume must, it seems, recognize *some* force in this attempt to accord to all the co-operating members of an agent's society the status of those who are, in Hume's expression, the agent's 'nearest friends' (T 492).[19] He could, however, easily recast his claim about public benevolence in terms of normal differences between the degree of an individual's concern for the interests of her 'nearest friends' and the degree of her concern for the others (her more distant friends?) in her society. Whatever be the merits of this suggested reply, the objection itself can do no damage to Hume's case specifically for the artificiality of justice. The suggested extension of the range of an agent's non-moral benevolence *presupposes* the presence of artifice or convention. The agent's more distant friends are friends, so far as they are, simply in virtue of their participation in the social practices constitutive of the society in question.

Is Hume's own constructive doctrine concerning the generality and impartiality of moral sentiments, or his doctrine of corrected sympathy, compatible with his rejection of a 'universal affection to mankind'? Isn't 'humanity', the fundamental moral desire, just such a universal affection? Provided one does not confound specifically moral with non-moral desires, it will be clear that 'humanity' cannot be the *non-moral* desire that C_1 and C_2 call for. In Hume's view, it is plain, the partiality and limited scope of non-moral benevolence is perfectly compatible with the generality and impartiality of the benevolence that is constitutive of the moral point of view.

Hume's third candidate non-moral desire, somewhat misleadingly named, is *private benevolence*. It is not to be confused with 'confin'd generosity' (T 499) or a concern for 'our nearest friends' (T 492). It is not, that is to say, to be confused with the *partial benevolence* that love has as its consequence. It involves 'a *regard to the interests of the party concern'd*' (T 482) in the sense, specifically, of the person to whom a promise has been made, the person who has made the loan that is to be repaid, the person whose property one must refrain from stealing. The concerned party towards whom a given individual has some quite particular obligation (the obligation, say, to repay a particular loan) need not be, and will in general not be, some friend of hers, some person towards whom she feels any partial benevolence. At least typically, the concerned party will be just one of the many members of the individual's society—the one, say, who actually made the loan. Having rejected public benevolence as the needed non-moral desire implicated by moral sentiments concerning justice, Hume remarks, not surprisingly, that private benevolence is 'much less' likely to provide the desire that C_1 and C_2 call for (T 482).

---

[19] We shall examine the generation of increasingly more comprehensive modes of non-moral benevolence in Chap. 6.

Hume's two-pronged argument against private benevolence parallels that directed against public benevolence. Neither unrestrained nor restrained private benevolence fits the theoretical bill. Considered apart from convention, and so as unrestrained, acts of justice are not, quite generally, in the interests of the party concerned:

What if he [the party concerned] be a miser, and can make no use of what I wou'd deprive him of? What if he be a profligate debauchee, and wou'd rather receive harm than benefit from large possessions? (*T* 482)[20]

In any event, normal agents do not quite generally find, in the fact that a person is a 'party concern'd' (a person to whom a promise has been made, say), non-instrumental reason to do what is in that person's interests:

what if he be my enemy, and has given me just cause to hate him? What if he be a vicious man, and deserves the hatred of all mankind? ... What if I be in necessity, and have urgent motives to acquire something to my family? (ibid.)

The passage representing the second prong of this succinctly stated argument is less perspicuous than it needs to be. Is Hume's point that the mere fact that an individual is a 'party concern'd' would provide a normal agent with no (non-instrumental and non-moral) reason at all for doing what is in that individual's interests? Perhaps that is why private benevolence is a 'much less' plausible candidate than is public benevolence, for the fact that an individual is a human being can at least *seem* to provide a normal agent with some non-moral reason for seeking that individual's interests. This reading fails, however, to illuminate Hume's focusing on such facts as that the party concerned is the agent's enemy, or that he is vicious, or that his interests are in competition with the interests of those the agent loves. Perhaps Hume is simply calling attention to the fact that seeming instances of so-called private benevolence are not what they seem: a normal agent's apparent non-instrumental concern for the party concerned, where it occurs, is in fact an instance of concern for a friend. Hume may, however, just be thinking of his 'undoubted maxim' UM with its emphasis on the normal strength of virtuous motives. At the very least the agent has, so far as unrestrained sentiments

[20] In presenting his argument here Hume does not make plain that his counterexamples concern actions considered apart from convention. It should be clear, however, that this is precisely what the Artificiality Argument requires at this point. On this reading it remains open to Hume to say that, when the perspective of convention is introduced, misers and debauchees *are* in general benefited by the just actions of others. Of course, he can consistently combine recognition of this point with an insistence that concern for the parties involved is not the non-instrumental non-moral desire that prompts actions that serve their interests.

go, *stronger* non-moral motivation to disregard the interests of the party concerned than he has to advance them. This suggests that C1 and C2, in requiring a virtuous non-moral desire, require one that, for a normal agent, and for circumstances of the kind envisaged, would *dominate* competing non-moral desires.

Given the first prong of Hume's argument, so-called private benevolence, if it be the non-moral desire implicated by moral sentiments concerned with justice, must be an artificial desire, a desire resting, that is to say, on convention. Given the second prong, private benevolence is not, in fact, the needed non-moral desire. Hume appends to this two-pronged argument a set of further reflections whose point is, it seems, to draw attention to significant differences between moral sentiments concerning justice, on the one hand, and those concerned with the natural virtue of benevolence, on the other.

From the perspective of obligations of benevolence, depriving an individual of something he possesses is (with minor qualifications) commensurable with failure to assist him in his need. Obligations of justice, by contrast, look to the prevention of harm rather than the fostering of well-being (*T* 482). Obligations of benevolence vary with certain variations in relations between individuals: 'private benevolence towards the proprietor is, and ought to be, weaker in some persons, than in others: And in many, or indeed in most persons, must absolutely fail' (*T* 483).[21] Obligations of justice ignore such variations: 'A man's property is suppos'd to be fenc'd against every mortal, in every possible case' (ibid.). These differences in judged obligation must be explained. Hume is inexplicit here, but surely his point is that explanation must be sought in the differing ways (sans artifice, via artifice) in which normally motivated agents secure what they non-morally seek.

Even in their restrained, convention-presupposing, forms neither 'public benevolence' nor so-called 'private benevolence' can provide the non-moral desires that, according to C1 and C2, moral sentiments concerning justice require. In its *unrestrained* form 'self-love' also, as Hume has argued, fails to meet the conditions that C1 and C2 set. On the assumption that Hume's three-member list of candidate non-moral desires is exhaustive, shall we have him conclude that no coherent account can be given of moral sentiments concerned with matters of justice? Or shall we have him endorse the thesis that *restrained* self-love—self-love operating within the constraints of human conventions—will serve? The text of *Treatise*,

---

[21] Here 'private benevolence' must be read as what we have called 'partial benevolence', the benevolence consequent upon love.

III. ii. 1, is, as we shall see, less than helpful here. Hume's answer to the question should, however, be obvious.

Emphasizing the tie between restraint and convention he sketches the answer when he writes, well into *Treatise*, III. ii. 2 ('Of the origin of justice and property'):

> After men have found by experience, that their selfishness and confin'd generosity, *acting at their liberty*, totally incapacitate them for society; and at the same time have observ'd, that society is necessary to the satisfaction of *those very passions*, they are naturally induc'd to lay themselves under the *restraint* of such rules, as may render their commerce more safe and commodious. (*T* 498–9, emphasis added; compare *T* 492)

The framework provided by such rules bars the 'headlong and impetuous' pursuit of one's own interests (*T* 521); within it, self-love acquires 'a new and more convenient direction' (*T* 543). Given such a convention-presupposing framework of rules, one's interests are served not (or not necessarily) by actions 'consider'd apart' (by 'single acts of justice') but rather by 'the whole plan or scheme' (*T* 497). Provided self-interest, thus restrained, meets UM's normality condition—something about which, as we shall see, Hume has no doubts—it can provide the non-moral desire that C1 and C2 require.

Perhaps himself confounded by the ambiguity in his use of 'natural' that we noted at the start of the chapter, Hume writes confoundingly as he draws the Artificiality Argument to its close:

> From all this it follows, that [1] we have naturally no real or universal motive for observing the laws of equity, but the very equity and merit of that observance; and as [2] no action can be equitable or meritorious, where it cannot arise from some separate motive, [3] there is here an evident sophistry and reasoning in a circle. [4] Unless, therefore, we will allow, that nature has establish'd a sophistry, and render'd it necessary and unavoidable, [5] we must allow, that the sense of justice and injustice is not deriv'd from nature, but arises artificially, tho' necessarily from education, and human conventions. (*T* 483, numerals added)

Are we to take Hume's seeming commitment to [1] in this passage at face value? Does he, more than conditionally, subscribe to [5]? Does he view [1] and [5] as incompatible with one another, or as compatible? How, in any event, does he envisage [5] to provide protection against the antinomy—as we may term it—that appears to threaten? The representation of the Artificiality Argument at which we have already arrived enables us to decipher—even while acknowledging the element of misdirection in—this exceptionally puzzling passage.

Statement [1] appears—as it must, if subsequent talk of sophistry is to have any colour—to deny the possibility of meeting C1's and C2's conditions in the case of moral sentiments concerning justice. It appears, that is to say, to claim that we have no non-moral desires, but only specifically moral ones, that prompt acting as the rules of justice require.[22] What Hume writes when recasting the Artificiality Argument for the case of promises serves to reinforce this appearance: ''tis evident we have no motive leading us to the performance of promises, distinct from a sense of duty' (*T* 518). Read in this way, of course, statement [1] is incompatible with statement [2] which (while omitting the requirement that the non-moral desires be virtuous ones) in effect restates C1 and C2. Its constituents being incompatible, the conjunction of [1] and [2] constitutes 'an evident sophistry', as [3] has it. If committed, ineluctably, to both conjuncts of this 'sophistry', one's thinking about morality and justice is, one might say, radically antinomous: 'nature has establish'd a sophistry, and render'd it necessary and unavoidable', in the words of [4]. To subvert the antinomy that threatens, one must, endorsing [5], acknowledge the existence of *artificial* or *convention-presupposing* non-moral desires that are capable of prompting actions in accordance with the rules of justice, and that are thereby suited to be the non-moral desires implicated (according to C1 and C2) by specifically moral sentiments concerning justice.[23]

Why, if the antinomy is to be subverted, must one do that? Hume does not say in so many words. But his thought, it seems, is that, while holding firmly to [2], one must subscribe to [5] if one is to show that [1], read as we have read it, is *false* and so *not capable*—with [2]—of generating the antinomy he has described. One must—and Hume, despite some appearances, does—reject [1], as we have read it:[24] one is otherwise committed,

---

[22] Whatever it is Hume wishes to convey, just here, about the possibility of non-moral motivation and justice, he clearly assumes, here, that agents do sometimes act as justice requires from specifically moral motives. That Hume subscribes to the assumption is clear at *T* 484.

[23] For a defence of the claim that Hume is committed to the antinomous character of our thinking about the external world, see my *Hume's Philosophy of Mind*, 4–24. There is, however, no evidence whatever that he holds our thinking about morality and justice to be similarly antinomous.

[24] Harrison seems to have Hume subscribe to [1] read in the way we have read it here. In *Hume's Theory of Justice*, 1, he represents Hume as maintaining that 'where justice is concerned . . . there is no motive preceding the regard for justice itself, which by prompting men to perform just actions makes just actions meritorious' and that 'this motive cannot be self-interest, since this is the normal motive for injustice'. Later, however, he writes of 'modify[ing]' Hume's premise 'so that it states, not that there *is* no such motive, but that there *would be* no such motive were it not for human conventions' (7). Mackie, *Hume's Moral Theory*, 77, also seems to hold Hume to [1] as we have read it here: representing Hume, he

he claims, to the antinomous character of our thinking about morality and justice. In reckoning with what renders [1] false, one recognizes the artificiality, the convention-presupposing character, of justice. Provided one acknowledges genuine moral sentiments concerning justice one 'must', in the words of statement [5], 'allow, that the sense of justice and injustice ... arises artificially, tho' necessarily from ... human conventions'.[25] (More than the puzzling passage provides is, of course, needed if Hume is to secure his more determinate thesis that the non-moral desire in question is a convention-presupposing form of 'self-love' rather than either 'public benevolence' or 'private benevolence'.)

When fully elaborated, Hume's response to the threatening antinomy requires that restrained self-love be a *virtuous* desire. Can he—does he—subscribe to this surprising claim? Perhaps restrained self-love comports with UM's requirement of normality. But that, of course, is merely a necessary condition on a virtuous desire. Is there any reason to think that Hume can or does allow restrained self-interest to meet whatever further conditions he imposes on the virtuousness of non-moral desires? It is clear that (with a crucial qualification to be noted in just a moment) he does in fact take restrained self-interest to be the non-moral desire implicated in specifically moral sentiments concerning justice. Having provided his constructive account of '*the manner, in which the rules of justice are establish'd by the artifice of men*' (*T* 484), he writes: 'To the imposition then, and observance of these rules, both in general, and in every particular instance, they are at first moved only by a regard to interest' (*T* 499). In the same vein he writes: 'interest is the *first* obligation to the performance of promises' (*T* 523), and is presupposed by the *second*, the specifically moral obligation, that is constituted by the presence of specifically moral sentiments.

The crucial qualification just alluded to should dispel the air of paradox in Hume's contention that restrained self-love is the required virtuous desire. His use of the expression 'self-love', in the course of the Artificiality Argument, is importantly misleading. As his subsequent constructive theory of convention, justice, and morality makes plain, it is not 'self-love', construed narrowly, that he takes to provide the non-moral desire

writes that 'there can, after all, be no motive for honest actions except regard for honesty itself'.

Are other readings of [1] possible? Taking 'natural' not in the sense of 'non-moral' but in that of 'non-artificial' one perhaps secures a reading of [1] that Hume would take to be true. With [1] read in this way, however, no antinomy would even appear to threaten.

[25] Here, for simplicity's sake, we overlook the essentially secondary role that education plays.

needed for the case of justice. It is rather what he later terms 'selfishness and confin'd generosity', a concern 'for ourselves and our nearest friends' (*T* 492; compare *T* 489, 577, 586). This combination of self-interest (narrowly construed) and partial benevolence can, it is clear, meet the conditions imposed by C1 and C2 only within a framework of human conventions.[26] Unlike either so-called 'public benevolence' or so-called 'private benevolence', it is a combination of non-moral desires that Hume believes normal agents to have. It is a motivational combination that accords with what we have seen much earlier of his views both on psychological egoism and on the partial benevolence that is consequent upon love.

It seems that it is also a motivational combination that, if restrained, can meet the conditions other than normality that Hume imposes on the virtuousness of non-moral desires. Its selfish component is, after all, not the unrestrained self-love that is 'the source of all injustice and violence' (*T* 480). More importantly, it incorporates an appropriate measure of concern for 'our nearest friends' (*T* 492), and so an appropriate measure of altruism. The altruism is partial but *that*, for Hume, is normal, at the non-moral level, for human beings. Within a Humean framework, there can be nothing paradoxical in claiming that such a combination of desires is a virtuous one.

---

[26] Again, partial benevolence is not to be confused with what Hume confusingly calls 'private benevolence'.

6

From Convention to Moral Desire

When restrained by dependence on suitable conventions, it is the combination of 'selfishness and confin'd generosity'—that is, a concern for one's own interests and those of one's friends and relations—that meets the conditions that C_1 and C_2 impose on moral sentiments pertaining to matters of justice. It is—as for brevity's sake we may say—convention-dependent *narrow interest* that provides the virtuous non-moral desires that a moral sense of justice requires. So, as we have represented it, the Artificiality Argument maintains.

To secure this conclusion in more than a formal way, however, Hume must show that narrowly interested non-moral desires, thus constrained, can in fact meet C_1's and C_2's conditions. Crucially, he must show that the claims of narrow interest, when narrow interest functions within an appropriate framework of convention, correspond to the claims that 'the rules of justice' (T 534) make on an agent's conduct. Showing this is one of the two chief tasks of *Treatise*, III. ii. 2–6, which is devoted to an examination of 'the nature of the artifice, from which the sense of that virtue [i.e. justice] is derived' (T 477). The other is to set out the way in which specifically moral claims correspond to non-moral claims that are, equivalently, claims of convention-presupposing narrow interest or claims of justice. In the Artificiality Argument Hume proceeds analytically from reflection on the content of moral sentiment, including moral desire, to the thesis that the requirements of justice are a product of narrow interest operating within a framework of convention. At *Treatise*, III. ii. 2–6, reversing field, he employs an analysis of convention in an explication, first of the non-moral requirements of justice, and then of the sense of moral obligation that arises upon acknowledgement of those requirements.

Hume represents conventions as complex psycho-behavioural structures that have behavioural regularities, and complex patterns of expectation and attitude, as their intricately interrelated elements. He finds the rules of property or justice, just as the rules that govern promising, or political obedience, or certain aspects of sexual conduct, to be the product of such structures. Paying particular attention to the case of property or justice, he articulates a psychological profile that, when common, and recognized to be common, amongst the members of a given population, in an environment of a certain sort, involves a desire, on the part of members of that population, to act as justice requires. Persons with that profile, when in the circumstances envisaged, have reason to desire that the conventions constitutive of justice be in place. They have reason to be party to such conventions. They also have *some* non-moral reason to act in accordance with the rules of justice on any occasion when those rules apply. So, at least, Hume contends.

Such persons may also, of course, have competing non-moral reasons *not* so to act, for to act as justice requires may well be to act in a way that is, taken in itself, inimical to an agent's narrow interests. It is a further question, then, whether such persons always have non-moral reason, *all things considered*, to act justly, to eschew injustice. On the face of it, it is a further question still whether such a person, having non-moral reason, all things considered, to act justly rather than unjustly will in fact do what she has such reason to do. Arguing for a coincidence of the claims of justice and of narrow interest, Hume appears to hold that individuals with the psychological profile in question always have non-moral reason, all things considered, to comply with the rules of justice. He invokes weakness of will to explain the fact that they none the less at times act contrary to their narrow interest, thus contrary to the rules of justice. And he provides an explanatory sketch of the factors, psychological and environmental, that give rise to akratic irrationality.

The psychological profile the above account postulates—we may call those who fit it 'co-operators'—is not one that persons *must* fit. 'Knaves' differ from 'co-operators' in their conditional preferences. Co-operators prefer to conform to the rules of justice on condition that each of the other parties to the convention does. Knaves prefer to conform if the others do, but only if they can't get away with not doing so. Despite this element in his psychological profile the knave has *some* non-moral reason—indeed he has non-moral reason, *all things considered*—to act in accordance with the requirements of justice. So, at least, Hume holds. In the knave's case, it is specifically cognitive failures that explain irrational non-compliance.

In the case of co-operators, *specifically moral* desires *second* an agent's non-moral concern to comply with justice's requirements. Specifically moral desires, countering the effects of weakness of will, increase the likelihood of an agent's acting as narrow interest—equivalently, as her acknowledgement of the non-moral claims of justice—directs. Specifically moral desires *differ*, of course, from the non-moral desires that they second and that, given the Artificiality Argument, they implicate. They differ, that is to say, from the narrowly interested non-moral desires that prompt compliance with the rules of justice on the part of non-akratic co-operators. Specifically moral desires concerning justice are desire-implicating desires that display the generality and impartiality distinctive of the moral point of view. The non-moral desires of which, via sympathy, they are impartial variants are also, of course, themselves desire-implicating. But, being narrowly interested desires tied to the rules of justice peculiar to a particular society, they—just as the narrowly interested co-operators' desires that specifically moral desires here implicate— incorporate neither the impartiality nor the generality of morality.[1] The difference between narrowly interested non-moral, and impartial moral, desires corresponds to a difference between the non-moral rules of justice that are constitutive of a given convention and specifically moral rules that, in complex ways, presuppose them.

So far as justice is concerned morality presupposes convention. Morality is not, however, itself a matter of convention, and that for two principal reasons. First, morality is concerned not only with behaviours and motivations that presuppose conventions (the case of what Hume terms the artificial virtues) but also with behaviours, motivations, and other mental features that do not (the case of so-called natural virtues). In the latter case, neither the non-moral rules prescribing benevolence (to take but one example), nor the specifically moral rules that correspond to them, depend in any substantive way upon conventions. Second, joint adoption of the moral point of view is not properly to be understood as itself the product of a convention: the having of specifically moral desires originates, according to Hume, in a need to have intersubjective conative common ground; those who have such desires are none the less not constituted thereby as parties to some peculiarly moral convention, to a convention to view things impartially.

Hume's reflections on the interplay of morality and convention contribute substantially to his characterization of reasons for action, including specifically moral ones. They offer a representation of some of the many ways in which an agent's higher-order psychological states—his

[1] Amongst the many distinctions to be kept in mind here is that between Hume's conception of the non-moral desires that (some) specifically moral desires *implicate* (a conception he elaborates when developing the Artificiality Argument) and his conception of the non-moral desires of which specifically moral desires are *impartial variants* (a conception he deploys when displaying the origin of impartial moral desires in corrected sympathy).

higher-order beliefs and desires about his own and others' beliefs and desires, including his own and others' higher-order beliefs and desires—affect that agent's reasons for action. They point both to a place for probability assignments in the formation of reasons for action and to the role of weakness of will in the explanation of failures to act on such reasons. Emphasizing Hume's commitment to the centrality of desire, they provide occasion for the development of a doctrine of desire, both non-moral and specifically moral, of uncommon complexity. In doing these things in a thoroughly naturalistic fashion, they lend important support—as they are intended to do—to his case for an expanded moral conativism.

Being especially concerned with the contribution his theory of convention makes to Hume's moral psychology, we shall concentrate on his treatment of what he takes to be morally important conventions, but only in so far as that treatment reveals his thinking about reasons, including specifically moral ones, for action. We shall attend to his accounts of conventions governing property (or justice), promising, political obedience, and certain aspects of sexual conduct: these are the conventions, in Hume's view, of most importance to morality. But we shall not pause to assess the merits of his substantive claims about the contribution these conventions make to the narrow interests of those party to them. We shall leave unexamined the merits of his claims about the ineliminable social role of property, say, or about the rationale for differing prescriptions for men and for women in the matter of sexual behaviour. Concerned to uncover the central elements in his moral psychology, we shall focus narrowly on what, in the course of his discussion of such substantive questions, Hume has to say about such matters as reasons for having conventions, reasons for compliance with the requirements of one's conventions, irrationality in action, the motivational role of peculiarly moral concerns. Intent on his moral psychology, we shall simply allow his substantive claims concerning property and the rest to stand.

A caution must be entered as we turn to consider, as a contribution to his moral psychology, Hume's rendering of what is for him the most fundamental of morally significant conventions, that governing property or (as he is inclined to say) justice. Following Hume, we shall represent that convention as one that is in place *prior* to the introduction of specifically moral concerns. And we shall represent its 'rules of justice' as non-moral rules that have a role to play *prior* to the introduction of specifically moral rules that, in ways that we shall spell out, correspond to them.

1. AN ANALYSIS OF CONVENTION

Discussing the fundamental convention that establishes property Hume writes:

This convention ... is ... a general sense of common interest; which sense all the members of the society express to one another, and which induces them to regulate their conduct by certain rules. I observe, that it will be for my interest to leave another in the possession of his goods, *provided* he will act in the same manner with regard to me. He is sensible of a like interest in the regulation of his conduct. When this common sense of interest is mutually express'd, and is known to both, it produces a suitable resolution and behaviour. And this may properly enough be call'd a convention or agreement betwixt us ... since the actions of each of us have a reference to those of the other, and are perform'd upon the supposition, that something is to be perform'd on the other part. (*T* 490)

In the second *Enquiry* he is more succinct:

by convention ... [is] meant a sense of common interest; which sense each man feels in his own breast, which he remarks in his fellows, and which carries him, in concurrence with others, into a general plan or system of actions, which tends to the public utility. (*E* 306)

He says much the same of the conventions involved in promising (*T* 522–3) and in political obedience (*T* 535, 538), and he takes it that conventions, thus characterized, are at work in social practices governing sexual conduct, in the functioning of languages and systems of exchange, and even when two individuals co-operate in the rowing of a boat.

In characterizing a convention Hume is thinking of a behavioural regularity R on the part of the members of a population P when they are agents in a recurrent situation S.[2] The members of a given society act in property-claiming and property-respecting ways when opportunities for the respecting or violating of property occur. They accept, make, and

---

[2] David Lewis, in *Convention: A Philosophical Study* (Cambridge, Mass., 1969), offers an analysis of convention that is, he says, 'along the lines of Hume's' (3). Despite the absence, in Hume, of an explicitly game-theoretical framework for analysis, the similarities between Lewis's and Hume's accounts appear to be systematic and extensive. In attempting, in this and the next several paragraphs, to isolate the chief elements in Hume's general theory of convention, we shall be much aided by Lewis's presentation of his own modern-day, Humean, theory.

Other accounts of Hume's analysis of convention, that pay particular attention to its contribution to his theory of justice, are to be found in: Baier, *A Progress of Sentiments*, 220–54; David Gauthier, 'David Hume, Contractarian', *Philosophical Review*, 88 (1979), 3–38; Harrison, *Hume's Theory of Justice, passim*; Mackie, *Hume's Moral Theory*, especially 76–106; and Snare, *Morals, Motivation, and Convention*, 176–309.

keep promises when occasion provides. Each of two rowers strokes in such-and-such a way on each occasion for stroking. How regular must the behaviour constitutive of R be, if R is to be an element in a convention? Hume's usual practice is to write as if perfect regularity were required. He has much to say, however, about non-compliance on the part of persons who are party to what are none the less continuing conventions. And he acknowledges the possibility that a convention can continue despite violations of that convention by persons who seem to be, but in fact are not, parties to that convention. He strikes an appropriate note of realism for the cases of justice and promising when he writes, in the second *Enquiry*, of 'the whole scheme or system concurred in by the whole, or the greater part of the society' (E 304). For simplicity's sake, however, I shall for the most part follow Hume's usual practice and assume the stricter standard, that of uniform conformity, as I set out the remaining conditions on convention.[3] I shall lift the assumption later.

Within the framework of a convention the members of a population P 'regulate their conduct by certain rules'. Hume writes of 'the rules of justice, or the conventions of men' (T 506), perhaps suggesting that the regulation of their conduct by rules amounts to the existence, among the members of P, of a 'general plan or system of actions'. The possibility of non-compliance requires, however, a distinction between rule and behavioural regularity, a distinction perhaps intimated when Hume writes of 'an artificial convention for the establishment of these rules' (T 480) and of a 'convention for the observance of these rules' (T 526). What, then, are the conditions on the existence of the rules with which the members of P comply? If a general account is to be given, their existence cannot require explicit, public codification. One attractive, because minimalist, possibility is that they be understood in terms of the evaluative sentences that serve to express certain of the non-moral desires that, as we shall shortly see, are conditions on the existence of a convention.

The requisite conformity to R in S is a matter of interdependent decision on the part of members of P: 'the actions of each ... have a reference to those of the other[s], and are perform'd upon the supposition, that something is to be perform'd on the other part.' The behavioural regularity R in recurrent situation S is in the (narrow) interest of each member of P: Hume writes of a 'common interest' and, for the case of property, of a 'general plan or system of actions, which tends to the public utility'; and he remarks that '[t]his system [of conduct and behaviour] ... comprehend-

---

[3] For the difference between a stricter and a less strict standard compare the definition of convention at Lewis, *Convention*, 76, with the 'final definition' offered at Lewis, 78.

ing the interest of each individual, is of course advantageous to the pub-lic' (*T* 529). Each member of *P* recognizes that uniform conformity to *R* is in the (narrow) interest of each: Hume writes of 'a general sense' of their 'common interest'. In the circumstances, each member of *P* prefers to conform to *R* on condition that each of the others does. As Hume puts the point for the limiting case of two individuals: 'I observe, that it will be for my interest to leave another in the possession of his goods, *provided* he will act in the same manner with regard to me. He is sensible of a like interest in the regulation of his conduct' (*T* 490). Having such condi-tional preferences, each member of *P* is, we may say, a co-operator. For the cases described, each member of *P* expects each of the others to con-form to *R*.

Hume requires that the satisfaction of the above basic conditions be a matter of mutual knowledge amongst the members of *P* if *R*, in recurrent situation *S*, is to count as a convention. The heart of the requirement is that there be some state of affairs *A* which is such that, given that each member of *P* has reason to believe that *A* holds, each has reason to be-lieve that the basic conditions for the convention also hold. *A* is, we may say, the basis for the mutual knowledge in question. Under the mutual knowledge condition, each member of *P* has a variety of higher-order expectations. Each recognizes that conformity to *R* is in the (narrow) in-terest of each. Each recognizes that each prefers to conform to *R* on con-dition that the others do. Each 'remarks' the relevant attitudes 'in his fellows'; the presence of these attitudes in each 'is known' to each of the others. This mutual knowledge is part of the reason that the members of *P* are 'induce[d] . . . to regulate their conduct by certain rules', why each member of *P* is 'carrie[d] . . . in concurrence with others, into a general plan or system of actions'.[4]

On what is the mutual knowledge based? Hume writes of the relevant attitudes being 'mutually express'd', of the relevant interests being 'avow'd' (*T* 534, 544, 545). Presumably avowal is verbal: the members of *P* give voice to their expectations and interests.[5] On the face of it, explicitly evaluative expressions of desires would have a quite distinctive role to play. In addition to providing a basis for mutual knowledge they could, as noted earlier, serve for the articulation of the rules that structure the convention in question, rules to which each expresses a desire to conform.

---

[4] Lewis, *Convention*, 52–60, defends a common knowledge condition that is, as Ann Cudd has persuaded me, much stronger than anything to be found in Hume.

[5] Of course, it is not possible that verbal expression provide, quite generally, the basis for mutual knowledge: in Hume's view the use of language itself involves convention.

Of course, non-verbal behaviours, tentative essays in co-operation, may help generate the needed expectations as well. Hume has such a broader basis for mutual knowledge in mind when he writes, of 'the rule concerning stability of possession':

it arises gradually, and acquires force by a slow progression, and by our repeated experience of the inconveniences of transgressing it . . . [T]his experience assures us . . . that the sense of interest has become common to all our fellows, and gives us a confidence of the future regularity of their conduct. (*T* 490)

Expectations, including mutual expectations, of rationality must, of course, play a critical role here. Hume is clearest on this role when representing the collapse of convention, a matter to which we shall return.

It is tempting to allow explicit promises to serve as a basis for mutual knowledge, and so of convention. They can help make explicit the interests and expectations of each member of *P*; and by providing additional motivation for uniform conformity to *R* they can enhance the confidence of each member of *P* in the conformity of each of the others (see *T* 544). Hume recognizes that some conventions, in particular some conventions for political obedience, rest on promises (*T* 541–2). He insists, however, that not all conventions do: 'Two men, who pull the oars of a boat, do it by an agreement or convention, tho' they have never given promises to each other' (*T* 490). And, given his views about the conventional character of promising itself, he must reject the suggestion that promises *could* underpin all conventions.[6]

Hume's account of the formal conditions on convention requires a common interest, among the members of *P*, in uniform conformity to *R* in recurrent situation *S*. That each has a (narrow) interest in uniform conformity to *R* does not require each to have the same interest in that conformity. Hume adopts a version of the stronger assumption, however, when reflecting on those fundamentally important conventions that concern him, the conventions governing property, promising, political obedience, and sexual conduct.

Whose interests are of interest to each when such fundamentally important conventions are in question? As we have seen in effect already, Hume takes the members of the relevant population *P* to be mutually unconcerned. They are not moved by '*regard to publick interest*' (*T* 480) or

---

[6] It should be noted that, when actually discussing the links between conventions and promises, Hume focuses not on questions concerning the basis for mutual knowledge but on broader questions about the reasons one has—in particular, the moral reasons one has—for acting as convention requires.

by a non-instrumental desire for the well-being of each of the other members of *P*. Nor are they non-instrumentally concerned for the interests of the particular individuals, in a given situation *S*, towards whom they are required, by the convention in question, to act in certain ways. That is to say, they are not non-instrumentally moved by '*private benevolence*, or a *regard to the interests of the party concern'd*' (*T* 482). To be sure, there is one clear sense in which each member of *P* must be concerned with the interests of each of the other members of *P*: each must recognize that the others would not be party to the convention unless their interests were served. But this is a merely instrumental interest in the interests of the others. Hume remarks, of the convention of justice: 'This system ... comprehending the interest of each individual, is of course advantageous to the public; tho' it be not intended for that purpose by the inventors' (*T* 529).

Three further qualifications must be noted. First, Hume recognizes that in an ongoing convention some of the members of the relevant population *P* may come to have a non-instrumental concern for the interests of the others: this would be a natural response to benefiting from the co-operative activity of the others (compare *T* 383). Second, the acquisition of specifically moral concerns introduces, as we shall see, a non-instrumental concern for each of the members of any given population linked by a convention of justice, and so for the members of the specific convention-linked population *P*. Third, the mutual unconcern of each of the members of *P* is compatible with each of them being non-instrumentally concerned with the interests of some other persons. Though mutually unconcerned, each may none the less be concerned for the interests of her friends and relations. The combination of self-interest and partial benevolence that Hume terms 'selfishness and confin'd generosity'—and that we earlier termed 'narrow interest'—is, that is to say, perfectly compatible with the mutual unconcern that his theory of convention assumes.[7] As we have already seen, it is this motivational combination that Hume takes to be implicated by specifically moral sentiments pertaining to justice. It is this combination of desires that he takes to lie behind each co-operator's participation in the fundamentally important conventions we are examining.

[7] Here it is assumed that an individual, *A*, can be kin to, or friend of, an individual, *B*, who can benefit from *A*'s participation in a convention but who is not himself a participant in that convention. Even if *B* were a co-participant, however, the other co-participants need be neither friend nor relation of either *A* or *B*. If motivationally more complicated, this case would none the less provide for the measure of mutual unconcern that, method-ologically speaking, Hume's theory of fundamental conventions requires.

What has Hume to say concerning *membership* in these fundamental conventions? The most important point is that these conventions involve restricted populations, the members of the society in question. Though Hume occasionally mentions 'mankind' in this connection (as at E 192), it is a more restricted set of individuals, those whose actions and attitudes refer, in the ways specified earlier, to the actions and attitudes of each of the others, that constitutes the relevant population P. Membership may change, of course: individuals may enter or leave the population in question; they may leave one such population and join another. Hume notes one of the many possibilities when remarking 'that several persons, being by different accidents separated from the societies, to which they formerly belong'd, may be oblig'd to form a new society among themselves' (T 503).

Membership is restricted to individuals possessing the capacity to form the expectations and preferences detailed earlier. Each member must be 'rational' (E 190). Each must be capable of grasping the intricate connections between convention and interest (see E 307). Most controversially, perhaps, each must also have the capacity to act in ways inimical to the common interest served by the convention. In a multi-faceted passage in the second *Enquiry* Hume insists that, to be party to a convention for property, an individual must have sufficient 'strength, both of body and mind' (E 190), to make it costly for others not to act towards him as a party to that convention. Unless an individual has the capacity to disrupt the peace and order that the property convention is designed to ensure, there is no room for the thought that that individual is party to the convention. '[I]ntercourse' with such individuals 'could not be called society, which supposes a degree of equality' (ibid.); the members of the society in question would 'not, properly speaking, lie under any restraint of justice with regard to them, nor could they [i.e. the powerless individuals] possess any right or property' (E 190). The conduct of such powerless individuals might well accord, in certain respects, with the requirement of conformity to a given regularity R: the individuals might, for example, regularly refrain from seizing the property of the members of the society. But the power of the society's members, and not any convention linking the powerful and the powerless, would explain that conduct. The powerless person's reasons for acting would not make the right sort of reference to the convention in question, would not incorporate higher-order expectations and attitudes of the sort sketched earlier. The point is an analytical one, and it has to do specifically with non-moral reasons for action. It contributes to an understanding, or so Hume suggests, of the conduct of humans towards animals, of invading Europeans towards the native peoples of the Americas, and of men towards women in many situations.

The suggested analytical framework contributes as well to an explanation of fundamental changes in the membership of a given convention-defined population *P*. Acquisition of power can bring membership in its train. Hume's example concerns the status of women:

In many nations, the female sex are reduced to . . . slavery, and are rendered incapable of all property, in opposition to their lordly masters. But though the males, when united, have in all countries bodily force sufficient to maintain this severe tyranny, yet such are the insinuation, address, and charms of their fair companions, that women are commonly able to break the confederacy, and share with the other sex in all rights and privileges of society. (*E* 191)

The perspective, it is plain, is explanatory, not normative. The thought is that, specifically moral considerations apart, rational agents fitting the psychological profile Hume has outlined could have no reason to enter into conventions with the powerless, but would have every reason to do so should the latter become able to make their weight felt.

Children form a special class of the powerless. We shall consider their standing with respect to Hume's fundamental conventions when we investigate conventions governing sexual conduct. And when considering irrationality we shall in effect look to the membership status of individuals who fail to comply with the conventions of what (begging the question) we may call their societies.

How, precisely, do conventions serve the narrow interests of the members of a given population *P*? The makings of a general answer to the question can be gleaned from Hume's accounts of the reasons for having the fundamental conventions governing property (including the transfer of property), promising, sexual conduct, and political obedience.

The point of the convention for the establishment of property is, in the lapidary words of the second *Enquiry*, to 'procure happiness and security, by preserving order in society' (*E* 186). More explicitly, that convention helps secure a necessary condition for social organization, namely, peace and order. Only with peace and order secured can the benefits be achieved that the existence of society alone makes possible. Conventions governing property are instrumentally valuable, then, with a view to securing those further benefits.

Society's benefits are to be understood in terms of the remedying of three deficiencies to be found in non-social settings:

When every individual person labours a-part, and only for himself, his force is too small to execute any considerable work; his labour being employ'd in supplying all his different necessities, he never attains a perfection in any particular art; and as his force and success are not at all times equal, the least failure in either of these particulars must be attended with inevitable ruin and misery. (*T* 485)

Society remedies these deficiencies by enhancing the '*force, ability*, and *security*' of its members:

By the conjunction of forces, our power is augmented: By the partition of employments, our ability encreases: And by mutual succour we are less expos'd to fortune and accidents. (*T* 485)

Without 'peace and order', however, the social organization essential to the securing of such benefits is impossible (*T* 497). And that peace and order is threatened by the conjunction of our narrow interests—our self-interest and partial benevolence—with the scarcity and easy transferability of 'such possessions as we have acquir'd by our industry and good fortune' (*T* 487).[8] The rationale for a convention fixing property is, then, the fostering of peace and order by the elimination of the destabilizing instability of possessions. By the convention's workings individuals are made 'tolerable to each other' (*T* 520) and so—given the chain of dependencies just sketched—the common interest served.

　　The fundamental convention that possession be fixed must be supplemented by determinate conventions for the assignment of property rights. These in turn must be supplemented by a convention enabling the transference of property by consent, a convention viewed as a 'remedy' for the fact that, in its absence, 'persons and possessions must often be very ill adjusted' (*T* 514). If the convention establishing property makes individuals 'tolerable to each other', that governing the transfer of property makes them 'mutually advantageous' (*T* 520). The convention establishing the practice of promising makes individuals further 'serviceable' by providing both for the transfer of goods that are 'absent or general', and for the exchange not just of goods but also of 'services and actions, which we may exchange to our mutual interest and advantage' (ibid.).[9]

---

[8] Hume identifies three 'species of goods'—'the internal satisfaction of our mind, the external advantages of our body, and the enjoyment of such possessions as we have acquir'd by our industry and good fortune' (*T* 487)—and argues that only goods of the third type are such as to require conventions constraining action if peace and order are to be secured.

[9] Goods are 'absent' if they cannot be physically conveyed into the possession of the other party at the time of the agreement for exchange: 'One cannot transfer the property of a particular house, twenty leagues distant; because the consent cannot be attended with

Hume identifies similarly complex, if rather more surprising, chains of dependencies for the case of conventions governing sexual conduct. He depicts a convention imposing differing requirements on men and women, the differences a product of the different relations of the sexes to the generation and rearing of children.[10] The convention serves 'the interest of society' (*T* 570), is 'founded on the public interest' (*T* 573); as such it must be taken to serve the interests of each party to the convention, each member of the relevant population *P*. The purported links between convention and interest are, it must be said, difficult to make out. Hume focuses on the convention's role in serving two interconnected interests of (some of) the parties to the convention: the interest parents have in fostering the interests of their children; the interest men have in not incurring the costs of caring for children other than their own. Hume writes both of 'the concern which both sexes naturally have for their offspring' and of 'the fatigues and expences' that are willingly incurred only if men 'believe, that the children are their own' (*T* 570). A condition on the several interests being served is that circumstances allow the correct pairing of parents and offspring. And the immediate point of the convention, in particular the constraints on the sexual conduct of women, is to provide just those circumstances. On this account, of course, children are not themselves parties to the convention. Moreover, the serving of their interests contributes to the common interest only in so far as the relevant second-order interests of their parents are thus served. There is no intimation of the idea that children are prospective parties to conventions of which their elders are at present party.[11] Within Hume's stated framework, we may say, children are non-participant beneficiaries of sexual conventions designed to serve their parents' interests; this, despite the fact that they are objects of their parents' non-selfish concern.

Conventions of political obedience establish rules for the selection and conduct of rulers and the conduct of their subjects. They serve the

---

delivery, which is a requisite circumstance' (*T* 520). Goods are said to be 'general' if the agreed exchange concerns some item of a type but not a particular of that type: one cannot 'transfer the property of ten bushels of corn, or five hogsheads of wine, by the mere expression and consent; because these are only general terms, and have no direct relation to any particular heap of corn, or barrels of wine' (ibid.).

[10] The text can give the appearance of *two* conventions governing sexual conduct, one for women, one, less onerous, for men. It seems clear, however, that Hume intends the parties whose interests are here in question, and whose co-operative action is to secure those interests, to include both men and women. For further reflections on conventions governing sexual conduct, see Hume's 'A Dialogue'.

[11] For an illuminating discussion of the question of intergenerational relations that takes *this* idea seriously, see David Gauthier, *Morals by Agreement* (Oxford, 1986), 298ff.

interests of each, and so the common interest, in two ways. By blunting the effects of the short-sighted irrationality of the members of a society (of which more below), and so prompting action conforming to the pre-supposed conventions governing property, they help secure what we have seen to be a necessary condition for social organization—peace and or-der—and so society's benefits.[12] They promote the conditions, as well, for otherwise unachievable mutual advantages by the promotion of fur-ther conventions. Hume recognizes the double contribution of political convention to common interest when he writes:

> men acquire a security against each others weakness and passion, as well as against their own, and under the shelter of their governors, begin to taste at ease the sweets of society and mutual assistance. But government extends farther its beneficial influence; and not contented to protect men in those conventions they make for their mutual interest, it often obliges them to make such conventions, and forces them to seek their own advantage, by a concurrence in some common end or purpose. (*T* 538)

It is in virtue of such further conventions, such novel modes of concerted action, that 'bridges are built; harbours open'd; ramparts rais'd; canals form'd; fleets equip'd; and armies disciplin'd' (*T* 539).[13]

This is not the place to make a substantive assessment of Hume's de-terminate views about the rationale and fundamental role of the specific conventions governing property, promising, sexual conduct, and political obedience. Our purpose in characterizing them has been simply to se-cure, thereby, a clearer grasp of his views about the ways in which con-ventions can serve the narrow interests of the members of a population *P*, and so of his views about the general structure of the reasons the parties

---

[12] In Gauthier's succinct phrase, Hume's political conventions give rise to 'systems of rules for the enforcement of rules which determine possession and use'. See 'David Hume: Contractarian', 5.

[13] To appreciate the place of specifically political conventions within Hume's overall account it is helpful to note his four-part classification of social groups. *Family* groups, the members of which are moved by benevolence towards each of the others, function without Humean conventions for property (see *T* 486). *Small* societies, the 'narrow and contracted' societies that arise 'on the first formation of society' (*T* 499), comprise persons who are mutually unconcerned; they function smoothly on the basis of conventions governing property, promising, and sexual conduct. *Large but unpolished* societies require specifically moral motivation to second the combination of self-interest and partial benevolence that lies behind conventions for common interest: morality comes into play, Hume suggests, 'when society has become numerous, and has encreas'd to a tribe or nation' (*T* 499). Specifically *political* societies, those depending on specifically political conventions, are, by contrast, 'large and polish'd' (*T* 543) or 'large and civiliz'd' (*T* 546). The need for political conventions is linked to the development of societies 'where there are so many possessions on the one hand, and so many wants, real or imaginary, on the other' (*T* 544).

to a convention have for their conventions. As the discussions of property, promising, sexual conduct, and political obedience make plain, Hume takes the existence of behavioural regularities of the sort envisaged, in material and psychological surroundings of the sort specified, to provide essential conditions on the securing of further essential conditions on the satisfaction of narrowly interested desires of any given party to that convention. As these discussions also make plain, one such behavioural regularity may well be a condition, in any of a variety of ways, on the existence of some other such regularity. The behavioural regularities implicated in the conventions governing property are a condition on peace and order, which is a condition on social organization, which is a condition on a given person's securing society's benefits. And the conventions governing property are themselves intricately interdependent with those governing promising, say, or political obedience. Recognition of these chains of dependency, and of the complex conditions on securing the several links in the chains, gives individuals who have the requisite conative characteristics and beliefs (including, of course, the higher-order ones detailed earlier), reason to have, and to be party to, such conventions. Viewed as psychological states, such reasons are, it goes without saying, structures of quite extraordinary complexity.

It can readily be seen that they, and the actions that presuppose them, are, in Hume's expression, 'artificial'. Hume contrasts instinctive and conventional modes of social behaviour. The social behaviour of '[i]nferior animals' is instinctive (*E* 308 n.). So, too, is some of the social behaviour of humans: the 'social virtues of humanity and benevolence', Hume writes, 'exert their influence immediately by a direct tendency or instinct' (*E* 303).[14] By contrast, conventional modes of social behaviour such as those implicated in the making of promises, say, or in political obedience, require 'reason and forethought' of a quite special sort (*E* 308 n.). In their case, the desires that prompt action presuppose the devising of a 'scheme or system' (*E* 303) for the mutual securing of goals, schemes or systems of the sort we have just described, and so the desires and actions in question are, as Hume has it, 'artificial'.[15]

A certain obliqueness in the route to benefits is, Hume suggests, an ineliminable feature of actions embedded in such schemes or systems,

---

[14] The 'social virtue . . . of humanity' mentioned here, a virtue tied to a natural non-moral desire, must not be confused with the specifically moral desire Hume sometimes terms 'humanity'.

[15] Compare Hume's 'Of the Original Contract', in *Essays Moral, Political, and Literary*, ed. Milller, 479–80.

and so a mark of their 'artificial' character. He ties the obliqueness of this route to the non-instinctive character of convention-based social behaviour when he writes:

The only difference betwixt the natural virtues and [the artificial virtue of] justice lies in this, that the good, which results from the former, arises from every single act, and is the object of some natural passion: Whereas a single act of justice, consider'd in itself, may often be contrary to the public good; and 'tis only the concurrence of mankind, in a general scheme or system of action, which is advantageous. (*T* 579; compare *T* 497)

I shall attempt a characterization of this oblique route between convention-based action and benefit below.

Actions embedded in conventions in the way envisaged are conceptually dependent on their embedding conventions. In the absence of the relevant conventions, there could not be such actions as stealing or refraining from theft, as making or breaking a promise. In the absence of the relevant convention there can, Hume writes, be 'no such thing as property' and so 'no such thing as justice or injustice' (*T* 501). Without the conventions establishing property 'the distinction of *mine* and *thine* would be unknown in society' (*E* 311). There could be possession, of course, but possession is not to be confused with property (*E* 309 n.). In a similar vein, 'a promise wou'd not be intelligible, before human conventions had establish'd it' (*T* 516, emphasis deleted). An explication of the meaning of the terms for such actions, we may say, must make reference to suitable conventions. An especially interesting case is that in which such a convention-presupposing term is itself used to perform an action only possible given the convention in question, as when one promises by uttering the words 'I promise'. We have here, Hume writes, 'a *certain form of words* invented ... by which we bind ourselves to the performance of any action' (*T* 522). Such conceptual dependencies are a further sign of artifice.[16]

The artificiality of the convention-presupposing actions that concern Hume is further revealed by reflection on the rules to which they are subject. Individuals bound to fundamental social conventions such as those concerning property or justice are subject to 'general rules, which are

---

[16] Hume writes (*T* 500, 533–4) of the 'artifice of politicians' in the encouragement of a sense of obligation with respect to matters of justice. This is artifice of a secondary sort. In the case of justice such an artifice presupposes, but does not itself constitute, a convention. Even the presupposition of convention is not necessary for such artifices, however, for 'artifice and education' may be employed to encourage not only the artificial, but also the so-called natural, virtues (*T* 578–9).

unchangeable by spite and favour, and by particular views of private or public interest' (*T* 532), rules that are 'universal and perfectly inflexible' (ibid.), 'stedfast and immutable' (*T* 620). The rules in question are, of course, non-moral rules: they are rules adopted for the non-moral reasons that individuals have for devising, and for taking part in, such conventions. Though universal they can, it seems, accommodate exceptions or qualifications. Insisting that they do not 'allow of many exceptions' (*T* 531), Hume suggests that they do allow some; and he offers an account of promising that in effect identifies several classes of exceptions to the rule that promises be kept. While admitting exceptions, the rules in Hume's conventions are presumably universal in the formal sense that they deal with classes of cases, including classes of exceptions.[17] But he seems to have something further in mind when insisting that the rules in the conventions that concern him—rules that may, it seems, allow classes of exceptions—are none the less 'perfectly inflexible' or 'stedfast and immutable'. Perhaps his point is simply that, once satisfactorily framed, they impose requirements on conduct that may not be outweighed by any other concerns that an agent may have.

Why have rules with the properties just specified? Parties to such pivotal conventions as that governing property must recognize that the absence of rules with these features 'wou'd produce an infinite confusion in human society, and ... the avidity and partiality of men wou'd quickly bring disorder into the world' (*T* 532; compare *T* 533). What is true of the form of the rules governing property is true of their substance as well. If they are rational, prospective parties to conventions governing property must reject initially tempting rules that assign property rights according to some purported 'relation of fitness or suitableness' between owner and object owned (*T* 514), or in terms of some public utility purportedly consequent upon such a principle of distribution. In Hume's view, such initially tempting rules would generate controversy and disorder, not order and peace. They would, that is to say, subvert, not serve, the convention's purposes.

Hume hints, as we have seen, at an identification of a convention's rules with the behavioural regularity *R* that in part constitutes that convention, an identification that brings the benefits of ontological austerity. But he also hints at a distinction between rule and regularity, a distinction that is needed if one is to represent, in satisfactory fashion, the possibility of non-compliance on the part of parties to a convention. If rule

---

[17] Hume alludes to the formal properties of such rules at *T* 551.

and regularity are distinct, however, how is one to accommodate, in economical fashion, the existence of a convention's rules?

Hume offers no account, but the materials for a suitably minimalist one are ready to hand. Conventions of the kind that concern Hume incorporate complex linguistic practices. Parties to such conventions give voice to their mutual expectations. They give their reasons for doing what they do, including, on occasion, their reasons for failures to comply. They criticize one another's failures to comply. They countenance, or they reject as inappropriate or unavailing, reasons offered for non-compliance. In particular, they reject, as considerations justifying non-compliance, claimed exceptions or qualifications for which the conventions, designed for certain purposes, have not made, and cannot reasonably make, provision.[18]

The rules of such a convention are represented by the reasons that could be given, and that would be accepted, in such attempts at justification. More precisely, they are represented by the explicitly evaluative sentences that would provide the major premises in mutually acceptable arguments in support of claims to have complied with the convention's requirements, or to have been justified in acting in ways that, on the face of it, the convention proscribes. Provision made for the incorporation of classes of exceptions, they are represented by explicitly evaluative sentences of the form: 'Parties to convention C ought to act in such-and-such a way save in circumstances of such-and-such a sort.' If the convention's rules are *represented* in this way they are *constituted*, it may then be said, by the existence of the convention-presupposing desires that find expression in such explicitly evaluative sentences. A convention's rules are *realized*, that is to say, in appropriate conative states of those who are party to the convention.

Understood in this ontologically economical way, a convention's rules are tied to behavioural regularities by the presence of common, and commonly efficacious, convention-supporting desires. Their existence is none the less compatible with the possibility of non-compliance given the possession, by the several parties to the convention, of competing desires that on occasion overcome convention-supporting ones. On this minimalist reading, rules are tied to behavioural regularities while yet being distinguishable, as they must be, from those regularities. They may intelligibly require a regularity greater than that which actually obtains.

---

[18] This is not, of course, to rule out *revision* of conventions in light of novel, or newly impressive, considerations that are, in such a fashion, brought to the attention of the participants.

Convention-presupposing desires find expression, as other desires do, in explicitly evaluative sentences. Such evaluative sentences will employ convention-presupposing terms displaying the conceptual dependency we identified a few paragraphs back: 'Parties to convention *C* ought to keep their *promises* (pay their *debts*, obey their *sovereign*) save in circumstances of such-and-such a sort.' When such convention-presupposing desires are assigned their descriptive contents the very same convention-presupposing terms will have yet another crucial role to play. Parties to convention *C* will desire that they keep their *promises* (pay their *debts*, obey their *sovereign*) save in circumstances of such-and-such a sort. Their descriptive contents, just as their explicitly evaluative expressions, will display the convention-dependent, and so artificial, character of their desires.

2. REASONS FOR COMPLIANCE

Hume takes it to be obvious that, in the psychological and external circumstances he envisages—in the 'circumstances of justice'[19]—each of the narrowly interested members of a population *P* has compelling interests that can, and can only, be served given the existence of some convention, *C*, of property or justice. He takes it as equally obvious that each member of *P* has, in consequence, compelling reason to stand to that convention, *C*, in a way that ensures, so far as possible, the furtherance of her compelling narrow interests. Let us assume Hume right on both points. Let us ignore the difficulties posed by the possibility of differing determinate conventions that could serve the compelling interests of the members of *P*. Does it follow that each member of *P* has compelling narrowly interested reason to *comply*, on any given occasion, with the rules of justice to which the convention, *C*, gives rise? Surprisingly, perhaps, and with every show of confidence, Hume appears to hold that it *does* follow. Defending this claim he distinguishes the case of the *co-operator*, who may be described as party to the convention, *C*, from that of the *knave*, who in an important sense stands apart from *C*.[20] Whether for co-operator or knave, the convention, *C*, 'create[s] a new motive' (*T* 522). Whether for co-operator

---

[19] John Rawls, whose phrase it is, discusses 'the circumstances of justice' in *A Theory of Justice* (Cambridge, Mass., 1971). Hume's account is to be found at *T* 484 ff. and *E* 188 ff.

[20] The term 'co-operator' is not Hume's.

or knave, or so Hume seems to claim, the motive is a compelling one. Let us consider, first, the case of the co-operator.[21]

If a co-operator has *compelling* narrowly interested reason to comply with the convention's rules of justice, he must, trivially, have *a* reason to comply. To have *a* narrowly interested reason to comply he must have non-moral desires with appropriate descriptive contents, desires whose explicitly evaluative expression corresponds in a suitable way to the convention's rules. So much follows from Hume's conativism, as we have represented it. To have *a* narrowly interested reason to comply is, however, compatible with also having reasons—narrowly interested reasons—for acting in ways that would constitute non-compliance with convention C's rules. The possibility of competing reasons for action is, as we have seen, one of which Hume is well aware. He has every reason to acknowledge the presence of competing narrowly interested reasons when characterizing the co-operator's reasons for compliance.[22]

Hume also has reason, of a kind intimated earlier, to acknowledge the prima facie character of the co-operator's convention-dependent desires, to take them as expressible in explicitly evaluative sentences that are prima facie in form, and so to have co-operators take the convention's rules as, in effect, prima facie rules. He must do so if he is to model, in coherent fashion, the situation of a co-operator who deliberates in the face of competing considerations. To be sure, Hume appears to assume that the rules of justice that correspond to the co-operator's narrowly interested desires make explicit provision for classes of exceptions. Given the point and character of such a convention, *C*, co-operators have reason to introduce explicit, mutually countenanced, classes of exceptions as they establish

---

[21] To frame the problem as narrowly as we have is not, of course, to deny that there may be room for revision of conventions. Nor is it to deny that, were the envisaged circumstances to alter in any of a number of ways—because of a dramatic change in the material circumstances of the population in question, say, or because of a widespread change of heart, or because of a sapping failure in the mutuality of expectations—someone party to the convention would cease, with the collapsing of the convention, to have reason to comply with the convention's rules. 'Suppose', Hume writes, 'a society to fall into such want of all common necessaries, that the utmost frugality and industry cannot preserve the greater number from perishing, and the whole from extreme misery; it will readily, I believe, be admitted, that the strict laws of justice are suspended, in such a pressing emergence, and give place to the stronger motives of necessity and self-preservation' (*E* 186). The thesis being examined in the text is simply that, given the existence of a convention of property or justice that co-operators have compelling reason to have, and to be party to, they also have compelling reason, on every occasion, to comply with the convention's requirements.

[22] Throughout the present section only an agent's narrowly interested, and so non-moral, reasons are in question. Discussion of the interplay of non-moral and specifically moral reasons for just actions is reserved for Sect. 3.

the convention's impositions. He also describes these rules as 'perfectly inflexible' (*T* 532), as 'stedfast and immutable' (*T* 620). For a co-operator with competing narrowly interested concerns, however, a given action may well be both desirable in so far as it accords with the convention's rule against theft, say, and undesirable in so far as it constitutes a failure to take a step that would assuage his hunger. Such convention-countering considerations may well not be ones that parties to the convention could build in as exceptions in the framing of the convention's rules: those rules may well, in *that* sense, be 'inflexible' or 'stedfast' or 'immutable'. Of course, their being *taken* as prima facie in character is compatible with the convention's rules being heavily weighted rules, and with the desires to which they correspond being similarly weighted. Those desires must be so weighted if a co-operator is to have, as Hume claims he will have, *compelling* reason to comply with the rules of justice.

Given this picture of the narrowly interested co-operator, he may have both *compelling* reason, originating in narrow interest, to comply with the rules of justice on a given occasion, and *some* reason, also originating in narrow interest, to act in a way not consonant with those rules. ''[T]is easily conceiv'd', Hume remarks, that 'a man may impoverish himself by a signal instance of integrity' (*T* 497). It is 'evident', he claims, 'that the particular consequences of a particular act of justice may be hurtful' (*E* 306); 'single instances of justice are often pernicious in their first and immediate tendency' (*E* 286); '[t]aking any single act, my justice may be pernicious in every respect' (*T* 498).[23] A co-operator, faced with such a prospect, must have *some* narrowly interested reason to act in unjust ways. That he should find himself faced with such challenges to the narrowly interested claims of justice should, of course, come as no surprise: the parties to the convention must recognize that ''[t]is impossible to separate the good from the ill' (*T* 497), that one cannot 'prevent all particular hardships, or make beneficial consequences result from every individual case' (*E* 305).[24] Co-operators adopt conventions with a view to narrow interest, fully cognizant, none the less, of the costs to be incurred thereby. And despite the prospect of such costs, the co-operator's narrow interests will dictate compliance with justice's rules. '[E]very individual person must find himself a gainer', Hume writes, 'on ballancing the account' (*T* 497; compare *E* 305). Despite the costs of compliance every co-operator

[23] The last-quoted passage must be read in the light cast by Hume's contrast, discussed below, between an 'enlarged' and a 'limited' view of an action.

[24] Anticipating later discussion, we may take the quoted passage to claim that one cannot make *only* beneficial consequences result from every individual case.

must in every case have compelling narrowly interested reason to do as justice demands. So, at least, Hume seems, with untrammelled confidence, to claim.

He makes frequent reference, in passages such as those just cited, to the particular consequences of particular actions. On the face of it, however, his untrammelled confidence neither rests nor could, with any convincing show of plausibility, be made to rest on a rational co-operator's comparative calculations of the effects, on narrow interest, of particular acts of compliance and non-compliance. Hume rests his case neither on the damaging effects of detected non-compliance on the interests of the non-complying co-operator nor on estimates of the likelihood of detection. His co-operators are aware, of course, of the enormous damage that would be done to their narrow interests were they ostracized or shunned, as also of the more tractable damage that would be done by their diminished credibility, or by their having to pay penalties of some sort or other. Hume does not, however, fasten on such considerations when discussing the case of co-operators. This is to the good, for it seems he could have little hope of showing that the expectation of *such* damages must in every case outweigh the losses surely to be incurred by some instances of compliance.

He can have even less hope of resting his case on a calculation of the damage done, by a single instance of non-compliance, to the convention itself, and thus to the convention's ability to contribute to a co-operator's narrow interests. But if, eschewing an unavailing consultation of the consequences of particular unjust actions, Hume were simply to point to a comparison of the consequences of having, and of failing to have, the convention itself, he would—nothing more being said—be no further forward. How can the convention's admittedly crucial contribution to his narrow interests give a co-operator compelling reason to comply with the convention on a given occasion even though non-compliance would, on that occasion, secure him from losses that would not themselves be outweighed by expected damage to the convention, or to his own standing with respect to the convention, or in other, more incidental, ways?

Does Hume's untrammelled confidence perhaps rest on a conviction that the costs to be incurred by compliance could never be so high as we—influenced, of course, by his own illustrations—have imagined? No rules of justice that rational and narrowly interested co-operators would adopt would, it might be said, be such as to require, even if only on occasion, the acceptance by co-operators of catastrophic losses. Rules of justice can, as we have seen, accommodate the specification of classes of exceptions. To be sure, a class of exceptions could be allowable only if the resultant rule would be consonant with, perhaps would enhance the prospects for, the mutually attractive goal of fostering peace and order and thereby the generation of society's many benefits. A rule imposing no burdens on a co-operator that, when shouldered, would prove in some way costly to the agent would transparently fail to meet this condition. Provisions *limiting* the losses to be incurred when respecting the possessions of others could conceivably, however, have a legitimate role to play. For one thing, co-operators must be reasonable in the mutual expectations they form about the efficacy of each other's motives: they must not expect the motivationally impossible, whether of others or of themselves. For another, they could—it might be said—have no reason, in their reflections on the appropriateness of candidate classes of exceptions, to adopt rules compliance with which might ensure, for a given complying co-operator, an inability to benefit at all from the convention's fruits. Arguably, then, Hume's co-operators would not adopt rules compliance with which would require, in envisageable circumstances, the acceptance by an agent of some catastrophic loss.

Such considerations, if sound, would limit the costs a co-operator could incur by compliance. Offering protection only against catastrophic loss, however, they provide no help towards the characterization of more run-of-the-mill situations. The problem of catastrophic losses safely to one side, what gives a co-operator compelling reason for compliance, no matter the occasion, even if faced with the prospect of substantial, albeit not catastrophic, damage to his narrow interests? What, for run-of-the-mill cases, supports Hume's untrammelled confidence in the coincidence of narrow interest and compliance?

Hume's confidence must, it seems, derive directly from his representation of the psychological profile of those who are party to the convention, those we have called co-operators. He contrasts a limited and an 'enlarged' (*E* 305) view of an action that conforms to the convention. Taking an 'enlarged' view of a prospective action, a given co-operator sees that action as embedded within 'a general plan or system of actions, which tends to public utility' (*E* 306), and thus 'tends', in the deeply important way detailed earlier, to his own narrow interests. He sees that 'general plan or system of actions'—that convention—to be 'to the highest degree, advantageous' (*E* 304) to its beneficiaries, to be 'highly conducive, or indeed absolutely requisite' (*T* 497) to their well-being and that of their friends and relations, to be, in fact, 'infinitely advantageous' (*T* 498), a condition on securing society's 'infinite advantages' (*T* 489). Taking an 'enlarged' perspective he views the action from within a framework formed by the shared and mutually acknowledged attitudes and expectations – including the conditional preferences—that Hume, in offering his analysis of convention, has described. From within that framework the co-operator is cognizant in particular that—and he takes the others to be cognizant that—the mutually beneficial convention rests on the confident expectation, on the part of each, that each of the others has an appropriate attitude towards compliance, a pre-emptively weighted conditional preference for compliance with the convention's rules. He is cognizant as well—and he takes the others to be similarly cognizant—of the conditions on the confident expectations thus required. Psychologically situated within this intricate causal setting of expectations and attitudes, thinking of himself as one party to a convention that is so deeply implicated in the securing of his narrow interests, he must think of the prospective action as one that, consulting those interests, he must perform. To think of his prospective action in this way, however, is to have a compelling narrowly interested desire to do it. For co-operators such as he, the coincidence of narrow interest and compliance is—so, it seems, Hume thinks—assured.

When taking an 'enlarged' view of a prospective action required by the rules of justice, a co-operator must desire—indeed, must have a pre-emptively weighted (albeit conditional) desire—to perform that action. Taking that 'enlarged' view is, however, compatible with a co-operator's also taking a 'limited' view of that very action. It is compatible with his finding that very action, when 'consider'd apart' (T 497) or 'consider'd in itself' (T 579), to be inimical to his narrow interests. It is compatible with his having a competing reason *not* to act as justice requires. As a co-operator cognizant of the profound connection between the convention and his narrow interests, however, he must nevertheless—so, it seems, Hume claims—have compelling narrowly interested reason to comply with justice's demands.

A 'sensible knave', as Hume terms him, differs radically from the co-operator in psychological profile. Not having the co-operator's conditional preferences, he recognizes no compelling reason, akin to the co-operator's, to comply in every instance with the rules of justice. No party to a convention of justice, the knave nevertheless has, as Hume represents him, compelling reason to appear to be party and so to appear to comply with justice's rules. On the assumption that he can maintain the appearances, however, he often has, or at least takes himself to have, compelling reason to escape, or to shift, the burdens the co-operator shoulders. Hume represents the cunning cast of his mind:

though it is allowed that, without a regard to property, no society could subsist; yet according to the imperfect way in which human affairs are conducted, a sensible knave, in particular incidents, may think an act of iniquity or infidelity will make a considerable addition to his fortune, without causing any considerable breach in the social union and confederacy. That *honesty is the best policy*, may be a good general rule, but is liable to many exceptions; and he, it may perhaps be thought, conducts himself with most wisdom, who observes the general rule, and takes advantage of all the exceptions. (*E* 282–3)

For the most part he complies, aiming thus to keep up appearances and so not be barred from the convention's benefits. He is clear that his occasional non-compliance will not subvert the convention. He is confident that, with due caution, he can on particular occasions—Hume writes of calculations made 'in particular incidents'—both violate justice's rules and avoid the losses that he would incur were he to be ostracized or shunned, or were he to be penalized in some way, or punished. Selecting his opportunities with care, he finds occasional quite compelling reason to make unilateral 'exceptions' in his own favour. He intends thereby to secure the advantages of parasitism and free-riding, advantages that presuppose the existence of the convention to which he strives to appear to be party.[25] His objective is to combine the convention's benefits with those of undetected non-compliance. Not a co-operator, he prefers to conform if the others do, but only if he can't get away with not doing so.[26]

He hasn't the co-operator's compelling reason for compliance in every case. Given his narrow interests, however, he has, if thinking clearly, compelling reason none the less. The likelihood of his escaping detection is low: Hume remarks the frequency with which knaves are, 'with all their pretended cunning and abilities, betrayed by their own maxims' (*E* 283). So, in particular, is the likelihood of his sustaining his policy of coolly calculated cunning: 'while ... [he] purpose[s] to cheat with moderation and secrecy, a tempting incident occurs, nature is frail, and ... [he] give[s] into the snare' (ibid.). The losses he faces upon detection are amongst the

[25] Gauthier offers the following characterization and contrast in *Morals by Agreement*, 96: 'A free-rider obtains a benefit without paying all or part of its cost. A parasite in obtaining a benefit displaces all or part of the cost on to some other person.' In a narrower context Hume gives an example of an individual who 'seeks a pretext to free himself of the trouble and expence, and wou'd lay the whole burden on others' (*T* 538).

[26] Perhaps Hume has such knaves in mind when he writes of 'the whole scheme or system concurred in by the whole, or the greater part of the society' (*E* 304). Perhaps he thinks of knaves as members of a society but those who, when properly understood, do not, despite common appearances, concur in the schemes or systems that constitute the society's conventions. Hume says little about the bearing, on the attitudes and expectations of co-operators, of the possibility that they may have knaves in their midst.

most substantial. Were he to suffer 'a total loss of reputation, and the for-feiture of all future trust and confidence with mankind' (ibid.) he would, at the very least, lose many of the 'infinitely advantageous' (*T* 498) bene-fits that co-operators secure—and that he himself hopes to secure by the preserving of co-operative appearances. The knave must make calcula-tions of expected utilities, calculations into which assessments both of the possible losses and gains, and the probabilities of suffering those losses and securing those gains, must enter. He must factor in assessments of the probability that he will in fact be rational in his crucial calculations. With again untrammelled confidence, Hume holds that the would-be knave must, if rational in the seeking of his narrow interests, consistently act as justice requires. Even without the co-operator's conditional pref-erences, the knave can only be deluded, Hume maintains, in thinking he ever has compelling reason not to do so.[27]

They are irrational in doing so, if Hume is right, but knaves act knav-ishly none the less. Their acting irrationally is, however, intelligible enough: it's a matter, in large measure, of missteps in the calculation of consequences. But what of the co-operator's occasional non-compliance, an occurrence that is, as Hume would surely insist, a matter of common-place observation? Readily intelligible miscalculations may enter here as well, of course, as may a variety of other obviously cognitive failings. In addition, however, there appear to be more deeply puzzling, and more widely damaging, dimensions to the irrationality co-operators display in their occasional failures to do what they have every reason to do. At times they act contrary to justice's requirements while to all appearances know-ing themselves to be acting against their own narrow interests in doing so. They have, as we have seen, narrowly interested desires that compete with those, likewise narrowly interested in character, that constitute their conditional preference for compliance. These desires can provide the conative components in the reasons from which they act in acting akratically. As represented earlier, however, a co-operator's conditional

---

[27] Hume adds that the knave would, even if consistently successful in his cunning venture, suffer the loss of benefits that, while not recognized as such by the knave, are none the less benefits of substance. He is thinking of 'the invaluable enjoyment of a character' (*E* 283), of enjoyments consequent upon 'the peaceful reflection on one's own conduct' (*E* 284). The knave would, it seems, have *something* to say in reply.
    Hume's response to the knave, treated so briefly here, has been discussed with great care and subtlety, but to widely differing effect, in: Gauthier, 'Artificial Virtues and the Sensible Knave'; Annette Baier, 'Artificial Virtues and the Equally Sensible Non-Knaves: A Response to Gauthier', *Hume Studies*, 18 (1992), 429–39; and Gerald J. Postema, 'Hume's Reply to the Sensible Knave', *History of Philosophy Quarterly*, 5 (1988), 23–40.

preference for compliance is pre-emptively weighted. How, then, can he fail to follow justice's rules?

Hume is less than pellucid when he adverts to the intersection of akrasia and convention:

> as this interest, which all men have in the upholding of society, and the observation of the rules of justice, is great, so is it palpable and evident, even to the most rude and uncultivated of human race; and 'tis almost impossible for any one, who has had experience of society, to be mistaken in this particular. Since, therefore, men are so sincerely attach'd to their interest, and their interest is so much concern'd in the observance of justice, and this interest is so certain and avow'd; it may be ask'd, how any disorder can ever arise in society, and what principle there is in human nature so *powerful* as to overcome so strong a passion, or so *violent* as to obscure so clear a knowledge? (*T* 534)

The passage reveals an obscurity in Hume's representation of akratic agency. He writes without flinching that co-operators 'so often act in contradiction to their known interest' (*T* 535). Comparing the claims, from the side of narrow interest, of a prospective violation of the rules of justice with those of relevant conformity to those rules, a co-operator may well be 'fully convinc'd, that the latter object excels the former' (*T* 535). The claims of the latter, from the side of narrow interest, may well be 'certain and avow'd' (*T* 534). The co-operator may none the less, on occasion, 'not [be] able to regulate ... [his] actions by this judgment' (*T* 535) and so may, while acting intentionally, pursue what he acknowledges to be a substantially less satisfactory course. In doing so he will fail to do what justice demands. When representing akratic agency in this fashion, Hume highlights its seeming intractability within a theory of action.

At times he tones down akrasia's apparent intractability. At times, that is, he represents the akratic co-operator's knowledge, though 'certain and avow'd', as somehow compromised, and so rendered unmysteriously in-efficacious. '[P]resent interest', he writes, 'may ... blind us with regard to our own actions' (*T* 545; compare *T* 499). And he seeks the 'principle' that works 'to obscure so clear a knowledge' (*T* 534).

Hume's proffered explanation of the occurrence of action against acknowledged interest does not eliminate the obscurity in these remarks. That explanation invokes three things: variability in the imaginability, and so the concreteness of conception, of expected effects of actions, where that variability is a function of the expected effects' spatial or temporal distance from the agent; a positive correlation between the concreteness of conception of expected effects and the degree of emotional excitation (the degree of 'violence') associated with the desire for those effects; and a positive (but not uniform) correlation between the degree of excitation of a desire and the motivational force (the degree of 'strength') of that desire (see T 534–7). From the co-operator's vantage-point, the benefits of compliance, being long-term benefits, are less concretely imaginable than the more immediate benefits she might secure by non-compliance. The thought of the latter benefits must, then, generate a greater degree of excitation and so (in some cases, at least) the enhanced motivational strength that explains the agent's intentional, but akratic, act of non-compliance. Because of the effects on the imagination, the proximity of such immediate benefits 'has a proportional effect on the will and passions' (T 535). '[M]en are', Hume suggests, 'mightily govern'd by the imagination, and proportion their affections more to the light, under which an object appears to them, than to its real and intrinsic value' (T 534).

What, precisely, is the envisaged causal route from effect on imaginability to effect on motivational force? Hume is inexplicit, but three arguably Humean—if unprepossessingly official—accounts suggest themselves. One account has differences in the imaginability of the expected effects of actions generate differences pro tem in the agent's assignments of probability to those expected effects, and thus differences in the motivational strength of desires that are affected by those probability assignments. Another traces a route from differences in the imaginability of the expected effects, through differences of degree of excitation in associated desires, to alterations (pro tem) in probability assignments made with respect to those expected effects, and thus to changes in the motivational strength of desires linked to those effects. On yet a third account, increases in the imaginability of the expected effects, while having no impact (even pro tem) on the agent's probability assignments with respect to those effects, would have a belief-bypassing effect on the motivational strength of desires linked to those effects. On the first two of the three accounts, the agent's irrationality derives from specifically cognitive incompetencies affecting the procedures he employs in the formation of beliefs. On the third, the irrationality derives from the severance of required ties between belief and desire. The first two accounts sit uneasily with Hume's representing akratic action as 'in contradiction to . . . known interest' (T 535). The third comports poorly with his suggestion that the conjectured mechanisms serve to 'obscure so clear a knowledge' (T 534). Obscurity remains.

The three options just considered take the 'knowledge' against which the akratic agent acts as wholly a matter of descriptive beliefs. To treat the 'knowledge' against which the akratic agent acts as a matter of (what are commonly taken to be) explicitly evaluative, rather than of descriptive, beliefs would, given Hume's conativism, introduce a very different range of theoretical considerations. Most interestingly, it would raise the question how an akratic agent could act—intentionally, but irrationally, of course—against what he judges to be in his best (narrow) interests, which is to say, against what he most wants to do. Hume's conativist theory, as we have set it out thus far, makes no provision for akratic action *so conceived*. A conativist theory capable of accommodating akratic action conceived in this fashion requires a more complex model of the links between desire and volition than we have seen Hume to possess. It requires, too, the introduction of a notion nowhere to be found in Hume, that of semi-autonomous functional divisions within the mind of the akratic co-operator. The key to such a conativist theory of akrasia is to provide the theoretical room within which one can characterize a co-operator both as wanting, all things considered, to comply, and as wanting—effectively—not to do so. To find that theoretical room one must move past Hume.[28]

Co-operators can, akratically, fail to comply. In Hume's view, the likelihood of this happening increases with the increasing complexity of the societies within which they function. Akratic irrationality is relatively unlikely in small, more rudimentary, societies: in them 'regard to [long-range] interest' is 'sufficiently strong and forcible' (*T* 499). In larger, more complex, societies its incidence is much greater. '[W]hen society has become numerous, and has encreas'd to a tribe or nation', Hume writes, 'this [long-range] interest is more remote; nor do men so readily perceive, that disorder and confusion follow upon every breach of these rules [of justice], as in a more narrow and contracted society' (ibid.).[29] In such

---

[28] In 'How is Weakness of the Will Possible?' Davidson develops what, if transposed from a linguistic to a psychological setting, we may take to be the more complex model we require of the links between desires and volition. He assigns distinctive roles to prima facie evaluative judgements, including both all things considered ones and those they presuppose, and to unconditional evaluative judgements. His prima facie evaluative judgements express desires, and his unconditional evaluative judgements express states that play a role comparable to that we have had Hume assign to volitions. Davidson develops the notion that the mind, because it has parts that are to some extent functionally independent of one another, can harbour irrationalities of various sorts, in 'Paradoxes of Irrationality', in *Philosophical Essays on Freud*, eds. Richard Wollheim and James Hopkins (Cambridge, 1982), 289–305, and in 'Deception and Division', in Ernest LePore and Brian McLaughlin (eds.), *Actions and Events: Perspectives on the Philosophy of Donald Davidson* (Oxford, 1985), 138–48. See Chap. 2, n. 33, above, as well as my 'Locke, Hume and the Nature of Volitions', especially 29–33. [29] For Hume's important contrast between more rudimentary and more complex societies, and the contrast of each of these with both family groups and political societies,

societies 'we may frequently lose sight of that interest, which we have in maintaining order' (ibid.).

Hume explains this tie between social complexity and akratic action by invoking his unprepossessing doctrine of the connections between imaginability of expected effects and the motivational strength of linked desires. The point to fasten on, however, is that he invokes the tie between social complexity and akratic non-compliance with a convention of justice in order to point up the threat that social complexity poses for the continuance of that convention. Numbers alone can pose a problem by affecting the ease with which the parties to the convention may 'know each others mind' (*T* 538), thus diminishing the prospects for the mutual knowledge on which conventions rely. It is the increased likelihood of akratic non-compliance, however, that poses the threat on which Hume fastens:

as all men are, in some degree, subject to the same weakness, it necessarily happens, that the violations of equity must become very frequent in society, and the commerce of men, by that means, be render'd very dangerous and uncertain. You have the same propension that I have, in favour of what is contiguous above what is remote. You are, therefore, naturally carried to commit acts of injustice as well as me. Your example pushes me forward in this way by imitation, and also affords me a new reason for any breach of equity, by shewing me, that I should be the cully of my integrity, if I alone shou'd impose on myself a severe restraint amidst the licentiousness of others. (*T* 535)

Agents sufficiently rational to recognize their own and others' tendency to akratic irrationality, and to reckon the effects of such irrationality on expectations and attitudes, must thus far have reason to be wary about continuing as party to the convention of justice in question. The effect, unless countered, must be the unravelling of the convention itself. His pathology of the collapse of a social convention mirrors Hume's analysis of the conditions on the convention's existence.[30]

see n. 13, above. According to Hume, it is with the development of more complex societies— societies in which the incidence of akratic non-compliance with conventions increases— that specifically moral sentiments come into play. We shall look to morality's role in countering the effects of akrasia in Sect. 3, below.

[30] In sketching this scenario for the collapse of a convention Hume fastens on the effects of the akrasia of co-operators. He neglects the effects on convention of the possible presence of knaves. He neglects, too, the possibility of *near*-conventions, as we may call them, amongst knaves.

3. MORALITY AND CONVENTION

Morality has a pivotal role to play just here. Providing an independent source of motivation, specifically moral desires serve to *second* the narrowly interested desires that co-operators have with respect to compliance. In the normal run of things, perhaps, the motivational contribution a co-operator's moral desires make to his compliance is otiose: he has compelling narrowly interested reason to comply, and that reason is sufficient to prompt his doing what justice demands. Situated in complex societies, however, co-operators are liable to akratic failures to comply: thus situated, their narrowly interested reasons for compliance, even if acknowledged as compelling, are—for psychological reasons that Hume has attempted to identify—not consistently sufficient to secure their compliance. Without the introduction of independent—and independently compelling—sources of motivation, akratic co-operators must, with increasing frequency, fail to comply. Introduction of specifically moral desires provides, however, just the sort of independent source of additional motivation that is needed. If equipped with an independent, because impartial, desire to do what justice demands, an otherwise akratic co-operator—akratic so far as his narrowly interested concerns go—has additional reason, reason that may well prove to be efficacious, to conform to the convention's rules. His moral desires may help him to act as his narrowly interested desires would, were he not akratic, ensure his acting. They may enable him to act as—were he not subject to akratic lapse— his taking an 'enlarged' view of his prospective actions would regularly lead him to act.

Hume insists on distinguishing narrowly interested and specifically moral reasons in contexts of justice. '[S]*elf interest* is the original motive to the establishment of justice', he writes, but it is not to be confused with '*the moral approbation*, which attends that virtue' (*T* 499–500, emphasis altered). He highlights the seconding role of specifically moral desires when discussing compliance with a convention governing promising: 'interest is the *first* obligation to the performance of promises', he writes, but '[a]fterwards a sentiment of morals concurs with interest, and becomes a *new* obligation upon mankind' (*T* 523, emphasis added). He does the same, with emphasis, when writing of justice:

we are to consider ... [the] distinction betwixt justice and injustice, as having two different foundations, *viz.* that of *self-interest*, when men observe, that 'tis impossible to live in society without restraining themselves by certain rules; and that of *morality*, when this interest is once observ'd to be common to all mankind, and men receive a pleasure from the view of such actions as tend to the peace of society, and an uneasiness from such as are contrary to it. 'Tis the voluntary convention and artifice of men, which makes the first interest take place ... After that interest is once establish'd and acknowledg'd, the sense of morality in the observance of these rules follows naturally, and of itself. (*T* 533, some emphasis omitted)

Hume insists, as well, that morality's seconding role is peculiarly important as a counter to the weakness of will that threatens when co-operators face the demands that the rules of justice impose. Moral desires come particularly into play when we 'lose sight of that interest, which we have in maintaining order' (*T* 499). They supply absent motivational efficacy when we are tempted to 'follow a lesser and more present interest' than that which justice serves or when, in the face of justice's requirements, we are 'blinded by passion, or byass'd by any contrary temptation' (ibid.). Having moral desires correspondent to the non-moral rules of justice, otherwise akratic co-operators are helped to act as they have every narrowly interested reason to act.[31]

The essential difference between a co-operator's specifically moral desires and the narrowly interested ones they second is, of course, that between the impartial and the partial. From her narrowly interested point of view, a co-operator desires that she comply with the rules of the particular convention to which she is party. (She also desires that the other parties to the particular convention comply as well.) From the moral point of view, by contrast, she desires that individuals act as narrowly interested

---

[31] Hume is not Panglossian here. His theory of *political* obligation starts from a recognition, on the part of rational agents, of the effect of their occasionally akratic irrationality on fundamental social conventions. He presents the novel convention that gives rise to specifically political society, with its provision for political authority and procedures of punishment, as a rational solution to the problems that irrationality poses for social organization, and so for the securing of society's benefits (*T* 534f.). Other factors also have a role to play in the defence against irrationality: the artifices of politicians and educators; a concern for one's reputation; an acquired 'affection to company and conversation' (*T* 489). Despite insisting on its seconding motivational role, then, Hume does not think morality sufficient, by itself, to counter each of the many threats that a tendency towards akratic failures to comply poses for a narrowly interested co-operator.

Introducing akrasia in connection with a convention's non-moral rules, Hume makes plain that akratic actions are not necessarily actions that fail to accord with specifically moral requirements: an agent can be described as akratic with respect to issues exclusively of narrow interest. Of course, an agent can *also* be akratic in so far as he fails to act in ways in which, in adopting the moral point of view, he finds himself to have compelling *moral* reason to act. A sense of political obligation may be viewed as providing motivation that seconds a specifically moral concern for the requirements of justice, both in standard settings and when akrasia threatens.

parties to determinate conventions of justice, that they be co-operators who act as the rules of their convention require—whoever those individuals may be, and whatever concrete convention of justice their convention may be. Adopting the moral point of view, her impartial desires make no essential reference to the particular convention of justice to which she is herself party. Of course, the conduct of all those who are party to the determinate convention to which she is herself party will fall within the scope of her impartial desire: she will be *impartially* concerned that she herself, as well as each of the others in her convention, be narrowly interested co-operators who act accordingly. In the case of that particular convention, of course, she will also have a *partial*, a *narrowly interested*, concern for mutual compliance. In the case of that convention alone she will have both narrowly interested and impartial—both non-moral and specifically moral—reason to comply.

This doubling of perspective will display itself in a doubling of the kinds of rules to which she will subscribe, as well as in a doubling of the kinds of explicitly evaluative sentences with which she will give expression to her distinguishable desires. She will subscribe to the non-moral rules specific to the convention of justice to which she is party. She will subscribe, in addition, to specifically moral rules pertaining to an individual's compliance with those rules, whatever they be, that are constitutive of the convention of justice to which that individual is party. She will give voice to her narrowly interested desires in evaluative sentences indexed to her own convention. She will also find expression for her impartial moral desires in sentences wholly free of such indexing, sentences with specifically moral content.

Specifically moral desires pertaining to justice are desire-implicating ones. Adopting the moral point of view, and making impartial application to her own case, a co-operator impartially desires that she herself have and act from a co-operator's narrowly concerned desire to comply with justice's demands. Their desire-implicating character constitutes another difference between the moral desires here in question and the co-operator's non-moral, narrowly interested desire to comply with the convention. With that difference in content come further differences between non-moral rules of justice and counterpart moral ones, and between the evaluative sentences used to give voice to the co-operator's moral desires, on the one hand, and to her non-moral desire to comply, on the other.[32]

---

[32] Despite the many differences between moral and non-moral rules of justice, the non-moral rules of the convention to which a given co-operator is party will contribute to the

The co-operator's narrowly concerned desire to comply with the convention's rules constitutes the *virtuous* non-moral desire that, in accordance with C1 and C2, moral desires pertaining to justice implicate. That non-moral desire is, in Hume's view, suitably distributed amongst human agents, and suitably efficacious in its bearing on conduct. Not every agent has it, for there are knaves. It is not everywhere efficacious, for co-operators can be weak-willed. It falls, none the less, within the rough range of normality that Hume's 'undoubted maxim' UM sets as a necessary condition on a desire's being virtuous.[33] It satisfies, too, the requirement that it be either useful or agreeable to the individual who has it, or to others. It is useful to individuals who have it, for it enables those individuals to be party to a convention that is profoundly in their narrow interest. It is useful, as well, to others. It is useful, in virtue of its role in a convention from which they will derive enormous benefit, to an individual co-operator's friends and relations. It is equally useful to all those others who, though not objects of that co-operator's narrowly interested concern, none the less benefit from the part he plays in their mutually advantageous convention. It is, to be sure, a narrowly interested desire. But it is useful, both to any individual who has it, and to others, in a way that the knave's narrowly interested desires could not, in Hume's view, ever be.

Focusing as closely as we have on the intricacies of Hume's account of the intersection of justice and morality, one runs the risk of assuming without warrant that, allowance made for the difference between the partial and the impartial, moral matters are essentially matters of convention. Plainly, however, it is Hume's view that the convention-bound does not exhaust the morally significant. If not so obviously so, it is also his view that adoption of the moral point of view is not itself the product of some convention.

That for Hume the convention-bound does not exhaust the morally significant is readily seen if one attends to the doctrine of natural virtues he develops at *Treatise*, III. iii. 1–5. As natural rather than artificial virtues, these have, as Hume depicts them, no essential dependence on convention.[34] All moral desires, as we saw much earlier, are mind-implicating

content of the determinate moral requirements to which that co-operator is subject as a party to that convention. While insisting on *this* link, Hume would reject Gauthier's apparent *identification*, in *Morals by Agreement*, of the moral rules (of justice) to which an individual subscribes with the rules of the convention (of justice) to which she is party.

[33] See Chap. 5, Sect. 1, for principles C1, C2, and UM.

[34] Mackie attempts, *Hume's Moral Theory*, 120–9, to subvert Hume's efforts to distinguish natural from artificial virtues.

desires: their contents make essential reference to the mind-displaying actions and qualities—the conative characteristics, the traits, the intellectual talents and abilities—of individuals. Some are desire-implicating desires: their contents make essential reference to the desires that lead individuals to act. Examining Hume's views of justice,[35] we have focused on a special class of desire-implicating moral desires, those implicating desires that depend upon conventions. The non-moral desires implicated by certain other moral desires have, however, no such dependency. The non-moral desire of benevolence is one such; gratitude is another. Being virtuous non-moral desires, but being independent of convention, either of these constitutes, in Hume's terminology, a natural virtue.

Some moral desires, though of course mind-implicating desires, are not specifically desire-implicating ones. The mind-displaying characteristics to which their contents make reference include such proclivities as courage or magnanimity, such talents or capacities as intelligence, imagination, or wit. To be sure, there may well be incidental respects in which the possession or valuation of such mental features implicates conventions of some sort: what counts determinately as courage, or as wit, may well vary from one society or historical period to another. Neither an analysis of conduct displaying such qualities, nor an account of the virtuousness of the qualities displayed, requires, however, any tale of the behavioural regularities, recurrent situations, complex settings of mutual expectations and attitudes, and obliquely achievable mutual advantages, that talk of convention entails. Accordingly, Hume treats such mental proclivities and capacities as natural, not artificial, virtues.[36]

Not all moral matters are matters of convention. But is adoption of the moral point of view itself the product of convention? If so, then, despite his careful distinction of natural and artificial virtues, Hume would be committed to morality's being at bottom conventional. He would be committed to the thesis that specifically moral desires, whether or not they be directed towards mental qualities that presuppose convention, are themselves convention-dependent. He would be committed to a corresponding

---

[35] As also his views of promising, political obedience, and various aspects of sexual conduct.

[36] Hume treats courage as a natural, not an artificial, virtue. Nevertheless he writes: 'Courage, which is the point of honour among men, derives its merit, in a great measure, from artifice, as well as [i.e. just as does] the chastity of women; tho' it has also some foundation in nature' ($T573$). Perhaps the point is that the common interest is best served by a convention assigning differing requirements of courage for men and women, after the fashion of the differing requirements with respect to sexual conduct. But the remark is cryptic and one cannot be confident about its interpretation.

thesis about moral rules. Such rules may proscribe or prescribe both convention-dependent and convention-independent conduct and characteristics. That the rules count as specifically moral rules would none the less be a function of some convention to which those who subscribe to the moral rules are party.

Hume's rejection of this thesis is, it seems, unequivocal.[37] Writing of the 'whole scheme ... of law and justice' he says:

After it [i.e. that scheme] is once establish'd by these conventions, it is *naturally* attended with a strong sentiment of morals; which can proceed from nothing but our sympathy with the interests of society. (*T* 579–80)

In a similarly emphatic fashion he also writes:

Tho' justice be artificial, the sense of its morality is natural. 'Tis the combination of men, in a system of conduct, which renders any act of justice beneficial to society. But when once it has that tendency, we *naturally* approve of it; and if we did not so, 'tis impossible any combination or convention cou'd ever produce that sentiment. (*T* 619–20)

The rules of justice specific to a given convention are a product of that convention: their standing is wholly conventional. Specifically moral rules that pertain, impartially, to matters of justice are, in striking contrast, products not of convention but of corrected sympathy. The wants that underpin a given set of rules of justice are convention-presupposing, narrowly interested, ones. Those underpinning specifically moral rules concerning justice are impartial rather than narrowly interested—though they make explicit reference to narrowly interested desires—and they introduce no requirement of participation in some morality-introducing convention.[38]

To be sure, joint adoption of the moral point of view may be said to meet several of the conditions on convention that Hume sets. Joint adoption of that point of view is a matter of mutual advantage. It appears to rest upon a network of expectations and attitudes, including second-order expectations and attitudes, comparable in many ways to that identified in the case of justice. (Surely this must be so if, as Hume maintains,

---

[37] Mackie *seems* to attribute a strong moral conventionalism to Hume when he writes, purportedly explicating Hume: 'it is only by some artifice or invention that people have come to feel approval of this behaviour and this disposition [i.e. convention-dependent behaviour and the dispositions that prompt it] and disapproval of their contraries', *Hume's Moral Theory,* 77.

[38] One also, of course, has specifically moral desires pertinent to conventions of justice other than those to which one is oneself party.

adoption of the moral point of view must be understood as a response to the intersubjective predicament caused by conative (and consequent linguistic) variability.)[39] Arguably, too, there are limitations on the moral claims to which one is subject in the treatment of individuals who would not reciprocate the recognition of such claims.[40]

Despite these similarities, there are deep differences between adopting a convention, such as that of justice, and adopting the moral point of view. For one thing, the range of those with whom one shares the moral point of view is inclusive in a way no convention could countenance: one shares that vantage-point not only with those spatially and temporally near to oneself, but also with those in quite distant times and places, those party to cultures—and to fundamental conventions—other than, indeed vastly different from, one's own. The range of those for whom one is concerned is also vastly more inclusive, from the moral point of view, than the range associated with a convention for mutual advantage could be: from the moral point of view, one is concerned (non-instrumentally, it must be added) for the interests of anyone, near or far, in so far as those interests are affected by the mind-displaying features of human agents, themselves or others. This impartially altruistic concern, a product of corrected sympathy, is utterly different from the narrowly interested concern characteristic of agents in so far as they are co-operators in conventions. Given its origin in corrected sympathy, it cannot be a motive had prior to morality. It cannot, then, be viewed, as narrow interest is, as a pre-existent motive that simply takes on a new direction through the workings of convention; and it can play no role in an explanation of adoption of the moral point of view.

As noted just above, and as we have seen in detail much earlier, Hume holds that adoption of the moral point of view must be understood as a response to what we have termed the intersubjective predicament.[41] Joint adoption of morality's impartial standpoint provides a conative (and, in consequence, a linguistic) common ground that would otherwise, and intolerably, be absent. According to his *modest* thesis about objectivity and language, adoption of the moral point of view both counters conative variability and provides a language for intersubjectively available evaluations. According to the *bold* thesis at which, as we have seen, he sometimes hints, joint adoption of the moral point of view is a condition on individuals making *any* communicative use of language, a condition on

---

[39] See Chap. 4, Sect. 2.
[40] Compare Harman's discussion of judging outsiders, *The Nature of Morality*, 107ff.
[41] See Chap. 4, Sect. 2.

their having *any* linguistic capacity at all. On the un-Humean, but plausible, assumption of the mutual dependency of thought and language, the bold thesis would establish joint adoption of the moral point of view as a condition on agents doing any thinking or talking at all. Hume's bold thesis—and *a fortiori* its un-Humean elaboration—is, we have maintained, much too strong. Given either it or its more modest predecessor, however, would we have arrived at a *quasi*-conventional foundation for impartial morality, paralleling the conventional foundation for justice, in narrow interest?

One can give *some* colour to the suggestion: narrowly interested in avoiding the situation of conative (and consequent linguistic) variability, or that of linguistic incapacity, agents each have a narrow interest in joint adoption of the moral point of view. Even if this be said, however, it must be insisted that the resultant moral concern for the interests of each of the others is not, as it can only be in the case of justice, a merely instrumental one. If led by narrow interest to the moral point of view, the impartial concern that results is one that has left its narrowly interested origins behind. Of course, each morally concerned individual must want each of her fellows to be likewise concerned. Each must want that in part because, recognizing the role of conative objectivity as a counter to the intersubjective predicament, each sees that as needed if each is to secure what she most deeply wants. Allusion to such networks of higher-order attitudes and expectations will perhaps provide some purchase for an attenuated concept of convention. If in an attenuated sense a convention originating in narrow interest, however, morality is a convention in which the narrow interests of each must constitute 'ultimate end[s]' (*E* 293) for each.

Of course if Hume's *bold* thesis were elaborated in the way envisaged morality *could not*, even in an attenuated sense, be a convention originating in narrow interest. For, were adoption of the moral point of view indeed a condition on the having of thoughts and language it would thereby be a condition on any agent's having the desires, self-interested or partial, in the having of which his having narrow interests resides.

7

Moral Agents

Let us introduce the technical notion of a *moral agent*,[1] defining such an agent as one who has, and who at times acts as the result of the promptings of, specifically moral desires. And let us reflect on the many properties that Hume assigns to typical agents of this type, and on the interrelations of those properties. Doing so will enable us to summarize, in perspicuous fashion, the central elements in the closely argued, and intricately articulated, moral psychology that Hume presents.[2] Doing so will also provide us with a theoretical setting within which to frame, in advantageous fashion, a number of further questions to which a Humean moral psychology must, and to which Hume to some extent does, attend.

A typical moral agent is, more primitively, a *non-moral* one. Her specifically moral desires (and so also her specifically moral affections) to one side, she is an individual with non-moral desires and affections, and with a host of other physical, psychological, and social features. She has a variety of cognitive capacities and incapacities, as well as a set of personal traits, whether short-lived or enduring, and traits of character. She has a complex network of descriptive beliefs, with their mind-to-world direction of fit, and a set of largely unconscious strategies for making adjustments to that network in response to experience and other factors. She has desires, with their world-to-mind direction of fit, and devices for securing their satisfaction. She has affections of various kinds consequent upon her success or failure in securing the satisfaction of her desires. She is cognizant of possessing features of the kinds we have enumerated, and that others are like or unlike her in the determinate features that they in their turn possess. And she is cognizant of changes, and of apparent possibilities and impossibilities of change, in some or other of these features, both in herself and in others.

Her non-moral desires, if Hume is right, are narrowly interested. Many of them (and so many of her affections) are person-implicating, or (more

---

[1] This interpretative term of art is not Hume's. For the relation between a *moral* agent, as here understood, and a *virtuous* one, see below.

[2] For an earlier effort at a summary representation of Hume's moral psychology see my 'Hume, Motivation and Morality', *Hume Studies*, 14 (1988), 1–24.

narrowly) mind-implicating, or (more narrowly still) desire-implicating. The implicated desires and other mental features may be her own or may belong to others. Some of the implicated desires presuppose her presence, with others, in a framework of convention. That framework presupposes, in ways we have detailed, her—and their—having complex arrays of higher-order expectations and attitudes concerning the expectations and attitudes of each. And the character of the framework's contribution to her narrow interests is such as to provide room for her failing, on occasion, and akratically, to pursue those narrow interests. The same holds for the others as well.

What renders her a *moral agent*, in the terminology introduced above, is the introduction of a further dimension to her conative (and so her affective) life—her having specifically moral desires (and so specifically moral affections), and her being at times moved to action by those desires. What renders her a moral agent is her coming to have occasionally efficacious desires with the universality, impartiality, and mind-implicating character that we characterized earlier. In having such moral desires, as a product of corrected sympathy, she has impartial desires directed towards her own and others' desires, traits, and mental capacities. She is concerned with those desires, traits, and capacities in so far as they are, in Hume's formula, useful or agreeable to the individual who has them, or to others. She is concerned, that is to say, with those desires, traits, and mental capacities in so far as they are virtuous non-moral features of the individuals in question. She is cognizant of the differing ways in which desires—narrowly interested desires—constitute virtuous features of individuals in settings that involve convention, and in those that do not. She can be bolstered, in acting in ways she acknowledges to be in her narrow interest, by her moral desires. Commonly, she is in contact with others who are likewise moral agents in the sense defined, and who have the further features just identified. She thinks both of herself, and of such others, as moral agents. Having specifically moral affections, both person-directed and more generally person-implicating, that are dependent on her moral desires, she is, and thinks of herself and each of the others as, a moral critic as well as a moral agent. She shares with others a language of moral evaluation, a language with which she and they can give voice to moral desires and affections.

What makes her an *agent*? For Hume, an individual is an agent just in case that individual has reasons for action, and acts in light of those reasons. Given his conativist theory of reasons for action, of course, it follows that an individual is an agent just in case she has desires and beliefs that are causally implicated in her volitions, thus her actions, in the complex ways that Hume has set out. Given his moral conativism, an individual is a moral agent just in case she has specifically moral desires that stand in the requisite relations to her beliefs, volitions, and actions.

For Hume, what makes an individual an agent, whether non-moral or moral, makes her a *free* agent as well. This can be seen from a consideration of his views about *freedom to act* and about *free action*.

In the *Treatise* he distinguishes two notions of liberty or freedom, allowing the legitimacy of the first. '[L]iberty of *spontaniety*', he says, is 'oppos'd to violence' and is the 'only ... species of liberty, which it concerns us to preserve' (*T* 407–8). (This sense of the word 'liberty' is, he adds, 'the most common sense of the word', *T* 407.) '[L]iberty of indifference', by contrast, is an ersatz notion introducing a purported 'negation of necessity and causes' (*T* 407).

In the first *Enquiry* he offers an analysis of the legitimate notion. 'By liberty', he writes, 'we can only mean *a power of acting or not acting, according to the determinations of the will*; that is, if we choose to remain at rest, we may; if we choose to move, we also may' (*E* 95). This 'hypothetical liberty', as he calls it, 'is universally allowed to belong to every one who is not a prisoner and in chains' (*E* 95). It is 'opposed to ... constraint' (*E* 96) and is absent when a man's actions 'are derived altogether from external violence' (*E* 99). It is 'hypothetical' only in the sense that hypotheticals appear in its analysis.[3]

Regimenting somewhat, and eliminating redundancy, we may take Hume's analysis of freedom to act, or of the fact that an agent (*A*) has the power to act, or can act, in a certain way (*φ*), to go as follows:

(1) *A* can *φ* means that if *A* chooses to *φ A φ*s, and if *A* chooses not to *φ A* does not *φ*.[4]

Introducing Hume's conception of volitions and their role in intentional actions[5] this becomes:

(2) *A* can *φ* means that if *A* forms a volition to *φ* that volition causes an

---

[3] Hume's analysis of 'hypothetical liberty' is reminiscent of Locke's analysis of freedom in *An Essay Concerning Human Understanding*, especially II. xxi. 8 and 56. Hume's 'hypothetical liberty' must not be confused with 'the scholastic doctrine of *free-will*' he alludes to at *T* 312.

[4] This and subsequent Humean proposals for the analysis of freedom to act have been much influenced by, though they differ in their emphasis on choice and volition from, Davidson's analysis in 'Freedom to Act'. For a more detailed treatment of Hume's views see my 'Hume, Freedom to Act, and Personal Evaluation', *History of Philosophy Quarterly*, 5 (1988), 141–56.

[5] See Chap. 2, Sect. 2.

appropriate upshot, and if *A* forms a volition not to ϕ that volition causes an appropriate upshot.

In the case of a volition to move one's arm the appropriate upshot would be the arm's moving; in the case of a volition not to move one's arm the appropriate upshot would be the arm's remaining still.[6] On this causal analysis an agent's freedom to act is straightforwardly a causal power of the agent, the root idea being that one's freedom to act is a matter of the causal efficacy of one's volitions. This, it seems, is the idea behind Hume's use of his term 'spontaniety'.

An attractively austere analysis of freedom to act, (2) is none the less not austere enough. In its second conditional it appears to introduce, as a condition on *A*'s being free to ϕ, *A*'s having the power to do otherwise.[7] It is, however, not a condition on one's being free to ϕ that one would refrain from ϕ-ing were one to choose to do so. If it is true that one would ϕ were one to choose to do so (and would do so because one chose to do so) then, no matter what would happen were one to choose *not* to ϕ, one is free to ϕ. Against this it may be objected that one cannot be free to ϕ unless one can refrain from ϕ-ing: if one cannot refrain there must be conditions sufficient for one's ϕ-ing quite apart from one's choosing to ϕ. But, the objection continues, if one will ϕ willy-nilly (whether one chooses to ϕ or chooses not to ϕ) one's ϕ-ing cannot be in one's own hands, and so cannot be something with respect to the doing of which one is free. This objection, though tempting, is confused, for even in cases of overdetermination *something*—the crucial thing—is in the agent's hands, *viz.*, acting *intentionally*.[8]

A's freedom to ϕ does not require the power to do otherwise: *A* can ϕ even if she can't not ϕ. We improve on Hume's analysis, then, if we replace (2) with the more austere:

(3) *A* can ϕ means that if *A* forms a volition to ϕ that volition causes an appropriate upshot.

---

[6] A given neural event and a given rising of one's arm may equally be effects of one's volition to raise one's arm, but only the latter event (here called the volition's 'upshot') can, even by relaxed standards, count as 'the desired event [that] is produced' or 'the immediate object of volition' (*E* 66).

[7] Hume's second conditional echoes Locke's unambiguous claim at *Essay*, II. xxi. 8: 'Wherever any performance or forbearance are not equally in a Man's power; where-ever doing or not doing, will not equally follow upon the preference of his mind directing it, there he is not *Free*, though perhaps the Action may be voluntary.' See also *Essay*, II. xxi. 10 and 24.

[8] The argument in the text derives from Davidson's 'Freedom to Act', 74–5. In Davidson's words (75), the agent's 'action, in the sense in which action depends on intentionality, occurs or not as he wills'.

'ϕ' in (3), and in earlier formulations, is to be replaced by a verb of action. But what of the expression 'forms a volition to ϕ'? Is it (or does it contain) a verb of action? If so, then unless one makes the *ad hoc* move of denying that questions of freedom arise for the formation of volitions, it must be an intelligible question whether A can form a volition to ϕ. If A *can't* do so then it seems she can't ϕ either, even though it is true that if she does form a volition to ϕ she will ϕ, and so (3) would fail as an analysis of freedom to act.[9] Unfortunately, if A *can* form a volition to ϕ the question must arise whether she can form a volition to form a volition to ϕ, and it is not clear how the threatening regress is to be blocked.

One way out is to deny that volitions, or formings of volitions, are themselves actions. Hume does not take this way out: he neither notices the present difficulty for a causal analysis of freedom to act nor directly addresses the question whether volitions, or formings of volitions, are actions. But he can avail himself of this way out and he has compelling reason to do. Only so can he both understand an ordinary action in terms of the causation, by volition, of the volition's upshot,[10] and provide a causal analysis of freedom to act in the way suggested by (3). To signal the requirement that forming a volition not be construed as itself an action we may replace (3) by:

(4) A can ϕ means that if A comes to have a volition to ϕ that event causes an appropriate upshot.[11]

We saw above that freedom to ϕ does not require the power to do otherwise. Does it, as some have suggested, require the power to *choose* otherwise? If this is not the bootless requirement of second-order volitions or choices (volitions to form volitions, choices of choices) it can only be the requirement that an agent's beliefs and desires not be causally sufficient for the choices he makes. But this requirement is one that Hume's analysis of freedom to act, an analysis tied to his theory of reasons for action, is designed to subvert. In Hume's view the presence of just such

---

[9] Compare Davidson 'Freedom to Act', 63–4, 68, 72. The objection derives from R. M. Chisholm, 'J. L. Austin's *Philosophical Papers*', *Mind*, 73 (1964), especially 24–5.

[10] For some of the twists and turns here see my 'Hume's Volitions', 84–6.

[11] As Davidson notes, there are writers who would deny that the problem is solved by introducing antecedent conditions that are not actions: in the present connection it would be objected that A can ϕ only if A can come to have a volition to ϕ. Davidson, who takes desires and beliefs (not volitions) to be the antecedent conditions, disagrees in 'Freedom to Act', 73: 'I hold that there is a basic sense in which we are free to —— (can ——) provided all that is needed for the action (in addition to other present circumstances) is the right attitudes and beliefs. The question whether we can have those attitudes and beliefs in turn is (except in special circumstances) not relevant.'

causal dependencies is a condition on free, because a condition on intentional, action. It is a condition, too, on an intelligible conception of responsibility.

Hume combines, with his austere causal analysis of freedom to act, an equally austere conception of a *free action*. An action is a free action *if* – as well as only if – it is an intentional action. A can't have ϕ-ed intentionally if she was not, at the time of acting, free to ϕ.

An agent may, of course, intelligibly wonder whether he is free to ϕ. Indeed, Hume appears to hold that believing oneself capable of ϕ-ing is a necessary condition of one's ϕ-ing intentionally because it is a necessary condition of one's forming a volition to ϕ (E 66). Obviously it is not a necessary condition of one's being free to ϕ. As obviously, it is a sufficient condition neither of one's being free to ϕ nor of one's ϕ-ing intentionally.

Hume rejects what he terms 'liberty of *indifference*', with its 'negation of necessity and causes' (T 407). He takes psychological states and events to be on a par with 'the operations of external bodies' (T 399) so far as the crucial marks of causality go. There are regularities to be discerned, both on the psychological, and on the physical, sides. And our explanatory and predictive responses, with respect to the psychological, match, in ways that matter, those to the physical. '[O]ur actions', he argues, 'have a constant union with our motives, tempers and circumstances' (T 401); and 'the *union* betwixt motives and actions... [has an] influence on the understanding ... in *determining* us to infer the existence of one from that of another' (T 404). It must be objected that, in here pressing the parallels, Hume lets slip his own grasp on the peculiarities of the role that reasons play both in the explanation, and in the prediction, of actions. Intent on displaying reasons as causes, he here neglects what makes them rational causes. He is none the less right to insist that the psychological is causal and that psychological states and events, just as physical ones, are subject to causal law.

It follows neither that those laws must be, nor that they can be, statable in psychological (or in psychophysical) terms. Indeed, there is compelling reason to think that the requisite laws, if required to be strict, cannot be formulated using the psychological vocabulary of desires, beliefs, intentions, and volitions.[12] Hume envisages a route from rough-and-ready psychological (or psychophysical) generalization to serious law through

---

[12] Davidson argues for the anomalism of the mental in 'Mental Events', 'Psychology as Philosophy', and 'The Material Mind', all in *Essays on Actions and Events*. For an exploration, by many hands, of some of the difficulties in the concept of mental causation, see John Heil and Alfred Mele (eds.), *Mental Causation* (Oxford, 1993).

the specification, always in psychological terms, of ever more complicated sets of conditions (compare *T* 403–4). As it seems, however, that
route is blocked by just those features of rational causes that Hume neglects when, at *Treatise*, II. iii. 1 ('Of liberty and necessity'), and again in the
first *Enquiry* section of the same name, he makes his case for causal regularities of a psychological sort.

Fortunately, he attends to these neglected features when elaborating
his conativist account of reasons for action. Indeed, in developing his
conativism he offers what must count as an independent argument for
psychological causation, and in particular for the presence of causal ties
between beliefs and desires, on the one side, and intentions and volitions,
on the other. '[A]ll actions of the will', he writes, 'have particular causes'
(*T* 412). The causes he has in mind are rational causes, causes constituted
by the reasons from which agents act.

Hume's austere analysis of freedom to act, and his minimalist conception of free action, comport nicely with—indeed, compel—the thoroughly naturalistic, because thoroughly causal, approach to human conduct
that he advances. In his view, they contribute, as well, to the articulation
of an intelligible conception of responsible agency, one that helps explain
several aspects of exculpation.[13]

Hume writes, in the *Treatise*: 'Men are not blam'd for such evil actions
as they perform ignorantly and casually [i.e. accidentally], whatever may
be their consequences. Why? but because the causes of these actions are
only momentary, and terminate in them alone' (*T* 412). Of course, the
volitions implicated in intentional action are themselves 'momentary',
and they too can be said to 'terminate alone' in the particular events that
are their upshots. Hume's point is that actions, in so far as performed
'ignorantly and casually', do not have their causal origin in the agent's
desires, these here being taken both to endure (they are not 'momentary') and to be general (they do not—or not necessarily—'terminate
alone' in the particular action performed on a particular occasion).

In a similar vein he writes:

repentance wipes off every crime, especially if attended with an evident reformation of life and manners. How is this to be accounted for? But by asserting that
actions render a person criminal, merely as they are proofs of criminal passions
or principles in the mind; and when by any alteration of these principles they
cease to be just proofs, they likewise cease to be criminal. (*T* 412)

---

[13] For a more extensive treatment of Hume's views on exculpation than that provided
here, see Michael Bayles, 'Hume on Blame and Excuses', *Hume Studies*, 2 (1976), 17–35.

The person's past criminal actions were properly a basis for negative person-directed affections directed towards him because, as intentional, they revealed the person to have enduring conative qualities of a certain undesirable sort. If he has reformed—if, that is, he no longer has those 'criminal passions or principles in the mind'—his past criminal actions reveal nothing of the person he now is, nothing, that is, of his present enduring desires and motivation. Hume stresses 'evident reformation of life and manners'. The man's more recent intentional actions are the product of his latter-day desires: only so can they reveal him in his newer, now shining, colours.

Hume returns to the theme of the enduringness of the desires that lie behind intentional actions when he writes:

Men are less blam'd for such evil actions, as they perform hastily and unpremeditately, than for such as proceed from thought and deliberation. For what reason? but because a hasty temper, tho' a constant cause in the mind, operates only by intervals, and infects not the whole character. (T 412)

Granted that hastiness is itself an undesirable enduring quality of the agent, the passage must be puzzling. On two central points, however, Hume's position is passably plain. First, hastiness and undesirable desires are action-affecting qualities of quite different kinds. Undesirable desires, unlike hastiness, 'infect the whole character'; being desires, they are 'durable principles of the mind, which extend over the whole conduct, and enter into the personal character' (T 575). Second, an agent's desires have a peculiarly central role to play in affective responses prompted by an agent's actions. When actions are in question, it's his motives that make the man.

Even in the absence of action this can be so:

Where a person is possess'd of a character, that in its natural tendency is beneficial to society, we esteem him virtuous, and are delighted with the view of his character, even tho' particular accidents prevent its operation, and incapacitate him from being serviceable to his friends and country. Virtue in rags is still virtue; and the love, which it procures, attends a man into a dungeon or desart, where the virtue can no longer be exerted in action, and is lost to all the world. (T 584)

Two types of cases may be distinguished. In the one, the agent forms a volition but the volition is ineffective; in the other, the agent, believing himself incapable of acting in the way in question, fails to form a volition that, without that belief, he would have formed. In either case his desires, ineffective though they be, constitute their possessor an admirable individual. Neither one's being free to act in a certain way, nor one's believing that one is free to act in that way, is a necessary condition on one's being assessed as a person inclined to act in that way.

From the standpoint of person-implicating affections, the significance of intentional action, thus of free action, lies in what it reveals of the relatively enduring conative character of the agent, what it reveals of the agent's enduring desires. Its significance derives from the fact that, as intentional, it is 'connect[ed] ... sufficiently with the person', is 'deriv'd from a particular fore-thought and design', is linked with 'the sensible and thinking part' (*T* 349). '[A]n intention', that is to say, 'shews certain qualities, which remaining after the action is perform'd, connect it with the person' (*T* 349). Free, because intentional, actions have their causal origin in enduring conative qualities of their agents, qualities that, precisely because of their enduringness, and because of the distinctive contribution they make to the agent's character, bear centrally on affective responses towards that agent. The intentional actions that an agent would perform were she free to do so bear in a similarly central way on such person-directed responses.

There is room for misgiving here. Surely there are transient desires, momentary hankerings, say, to kick off the traces? And surely one cannot, with *no* further ado, identify causally efficacious desires with enduring dispositional properties of the agents who have them? But Hume can insist that the desires that matter in our affective responses to an individual are relatively long-standing ones, desires that help constitute, as one might say, that individual's personality. He can insist, too, that the very idea of an agent requires the kind of structuring of motivation that only enduring conative states can provide. And he can plausibly hold that, if negligent in their deployment, he has available the materials for the development of a coherent realist theory of mental dispositions, a theory that not only can countenance a causal role for enduring desires but also can permit the devising of statements, used for the attribution of desires to agents, that are at least lawlike in character.[14]

According to Hume, proponents of 'the doctrine of liberty or chance' (*T* 411)—where the so-called 'liberty of indifference' is in question—can make no sense whatever of the significance of intentional action for affective valuation. Their doctrine implies, says Hume, that a man's actions reveal nothing of the man, that 'a man is as pure and untainted, after

[14] See Chap. 3 ('Mental Dispositions') in my *Hume's Philosophy of Mind*. See, too, Davidson's 'Hempel on Explaining Action', *Essays on Actions and Events*, 261–75.

having committed the most horrid crimes, as at the first moment of his birth' (ibid.). It implies that a man is no more accountable for his intentional than for his unintentional actions: he is not 'more accountable for those actions, which are design'd and premeditated, than for such as are the most casual and accidental' (ibid.). Why? Because, by denying the causal tie between action and enduring desire, it cannot link what is done with the 'person or creature endow'd with thought and consciousness' (ibid.) who is the proper object of person-directed affections. Unable to effect that link, it has no coherent account to offer either of free, because intentional, action or of the purported agent's agency, and so can provide no intelligible account of affective responses to the purported agent as an agent.[15]

We have been led, by attending to his views on freedom to act, and on free action, to register the place, in Hume's theory of agency, of a person's enduring conative characteristics, her 'durable and constant' desires. We have been led, by accompanying reflections on his doctrine of exculpation, to mark the central place that he assigns to such enduring desires in his account of person-directed affective responses. Of course, other enduring qualities have roles to play in Hume's accounts both of agency and of affective response. Agents have, as we have seen, a host of enduring cognitive and affective, as opposed to conative, features. As we have also seen, their cognitive and affective features complement their conative ones in constituting the basis for affective responses, whether non-moral or moral, whether their own or others', to these agents. Given Hume's com-

---

[15] According to 'the doctrine of liberty or chance', Hume writes, a man's 'character [is not] any way concern'd in his actions' (*T* 411). In Hume's own view, if actions 'proceed not from some cause in the characters and disposition of the person, who perform'd them, they infix not themselves upon him' (ibid.; compare *T* 575). Does this commit Hume to the claim, surely unconvincing, that an agent is responsible only for his characteristic actions? Surely not. Hume is here concerned with two now-familiar theses: that intentional actions have their causal origins in the agent's desires or motives; and that his desires are 'durable and constant' (*T* 411) qualities of the agent. Neither thesis requires the actions for which he is responsible to be characteristic actions, actions that he characteristically or typically performs. The first thesis patently does not. That the second does not can be seen by reflecting on the fact that the agent's acting or not from some desire depends not only on his having that desire but also on his beliefs, his other desires, the circumstances in which he finds himself, and other factors as well. He may have a desire for a length of time, while not acting from it, or while rarely acting from it. His occasional actions prompted by that desire would then, in the sense intended, be *un*characteristic actions. Revealing, none the less, the desire that lies behind them, they would reveal something of the sort of person he is, thus would contribute to the basis for person-directed affective responses of which he is the object. In the sense Hume intends, any intentional action, characteristic or uncharacteristic, originates in the agent's character. Contrast Philippa Foot, 'Free Will as Involving Determinism', *Virtues and Vices and Other Essays in Moral Philosophy* (Oxford, 1978), 62–73, and Paul Helm, 'Hume on Exculpation', *Philosophy*, 42 (1967), 265–71.

mitment to the centrality of desire, such affective responses, whether moral or non-moral, presuppose appropriate mind-implicating desires with respect to enduring mental qualities of any of these sorts. Non-moral mind-implicating desires are narrowly interested desires concerned with enduring mental qualities, conative, cognitive, and affective, of the desirer herself, and of some others. Specifically moral desires are their impartial variants.

Not being actions or events, however, such enduring desired qualities are not properly within the province of an agent's freedom to act. So far as his mind-implicating desires go, an agent desires that agents, himself and others, have and act from such-and-such desires, and that they have such-and-such capacities and affective responses. And he has affective responses consequent upon his determination that agents, himself or others, act in the manner desired, have, or fail to have, the desired desires, capacities, and responses. But what, thus described, he desires of himself—or of them—is not something that it is in his power—or in theirs— to do. Not being actions, his desires, say, or his intellectual capacities, or his proclivities to certain affective responses, are not possible free actions of his, not things he can—that he is free to—do.

It doesn't follow that his desires and the rest are not within his control, for it could be argued that, by performing actions that he is free to perform, he can intentionally, if in necessarily oblique ways, effect changes in his desires, his capacities, his affections. Hume is highly restrictive, however, when he represents the prospects for such purported control. Natural abilities, he writes, 'are almost invariable by any art or industry' (*T* 609). Characteristics such as 'constancy, fortitude, magnanimity' are 'equally involuntary and necessary, with the qualities of the judgment and imagination' (*T* 608); and it is 'almost impossible for the mind to change its character in any considerable article, or cure itself of a passionate or splenetic temper, when they are natural to it' (*T* 608). Desires and other sentiments 'must be excited by nature ... and must arise from the particular situation, in which the mind is placed at any particular juncture' (*E* 48); it is 'certain we can naturally no more change our own sentiments, than the motions of the heavens' (*T* 517).[16]

There is *some* scope for control even so. Agents can have *some* effect on the desires and affections, say, of others. There is *something*—if not what is usually thought—to the educative and other efforts of 'legislators, and divines, and moralists' (*T* 609; compare *T* 533–4). At least this can be said: 'moral

---

[16] It follows that there are other impediments to freedom, other limits to effective volition, than 'force, and violence, and constraint' (*T* 407).

qualities... or at least, the actions, that proceed from them, may be chang'd by the motives of reward and punishment, praise and blame' (*T* 609). Can agents, non-moral or moral, have such effect on their own desires and affections? Hume has little to say to the question. Surely, however, he can allow *some* measure of indirect control over one's own sentiments, control exercised by the doing of things one thinks will generate or eliminate, dampen or encourage, those sentiments. As noted earlier, he countenances the case of a parent, devoid of parental benevolence, who acts towards his child out of a sense of moral obligation, and who hopes, thereby, to come to have the non-moral desire he morally values.[17] (In what Hume presumably takes to be the standard case, of course, specifically moral desires *second* the motivational contribution of virtuous non-moral desires the agent already has.)

Hume's moral agents are free agents fully subject to nature's causal laws. Are they also *single* agents? Are they also *enduring* agents, agents who maintain their identity through time and change? As represented here, they appear to be *mis*represented by the official theory of the unity and identity of persons, and of the consciousness that persons have of their own unity and identity, that Hume offers at *Treatise*, I. iv. 6 ('Of personal identity'). As represented here, they are more than bundles comprising perceptions (these construed in Hume's official way) that stand in suitable causal and similarity relations to one another; and their sense of self, and of self-identity, seems to demand more than the associative machinery Hume's official theory provides.[18]

To be sure, they do have Humean perceptions, at least if these are construed, in non-official fashion, as occurrent sensations, images, recollections, thoughts, desires, and affections. And arguably their perceptions do—though the details are notoriously difficult to get quite right—stand in relations of causality and resemblance that help constitute them the

---

[17] Locke appears to allow far greater scope than Hume does in such matters. In particular, he allows the voluntary suspension of the securing of desire, as well as the possibility of an agent's choosing his goals. For an examination of Humean responses to these and related Lockean claims, see my 'Locke, Hume and the Nature of Volitions', 41–8.

[18] For a detailed examination of Hume's official theory, see Chap. 5 ('The Idea of One's Self') in *Hume's Philosophy of Mind*; for a briefer account, concentrating on the difficulties, see my 'Hume on Self-Identity, Memory and Causality', in *David Hume: Bicentenary Papers*, ed. George Morice (Edinburgh, 1977), 167–74. David Pears's *Hume's System: An Examination of the First Book of his Treatise* (Oxford, 1990), 120–51, is very helpful on this vexed topic, as is a series of essays by Terence Penelhum including: 'Hume on Personal Identity', in *Hume: A Collection of Critical Essays*, ed. V. C. Chappell (Garden City, NY, 1966); 'Hume's Theory of the Self Revisited', *Dialogue*, 14 (1975), 389–409; and 'The Self in Hume's Philosophy', in Kenneth R. Merrill and Robert W. Shahan (eds.), *David Hume: Many-sided Genius* (Norman, Okla., 1976), 9–23.

single, and enduring, persons they are. But they are, in addition, physical entities, with determinate physical capacities and limitations. And they are individuals whose psychological lives are intricately structured in the many ways we have seen. They have complex networks of variously interdependent beliefs, desires, and affections, these networks depending on the contents of the beliefs, desires, and affections in question, on their differing functional roles, and on a host of content-dependent causal dependencies. They come to have, and they continue in the possession of, a variegated collection of enduring psychological abilities, capacities, dispositions, proclivities, and traits. Centrally, they have 'durable and constant' desires, desires with the extraordinarily complex contents that we have attempted to detail, and that play a critical causal role—what we earlier called the major role—in their conduct. They are subject to occasional akratic lapses, lapses that reveal, perhaps, divisions. At a given time, however, and over time, their mental lives—and the physical lives in which these are embedded—display an integration amidst complexity that is (save that it must be this way) quite extraordinary.

Hume's moral agents not only are, but also think of themselves and the others as, entities of the sort just described. They cannot have the person-implicating desires, whether natural or artificial, whether nonmoral or moral, that they have, and they cannot have the affections that presuppose those desires, unless they do so. Their desire-implicating desires, whether moral or non-moral, are concerned with desires taken not in isolation but as located in complex structures of the sort just described, structures constituting the mental lives of particular individuals. So, at least, our reflections on sympathy, and on its correction, have suggested.[19] And in adopting the moral point of view they think of themselves, and the others, impartially but not abstractly. They think of themselves and the others in ways that abstract from partiality-generating ties to themselves, to be sure. But in doing so they none the less think of themselves, and the others, as distinct, unitary and enduring individuals, as individuals with narrowly interested as well as specifically moral desires, as individuals whose cognitive, conative, and affective lives reveal a daunting richness of interconnections.[20]

---

[19] Pursuit of questions raised by *this* element in our representation of Hume's theory of moral agents would require careful attention to arguments to be found briefly set out in Derek Parfit, 'Later Selves and Moral Principles', in Alan Montefiore (ed.), *Philosophy and Personal Relations* (London, 1973), 137–69, and much more elaborately in his *Reasons and Persons* (Oxford, 1984).

[20] For some of the issues raised by *this* element in our characterization of Hume's moral agents see Bernard Williams, 'Persons, Character and Morality', *Moral Luck*, 1–19.

Of course, some elements in this non-atomistic depiction of agents play a sufficiently prominent part even in Book I of the *Treatise*. The official theory of *Treatise*, I. iv. 6, is inadequate, then, even for individuals viewed, in the manner of Book I, as merely cognitive ones, and in abstraction from their conative and affective dimensions. The official theory's inadequacies come most forcefully into view, however, when we turn to the doctrines of Book II and especially Book III. '[W]e must distinguish', Hume writes, 'betwixt personal identity, as it regards our thought or imagination, and as it regards our passions or the concern we take in ourselves' (*T* 253). Some hint of the significance of making that distinction is already apparent in his discussion of the non-moral affections in Book II: 'pride and humility', Hume there writes, 'have the qualities of our mind and body, that is *self*, for their natural and more immediate causes' (*T* 303). Given the centrality of desire, however, inadequacies in the official theory of personal identity so far as the non-moral affections go must also be inadequacies, more fundamentally, so far as the treatment of non-moral desire, and so of intentional action and of agency, go. They must be particularly apparent when the non-moral desires in question are artificial ones presupposing conventions and their structures of higher-order expectations and attitudes. The inadequacies of his official theory of personal identity come fully into view, however, only when one reaches, in Book III, Hume's full-dress doctrine of moral agents whose impartial and person-implicating moral desires derive from the operations of corrected sympathy. Hume *displays* the inadequacies of his official theory as he develops his moral psychology. In doing so, however, he does nothing, in the way of explicit revision of theory, to remedy them.[21]

Hume's moral agents are free, and unitary, and enduring agents. Are they also *rational* ones? They act for reasons. They have reasons for acting—convention-presupposing ones—that demand the possession of particularly sophisticated calculative capacities. They have other reasons for acting—specifically moral ones—whose impartiality makes possible the intersubjectivity, indeed the objectivity, of valuations that find expression in the language of morals. Their specifically moral reasons, by seconding their virtuous narrowly interested desires, provide impediments against their acting, with akratic *ir*rationality, in ways other than those they judge

---

[21] For illuminating discussions of the bearing of Books II and III on the account of personal identity to be found in Book I, see: Baier, *A Progress of Sentiments*, 129–51; Jane L. McIntyre, 'Personal Identity and the Passions', *Journal of the History of Philosophy*, 27 (1989), 545–57; Terence Penelhum, 'Self-Identity and Self-Regard', in Amelie Rorty (ed.), *The Identities of Persons* (Berkeley and Los Angeles, Calif., 1976), 253–80.

best. They reason from their reasons to determinate courses of conduct. In doing so they do more than merely reason from ends to means; and they do more than reason about means to ends, or about the constitution of their ends. They weigh the competing considerations that make claims on their conduct—non-moral as well as moral claims—and in reaching conclusions form volitions and act. They have no statable algorithms for reaching their conclusions—none, at any rate, that Hume is prepared to acknowledge. They may none the less—indeed, it seems they must—have norms for proceeding from competing reasons to determinate action, from competing practical premises to practical conclusion. They value the capacity to proceed properly in practical deliberation, and they value their own and others' exercises of that capacity.[22] They have, that is to say, mind-implicating desires pertaining to the capacity for sound practical reasoning; they find that capacity useful to the agent who possesses it, and to others. That their doings and deliberations are to be modelled within the framework of an expanded moral conativism can, it seems, count not at all against their being construed as rational agents.

In the *Treatise* Hume offers an account of '[r]ules by which to judge of causes and effects' (*T* 173–6). This account is helpfully viewed as a contribution to what may be called a naturalized epistemology for causal reasoning.[23] The rules are presented as those that effective causal reasoners in fact employ; and their discovery is the product of a causal, specifically a psychological, investigation of the causal reasoning of such reasoners. He offers no similar list of rules by which to make practical judgements generally, or by which to make determinate moral judgements in the face of competing moral claims, or by which to decide amongst competing moral and non-moral claims. His more concrete exercises in moral reasonings in the *Treatise*, in the second *Enquiry*, and in many of his essays, surely serve, however, as illuminating illustrations of certain aspects, at least, of the norm-employing procedures of an effective practical reasoner. In so far as they are self-conscious exercises—and they are often so—they constitute contributions—exceptionally subtle and penetrating ones—to what may be called, without paradox, a naturalized

[22] Compare Páll S. Árdal, 'Some Implications of the Virtue of Reasonableness in Hume's *Treatise*', in Donald W. Livingston and James T. King (eds.), *Hume: A Re-Evaluation* (New York, 1976), 91–106.

[23] The *locus classicus* for the concept of a naturalized epistemology is W.V.O. Quine, 'Epistemology Naturalized', *Ontological Relativity and Other Essays* (New York, 1969), 69–90. Surprisingly, in his comments on Hume in that essay Quine appears to treat him as a partisan not of naturalized epistemology but of its non-naturalized predecessor.

moral epistemology, an epistemology that counts as a chapter in the psychology of morals.

Hume's free, unitary and enduring moral agents are rational agents. Are they, finally, *virtuous* ones as well? It seems that they must be, at least in so far as they possess, and act from, specifically moral desires. For such specifically moral desires must be among those that an agent, adopting the impartial moral point of view, desires herself and every other to have: she must desire them as useful—and, as Hume would insist, as agreeable—to their possessor and to others. Of course, if virtuous, a moral agent must also have the virtuous non-moral desires—the narrowly interested ones—that her specifically moral desires implicate. Hume's agents, if virtuous, must be more than merely moral agents.

WORKS CITED

Anscombe, G. E. M. *Intention.* 2nd edition. Oxford: Basil Blackwell, 1963.

Árdal, Páll S. *Passion and Value in Hume's Treatise.* Edinburgh: Edinburgh University Press, 1966.

—— 'Some Implications of the Virtue of Reasonableness in Hume's *Treatise*', in Donald W. Livingston and James T. King (eds.), *Hume: A Re-Evaluation.* New York: Fordham University Press, 1976.

Armstrong, D. M. 'Acting and Trying'. *The Nature of Mind and Other Essays.* Ithaca, NY: Cornell University Press, 1981.

Aune, Bruce. *Reason and Action.* Dordrecht: D. Reidel, 1977.

Austin, J. L. *How to Do Things with Words*, edited by J. O. Urmson. Oxford: Oxford University Press, 1962.

Ayer, A. J. *Language, Truth, and Logic.* 2nd edition. London: Victor Gollancz, 1946.

Baier, Annette. 'Artificial Virtues and the Equally Sensible Non-Knaves: A Response to Gauthier'. *Hume Studies*, 18 (1992), 429–39.

—— 'Hume's Analysis of Pride'. *Journal of Philosophy*, 75 (1978), 27–40.

—— *A Progress of Sentiments: Reflections on Hume's Treatise.* Cambridge, Mass.: Harvard University Press, 1991.

Bayles, Michael. 'Hume on Blame and Excuses'. *Hume Studies*, 2 (1976), 17–35.

Bennett, Jonathan. *Locke, Berkeley, Hume: Central Themes.* Oxford: Oxford University Press, 1971.

Blackburn, Simon. 'Moral Realism', in John Casey (ed.), *Morality and Moral Reasoning.* London: Methuen, 1971.

—— 'Reply: Rule-Following and Moral Realism', in Steven H. Holtzman and Christopher M. Leich (eds.), *Wittgenstein: To Follow a Rule.* London: Routledge & Kegan Paul, 1981.

—— *Spreading the Word: Groundings in the Philosophy of Language.* Oxford: Oxford University Press, 1984.

—— 'Supervenience Revisited', in Geoffrey Sayre-McCord (ed.), *Essays on Moral Realism.* Ithaca, NY: Cornell University Press, 1988.

Brandt, Richard. *Ethical Theory: The Problems of Normative and Critical Ethics.* Englewood Cliffs, NJ: Prentice-Hall, 1959.

Bricke, John. 'Emotion and Thought in Hume's Treatise'. *Canadian Journal of Philosophy*, Supplementary Volume 1 (1974), 53–71.

Bricke, John (cont.). 'Hume, Freedom to Act, and Personal Evaluation'. *History of Philosophy Quarterly*, 5 (1988), 141–56.

—— 'Hume, Motivation and Morality'. *Hume Studies*, 14 (1988), 1–24.

—— 'Hume on Self-Identity, Memory and Causality', in George Morice (ed.), *David Hume: Bicentenary Papers*. Edinburgh: Edinburgh University Press, 1977.

—— 'Hume's Associationist Psychology'. *Journal of the History of the Behavioral Sciences*, 8 (1974), 397–409.

—— *Hume's Philosophy of Mind*. Edinburgh: Edinburgh University Press, 1980.

—— 'Hume's Volitions', in Vincent Hope (ed.), *Philosophers of the Scottish Enlightenment*. Edinburgh: Edinburgh University Press, 1984.

—— 'Locke, Hume and the Nature of Volitions'. *Hume Studies*, Supplementary Volume (1985), 15–51.

Chisholm, R. M. 'J. L. Austin's *Philosophical Papers*'. *Mind*, 73 (1964), 1–26.

Davidson, Donald. 'Actions, Reasons, and Causes'. *Essays on Actions and Events*. Oxford: Oxford University Press, 1980.

—— 'Belief and the Basis of Meaning'. *Inquiries into Truth and Interpretation*. Oxford: Oxford University Press, 1984.

—— 'Deception and Division', in Ernest LePore and Brian McLaughlin (eds.), *Actions and Events: Perspectives on the Philosophy of Donald Davidson*. Oxford: Basil Blackwell, 1985.

—— *Expressing Evaluations*. Lawrence, Kan.: University of Kansas Lindley Lecture, 1984.

—— 'Freedom to Act'. *Essays on Actions and Events*. Oxford: Oxford University Press, 1980.

—— 'Hempel on Explaining Action'. *Essays on Actions and Events*. Oxford: Oxford University Press, 1980.

—— 'How is Weakness of the Will Possible?' *Essays on Actions and Events*. Oxford: Oxford University Press, 1980.

—— 'Hume's Cognitive Theory of Pride'. *Essays on Actions and Events*. Oxford: Oxford University Press, 1980.

—— 'Intending'. *Essays on Actions and Events*. Oxford: Oxford University Press, 1980.

—— 'Judging Interpersonal Interests', in Jon Elster and Aanund Hylland (eds.), *Foundations of Social Choice Theory*. Cambridge: Cambridge University Press, 1986.

—— 'Knowing One's Own Mind'. *Proceedings and Addresses of the American Philosophical Association*, 60 (1986–7), 441–58.

—— 'The Material Mind'. *Essays on Actions and Events*. Oxford: Oxford

University Press, 1980.

—— 'Mental Events'. *Essays on Actions and Events*. Oxford: Oxford University Press, 1980.

—— 'A New Basis for Decision Theory'. *Theory and Decision*, 18 (1985), 87–98.

—— 'Paradoxes of Irrationality', in Richard Wollheim and James Hopkins (eds.), *Philosophical Essays on Freud*. Cambridge: Cambridge University Press, 1982.

—— 'Psychology as Philosophy'. *Essays on Actions and Events*. Oxford: Oxford University Press, 1980.

—— 'Radical Interpretation'. *Inquiries into Truth and Interpretation*. Oxford: Oxford University Press, 1984.

—— 'Rational Animals'. *Dialectica*, 36 (1982), 317–27.

—— 'The Structure and Content of Truth'. *Journal of Philosophy*, 87 (1990), 279–328.

—— 'Thought and Talk'. *Inquiries into Truth and Interpretation*. Oxford: Oxford University Press, 1984.

—— 'Towards a Unified Theory of Meaning and Action'. *Grazer Philosophische Studien*, 11 (1980), 1–12.

—— 'True to the Facts'. *Inquiries into Truth and Interpretation*. Oxford: Oxford University Press, 1984.

—— 'What is Present to the Mind?', in Johannes Brandl and Wolfgang Gombocz (eds.), *The Mind of Donald Davidson*. Amsterdam: Rodopi, 1989.

Divers, John and Miller, Alexander. 'Why Expressivists about Value Should Not Love Minimalism about Truth'. *Analysis*, 54 (1994), 12–19.

Ewing, A. C. *Ethics*. London: The English Universities Press, 1953.

Foot, Philippa. 'Free Will as Involving Determinism'. *Virtues and Vices and Other Essays in Moral Philosophy*. Oxford: Basil Blackwell, 1978.

Gauthier, David. 'Artificial Virtues and the Sensible Knave'. *Hume Studies*, 18 (1992), 401–27.

—— 'David Hume, Contractarian'. *Philosophical Review*, 88 (1979), 3–38.

—— *Morals by Agreement*. Oxford: Oxford University Press, 1986.

Hare, R. M. *Freedom and Reason*. Oxford: Oxford University Press, 1963.

—— *The Language of Morals*. Oxford: Oxford University Press, 1952.

Harman, Gilbert. *The Nature of Morality: An Introduction to Ethics*. New York: Oxford University Press, 1977.

—— 'Practical Reasoning'. *The Review of Metaphysics*, 29 (1975–6), 431–63.

Harrison, Jonathan. *Hume's Moral Epistemology*. Oxford: Oxford University Press, 1976.

—— *Hume's Theory of Justice*. Oxford: Oxford University Press, 1981.

Heil, John and Mele, Alfred (eds.). *Mental Causation*. Oxford: Oxford University Press, 1993.

Helm, Paul. 'Hume on Exculpation'. *Philosophy*, 42 (1967), 265–71.

Horwich, Paul. 'The Essence of Expressivism'. *Analysis*, 54 (1994), 19–20.

Humberstone, I. L. 'Direction of Fit'. *Mind*, 101 (1992), 59–83.

Hume, David. *Abstract of a Treatise of Human Nature*, edited by J. M. Keynes and P. Sraffa. Cambridge: Cambridge University Press, 1938.

—— 'A Dialogue'. *Enquiries Concerning Human Understanding and Concerning the Principles of Morals*, edited by L. A. Selby-Bigge. 3rd edition with text revised by P. H. Nidditch. Oxford: Oxford University Press, 1975

—— 'A Dissertation on the Passions'. *Essays Moral, Political, and Literary*, vol. ii, edited by T. H. Green and T. H. Grose. London: Longmans, Green, 1889.

—— *Enquiries Concerning Human Understanding and Concerning the Principles of Morals*, edited by L. A. Selby-Bigge. 3rd edition with text revised by P. H. Nidditch. Oxford: Oxford University Press, 1975.

—— *The Natural History of Religion*, edited by A. Wayne Colver. Oxford: Oxford University Press, 1976.

—— 'Of the Original Contract'. *Essays Moral, Political, and Literary*, edited by Eugene F. Miller. Indianapolis, Ind.: Liberty Classics, 1985.

—— 'Of the Standard of Taste'. *Essays Moral, Political, and Literary*, edited by Eugene F. Miller. Indianapolis, Ind.: Liberty Classics, 1985.

—— *A Treatise of Human Nature*, edited by L. A. Selby-Bigge. 2nd edition with text revised by P. H. Nidditch. Oxford: Oxford University Press, 1978.

Hurley, Susan. 'Conflict, Akrasia and Cognitivism'. *Proceedings of the Aristotelian Society*, 86 (1985–6), 23–49.

—— *Natural Reasons: Personality and Polity*. Oxford: Oxford University Press, 1989.

Jackson, Frank, Oppy, Graham and Smith, Michael. 'Minimalism and Truth-Aptness'. *Mind*, 103 (1994), 287–302.

Jenkins, John. *Understanding Hume*, edited by Peter Lewis and Geoffrey Madell. Edinburgh: Edinburgh University Press, 1992.

Kenny, Anthony. *Action, Emotion, and Will*. London: Routledge & Kegan Paul, 1963.

Lewis, David. *Convention: A Philosophical Study*. Cambridge, Mass.: Harvard University Press, 1969.

—— 'Radical Interpretation'. *Synthese*, 27 (1974), 331–44.

Locke, John. *The Correspondence of John Locke*, vol. vii, edited by E. S. de Beer. Oxford: Oxford University Press, 1982.

—— *An Essay Concerning Human Understanding*, edited by P. H. Nidditch. Oxford: Oxford University Press, 1975.

MacIntyre, A. C. 'Hume on "Is" and "Ought"', in V. C. Chappell (ed.), *Hume: A Collection of Critical Essays*. Garden City, NY: Doubleday, 1966.

Mackie, J. L. *Ethics: Inventing Right and Wrong*. Harmondsworth: Penguin, 1977.

—— *Hume's Moral Theory*. London: Routledge & Kegan Paul, 1980.

McDowell, John. 'Are Moral Requirements Hypothetical Imperatives?' *Proceedings of the Aristotelian Society*, Supplementary Volume 52 (1978), 13–29.

—— 'Non-Cognitivism and Rule-Following', in Steven H. Holtzman and Christopher M. Leich (eds.), *Wittgenstein: To Follow a Rule*. London: Routledge & Kegan Paul, 1981.

—— *Projection and Truth in Ethics*. Lawrence, Kan.: University of Kansas Lindley Lecture, 1988.

—— 'Values and Secondary Qualities', in Ted Honderich (ed.), *Morality and Objectivity*. London: Routledge & Kegan Paul, 1985.

McGinn, Colin. *The Character of Mind*. Oxford: Oxford University Press, 1982.

—— *The Subjective View: Secondary Qualities and Indexical Thoughts*. Oxford: Oxford University Press, 1983.

McIntyre, Jane L. 'Personal Identity and the Passions'. *Journal of the History of Philosophy*, 27 (1989), 545–57.

Moore, G. E. *Principia Ethica*. Cambridge: Cambridge University Press, 1903.

Nagel, Thomas. *The Possibility of Altruism*. Oxford: Oxford University Press, 1970.

Norton, David Fate. *David Hume: Common-Sense Moralist, Sceptical Metaphysician*. Princeton, NJ: Princeton University Press, 1982.

—— 'Hume, Atheism, and the Autonomy of Morals', in Marcus Hester (ed.), *Hume's Philosophy of Religions*. Winston-Salem, NC: Wake Forest University Press, 1986.

Nowell-Smith, P. H. *Ethics*. Harmondsworth: Penguin, 1954.

Parfit, Derek. 'Later Selves and Moral Principles', in Alan Montefiore (ed.), *Philosophy and Personal Relations*. London: Routledge & Kegan Paul, 1973.

—— *Reasons and Persons*. Oxford: Oxford University Press, 1984.

Pears, David. *Hume's System: An Examination of the First Book of his Treatise*. Oxford: Oxford University Press, 1990.

Penelhum, Terence. *David Hume: An Introduction to his Philosophical System*. West Lafayette, Ind.: Purdue University Press, 1992.

Penelhum, Terence (cont.). *Hume*. London: Macmillan, 1975.

—— 'Hume on Personal Identity', in V. C. Chappell (ed.), *Hume: A Collection of Critical Essays*. Garden City, NY: Doubleday, 1966.

—— 'Hume's Theory of the Self Revisited'. *Dialogue*, 14 (1975), 389–409.

—— 'The Self in Hume's Philosophy', in Kenneth R. Merrill and Robert W. Shahan (eds.), *David Hume: Many-sided Genius*. Norman, Okla.: University of Oklahoma Press, 1976.

—— 'Self-Identity and Self-Regard', in Amelie Rorty (ed.), *The Identities of Persons*. Berkeley and Los Angeles, Calif.: University of California Press, 1976.

Platts, Mark. 'Hume and Morality as a Matter of Fact'. *Mind*, 97 (1988), 189–204.

—— 'Moral Reality and the End of Desire', in Mark Platts (ed.), *Reference, Truth, and Reality*. London: Routledge & Kegan Paul, 1980.

—— *Ways of Meaning: An Introduction to a Philosophy of Language*. London: Routledge & Kegan Paul, 1979.

Postema, Gerald J. 'Hume's Reply to the Sensible Knave'. *History of Philosophy Quarterly*, 5 (1988), 23–40.

Prichard, H. A. *Moral Obligation: Essays and Lectures*. Oxford: Oxford University Press, 1949.

Quine, W. V. O. 'Epistemology Naturalized'. *Ontological Relativity and Other Essays*. New York: Columbia University Press, 1969.

Raphael, D. D. (ed.). *British Moralists: 1650-1800*, vol. i. Oxford: Oxford University Press, 1969.

Rawls, John. *A Theory of Justice*. Cambridge, Mass.: Harvard University Press, 1971.

Ross, W. D. *Foundations of Ethics*. Oxford: Oxford University Press, 1939.

—— *The Right and the Good*. Oxford: Oxford University Press, 1930.

Sayre-McCord, Geoffrey (ed.). *Essays on Moral Realism*. Ithaca, NY: Cornell University Press, 1988.

Searle, John. *Expression and Meaning*. Cambridge: Cambridge University Press, 1979.

—— *Intentionality: An Essay in the Philosophy of Mind*. Cambridge: Cambridge University Press, 1983.

—— *Speech Acts: An Essay in the Philosophy of Language*. Cambridge: Cambridge University Press, 1969.

—— 'What is an Intentional State?' *Mind*, 88 (1979), 74–92.

Sellars, Wilfrid. 'Thought and Action', in Keith Lehrer (ed.), *Freedom and Determinism*. New York: Random House, 1966.

Smith, Michael. 'The Humean Theory of Motivation'. *Mind*, 96 (1987), 36–61.

—— 'Minimalism, Truth-Aptitude and Belief'. *Analysis*, 54 (1994), 21–6.

—— 'Why Expressivists about Value should Love Minimalism about Truth'. *Analysis*, 54 (1994), 1–11.

Smith, Norman Kemp. *The Philosophy of David Hume*. London: Macmillan, 1941.

Snare, Francis. *Morals, Motivation, and Convention: Hume's Influential Doctrines*. Cambridge: Cambridge University Press, 1991.

Stevenson, C. L. *Ethics and Language*. New Haven, Conn.: Yale University Press, 1944.

—— *Facts and Values: Studies in Ethical Analysis*. New Haven, Conn.: Yale University Press, 1963.

Stroud, Barry. *Hume*. London: Routledge & Kegan Paul, 1977.

Vesey, G. N. A. 'Volition', in Donald F. Gustafson (ed.), *Essays in Philosophical Psychology*. Garden City, NY: Doubleday, 1964.

Williams, Bernard. 'Internal and External Reasons'. *Moral Luck*. Cambridge: Cambridge University Press, 1981.

—— 'Persons, Character and Morality'. *Moral Luck*. Cambridge: Cambridge University Press, 1981.

Wittgenstein, Ludwig. *Philosophical Investigations*, translated by G. E. M. Anscombe. 3rd edition. Oxford: Basil Blackwell, 1958.

Wright, Crispin. *Truth and Objectivity*. Cambridge, Mass.: Harvard University Press, 1992.

—— 'Truth in Ethics'. *Ratio* (New Series), 8 (1995), 209–26.

INDEX

restrained, and justice 190–1, 193–4
unrestrained, and justice 183, 184–5
as a virtuous desire 193–4
sentiment, *see* affection; desire; moral affection; moral desire
sexual conduct, conventions governing 195, 198, 199, 207
Smith, Adam 131 n.
Smith, Michael 25 n., 32 n., 163 n., 168 n.
Smith, Norman Kemp 47 n.
Snare, Francis 6 n., 44 n., 160 n., 199 n.
society:
  benefits 205–6; of political 207–8; securing, and the convention of justice 206
  four-part classification of kinds of 208 n.
  political, and akrasia 208, 226 n.
Stevenson, C. L. 161 n.
Stroud, Barry 7 n., 160 n.
sympathy 128–48
  in absence of original desire 134
  and affection 129, 154
  and belief 129
  corrected, and correction of perception 140–1, 158; and moral affection 153–4; and moral desire 136–7, 146–7; and the moral point of view 107; and solution to intrasubjective and intersubjective predicaments 137–44
  correction of, 129
  and desire 129
  and disposition to sympathize 147
  extensive 133–5
  and initiation of concern 130
  naturalistic theory of 107, 147–8
  not itself a desire 129
  and original desire 129
  range of phenomena explainable by 135–6, 148
  and sympathetic desire 129
  thick theory of 130–1
  thin theory of 130, 131
  and type-identity 129, 132, 154

Tarski, Alfred 165
truth:
  asymmetrical treatment of 163–4
  and attenuated moral conativism 164–8
  desire-expressing *versus* (descriptive) belief-expressing 166, 167

differences in, for descriptive and evaluative sentences 164, 166
and direction of fit 25–7
and evaluative language 162–8
and Hume's second argument for conativism 21, 22, 23, 24–7
illusions with respect to 108, 162–3
moral, and Conformity Thesis 87–95; Hume's conativist rejection of 80, 81, 84; role of in moral cognitivism 80–2, 84
more-than-minimalist 91
other-than-substantive 163–4
and representational content 25–7
and sentences 164 n.
substantive 162–4; for evaluative sentences 164–7

undoubted maxim (UM) *see* Artificiality Argument

Vesey, G. N. A. 54 n.
virtue:
  artificial 115, 120, 121, 170, 182, 228–9
  and mental proclivities and capacities 229
  natural 115, 120, 121, 170, 182, 228–9
  and non-moral desire 229
volition 35–6, 49–59
  and action 54–6, 237
  as attitude to truth of proposition 51
  and basic configuration 36, 49, 69
  contrasted with desire 51–2, 60, 109
  Hume's official theory of, and its difficulties 49–51
  and intention 52–3
  linguistic expression of 58, 60
  as mode of conception 51
  non-evaluative content of 52, 60
  and practical reasoning 56–9
  as psychological primitive 53–4
  world-to-mind direction of fit of 35–6, 51, 60, 89 n.
  see also action
von Limborch, Philippus 54 n.

weakness of will, *see* akrasia
Williams, Bernard 34 n., 245 n.
Wittgenstein, Ludwig 54 n.
Wollaston, William 87, 89–91, 95
Wright, Crispin 163 n., 166 n.